ROYAL HISTORICAL SOCIETY

STUDIES IN HISTORY

New Series

WOMEN AND VIOLENT CRIME
IN ENLIGHTENMENT SCOTLAND

WOMEN AND VIOLENT CRIME IN ENLIGHTENMENT SCOTLAND

Anne-Marie Kilday

THE ROYAL HISTORICAL SOCIETY
THE BOYDELL PRESS

First published 2007

A Royal Historical Society publication
Published by The Boydell Press
an imprint of Boydell & Brewer Ltd
PO Box 9, Woodbridge, Suffolk IP12 3DF, UK
and of Boydell & Brewer Inc.
668 Mt Hope Avenue, Rochester, NY 14620, USA
website: www.boydellandbrewer.com

ISBN 978 0 86193 287 0

ISSN 0269–2244

A CIP catalogue record for this book is available
from the British Library

This publication is printed on acid-free paper

Printed in Great Britain by
Antony Rowe Ltd, Chippenham, Wiltshire

FOR MUM, DAD AND J. P.

Contents

List of Maps

Acknowledgements

Numerous people have helped in the writing of this book. Firstly, I would like to express my thanks to staff at the National Archives of Scotland, the National Library of Scotland and the Bodleian Library, Oxford, for their patience and helpful advice. Secondly, I would like to acknowledge the help and support of Tom Devine and Chris Whatley, both of whom encouraged me in the initial stages of this project, and who have retained an interest ever since. To my colleagues at Oxford Brookes University, especially Steve King and John Stewart, I owe a special debt of gratitude. Their comments, criticism and support were essential in the completion of this work. I would also like to acknowledge the help of the following individuals: Joanne Bailey, Katherine Bradley, John Finlay, Richard Finlay, Alex Friend, Pete King, Andrew Spicer, Katherine Watson and Clifford Williamson. In particular, I would like to thank Christine Linehan, David Nash and Alex Walsham. Without their patience, support and detailed advice, this book would simply not have been possible. Finally, I want to thank my parents and my brother John-Paul for all their love and constant encouragement.

Anne-Marie Kilday
January 2007

Abbreviations

Bodl. Lib.	Bodleian Library, Oxford
JC	Justiciary Court
JP	Justice of the Peace Court
NAS	National Archives of Scotland
SC	Sheriff Court
APS	*Acts of the parliaments of Scotland*, iii, xi, Edinburgh 1814, 1824
C&C	*Continuity and Change*
G&H	*Gender and History*
HJ	*Historical Journal*
JR	*Juridical Review*
JSH	*Journal of Social History*
P&P	*Past & Present*
SESH	*Scottish Economic and Social History*
SH	*Social History*

Introduction

It is clear that Scottish social and cultural history needs to be better integrated into the wider European picture. This book is a contribution to that process. Two major gaps exist in Scottish historical research on crime: the Scottish experience of crime after the early modern period, and the involvement of women in criminality. Although some research has been carried out into Scottish crime during this period by scholars such as Ian Donnachie, Kenneth Logue, Bruce Lenman, Geoffrey Parker and Deborah Symonds, their work has been either crime-specific or in the form of brief survey articles of a more general nature.[1] There has been no substantial study of Scottish women's involvement in illegal activity during the pre-modern period. Although English historians have gone much further than their Scottish counterparts in this kind of investigation, they too have paid less attention to the relationship of gender to crime and *vice-versa*.[2] The intention of this volume is to fill these historiographical gaps by providing a study of the nature and incidence of violent female criminality in lowland Scotland between 1750 and 1815. As well as contributing to Scottish and arguably wider international criminological research, this study also adds to the relatively limited amount of work on Scottish women's history in general in relation to the eighteenth century.[3]

This book is based primarily on an exhaustive study of the records of the Scottish Justiciary Court between 1750 and 1815. The indictments of more than 4,000 individuals have been examined, with the analysis focusing on those charged with violent offences, known as 'crimes against the person'. In total these individuals accounted for more than a third of the cases brought before the lowland Justiciary Courts during the eighteenth and early nineteenth centuries. The types of crime indicted were predominantly violent homicides, infanticides, assaults, popular disturbances and robberies. Detailed analyses of each of these offences are provided in chapters 3–7.

The comprehensive nature of Justiciary Court material allowed an in-

---

[1] See, for instance, I. Donnachie, '"The darker side": a speculative survey of Scottish crime during the first half of the nineteenth century', *SESH* xv (1995), 5–24; K. J. Logue, *Popular disturbances in Scotland, 1780–1815*, Edinburgh 1979; B. Lenman and G. Parker, 'Crime and control in Scotland, 1500–1800', *History Today* xxx (1980), 13–17; and D. A. Symonds, *Weep not for me: women, ballads and infanticide in early modern Scotland*, University Park, PA 1997.
[2] A notable exception would be G. Walker, *Crime, gender and social order in early modern England*, Cambridge 2003.
[3] For further discussion of the historiographical context of this book see chapter 1 below.

depth investigation of the nature of violent crime. Indictments were meticulously recorded in court books and contained detailed information relating to the circumstances of each case. At the outset of every indictment the applicability of the relevant statute was debated by the lawyers concerned. The plea offered by the accused, as well as witness testimony (for both the prosecution and the defence) and medical evidence was also documented. Finally, verdict and sentencing material was included to complete the picture of the judicial process. Each indictment thus generated a wealth of information. This meant that when it came to the examination of violent offences collectively by category, the analysis of each offence centred on five themes: the legal basis for the indictment, the incidence of the offence charged, the characteristics of the defendants involved, the methods used in the committal of the offence and the motives behind the alleged crime.

Despite the richness of Justiciary Court evidence, its use in the study of crime (and female criminality in particular) is not entirely unproblematic. In the first instance, court records are not a wholly representative indicator of criminal activity. Indictment rates tend to reflect the amount of crime reported rather than the amount of crime actually committed since the real incidence of crime can never fully be known.[4] Thus, in any study where court records predominate over other source materials, the picture of illegality will be incomplete. Just as many variables affected the reporting of crime as its perpetration. Consequently, data relating to prosecution rates often tell us more about socio-legal attitudes towards criminality, than about the incidence of law-breaking itself. For instance, the level of violent female criminality across lowland Scotland slightly increased during the period between 1750 and 1815. However, this does not necessarily reflect an increase in actual crime. Most of this increase could be explained by population growth, by changes in the nature of justice (more cases being indicted at the Justiciary Courts for example) or by an increase in the reporting of crime. The numerous difficulties and complexities associated with the evidence related to actual overall crime rates means that they cannot form a substantive part of the analysis found in this volume.[5]

An additional problem with indictment records is that in themselves they cannot tell the whole story of crime and those who perpetrated it. Little evidence, for instance, is provided about the backgrounds of the suspects accused of violent crime. Occupational references are commonly made in the indictment evidence, but it is often difficult to glean the particular social status of the men and women brought before the court. Certainly, the accused do not appear to have been individuals of high rank as was largely the case in

---

[4] The level of unreported crime is commonly referred to as the 'dark figure' of criminal statistics.

[5] For a more detailed exploration of trends in criminal activity in lowland Scotland see A.-M. Kilday, 'Women and crime in south-west Scotland: a study of the Justiciary Court records, 1750–1815', unpubl. PhD diss. Strathclyde 1998, ch. vii.

Scotland prior to 1650. Suspects were usually in some form of employment, but were rarely titled or described as being members of the landed gentry. The eighteenth-century concern with controlling the Scottish populace in the wake of the Jacobite rebellions suggests that 'ordinary' people were more likely to be brought to court and labelled 'criminal' than in earlier periods.[6]

As the supreme jurisdiction, the Justiciary Court was more likely than any other to indict violent offenders. It was more probable that aggressive women in particular would be brought before the Justiciary Court, as their actions were widely considered to be dangerous and abhorrent. This makes a study of this court essential for any investigation of violent female criminality and behaviour. However, it should be remembered that evidence from the Justiciary Court may well be unbalanced. As that court only dealt with the most serious offences, an analysis of its records might exaggerate the picture of violent crime in lowland Scotland, and in particular the involvement of women in that type of activity. The extent to which indictment evidence is a reflection of the particular concerns of the Scottish authorities of the day rather than representative of violent female criminality *per se* will be addressed throughout the book, but more especially in the conclusion. Subsequent studies, using other court records or alternative source material, might eventually qualify some of the findings of this book. Ultimately this volume analyses a significant proportion of the serious crimes indicted in lowland Scotland between 1750 and 1815.

Although the difficulties associated with the use of court records must be borne in mind, the study of crime remains important for the historian. Criminal history can provide us with a unique, double-edged perspective. On the one hand, this type of investigation provides access to the voices of the criminals themselves. It enables us to explore the multiple factors which influenced people in their daily lives and to speculate why some people reacted in an unlawful way to the circumstances they faced and others did not. This is perhaps particularly significant when considering women and their behaviour, as commonly they have been hidden from the histories of ordinary life, especially in a Scottish context. The other perspective provided by the study of crime relates to the reactions and responses of individuals towards criminal activity. Research can tell us much about why individuals chose to report or to ignore episodes of illegality. It can also tell us how criminals and certain crimes were regarded by society in various historical contexts and how and why these opinions changed. The study of crime can also provide us with an insight into how authority (in various guises) attempted to control and manage the populace (at both a local and national level) and how successful they were at doing so. Criminal history, then, can tell us much about the interplay between state and society, the circumstances which affected ordi-

[6] M. B. Wasser, 'Violence and the central criminal courts in Scotland, 1603–1638', unpubl. PhD diss. Columbia 1995, 1, 14, 295, 300.

nary men and women on a day-to-day basis and the reactions of individuals to the conditions they faced.

The year 1750 was selected as a starting point for this study as it was approximately from the middle decades of the eighteenth century that business at the Justiciary Court expanded to unprecedented levels. There were two principal reasons for this. First, and probably most important, the Heritable Jurisdictions Act of 1747 (which is discussed in more detail in chapter 2) made previously legitimate jurisdictions obsolete, with the result that the Sheriff and Justiciary Courts had greatly to expand in order to assimilate the extra work-load.[7] The second reason for the growth in court business after 1750, which makes it an excellent starting point for a study of Scottish crime, is related to changes in the perceived function of the criminal law. Before 1750, in the sixteenth and seventeenth centuries, the law was used to decide the degree of compensation that the allegedly guilty party should provide for his or her victim, or that victim's family. Frequently, cases were never even brought to court due to the expenses incurred but were settled through arbitration between the parties involved. Thus the ultimate function of the court was to raise money through the levying of fines and the confiscation of property. Increasingly, but especially after 1587 when the King's Advocate was authorised to do so, prosecutions 'in the public interest' could be made under Scots law against individuals, regardless of whether a settlement could be reached between the parties concerned. Furthermore, rather than compensation being the end result of a disputed litigation, specific penalties were created and varied according to the offence committed. As a result of all this, more cases were brought to court and, by an act of parliament in 1672, the High Court of Justiciary was established. By 1750, therefore, the transformation of society's perceptions and attitudes towards criminal justice in Scottish society was more or less complete and the abundance of indictments brought to the court demonstrates this.[8]

Another key factor in the selection of 1750 as the basis for this analysis is that it marked the zenith of Scotland's great intellectual revolution – the so-called age of Enlightenment. The advances in science, philosophy and culture in Scotland during this period have been well documented.[9] The effect of Enlightenment thinking on the legal process and attitudes to crime has, however, received markedly less attention. Did the growth of a more cosmopolitan and aesthetically aware society in lowland Scotland affect the nature

[7] For further discussion see chapter 2 below; Lenman and Parker, 'Crime and control', 17; and D. Walker, *The Scottish legal system: an introduction to the study of Scots law*, Edinburgh 1992, 123–4.
[8] For further discussion see chapter 2 below; Lenman and Parker, 'Crime and control', 15–17; and S. J. Davies, 'The courts and the Scottish legal system, 1600–1747: the case of Stirlingshire', in V. A. C. Gatrell, B. Lenman and G. Parker (eds), *Crime and the law: the social history of crime in western Europe since 1500*, London 1980, 147.
[9] See, for instance, A. C. Chitnis, *The Scottish Enlightenment: a social history*, London 1980.

and incidence of criminality and attitudes towards it? Was the long-standing notion that the Scots were a more brutal and hardened people extinguished by the 'humanising' developments of the Enlightenment era? Was the Scottish Enlightenment the end product of the 'civilising process' said to have encouraged the rise of manners, politeness and etiquette across Europe, or did 1750 merely mark the beginning of Scotland's modernisation process? These questions will be addressed throughout this study, but they will be particularly significant for its conclusions.

Making the study encompass the so-called 'long eighteenth century' and end in 1815 enables the volume to account for the legislative changes that occurred at the turn of the eighteenth century. Some of these affected the legal perception of crime and particularly that charged against women. For example, the statute 49 Geo. III C. 14, passed in 1809, altered penal policy in relation to infanticide, and made concealment of pregnancy a non-capital offence. The year 1815 also constitutes a good concluding point as it marked the culmination of the Revolutionary and Napoleonic Wars, the twilight of the Enlightenment and the beginning of a period of summary justice, when the indictment evidence presented to the Scottish courts became condensed and considerably less informative.

The geographical focus for this book is the lowland region of Scotland. This is the area below the Forth-Clyde valley outlined in maps 1 and 2 (pp. 6, 8). This region was chosen not least because it was the hub of economic and social modernisation, and was also the area where most of the Scottish population resided during the eighteenth and nineteenth centuries. As well as the High Court in Edinburgh, the Lowlands encompassed two circuit courts, the west and south, both of which covered a large geographical and jurisdictional area. A study of crime in this region facilitates an analysis of illegality in major cities (such as Edinburgh and Glasgow), middle-sized towns, smaller urban settlements and, of course, rural areas. This breadth of analysis would not have been possible for the Highlands during the 1750–1815 period as it was predominantly pastoral in nature.

In addition, a study of national crime statistics, available for Scotland from 1805 to 1814, reflects the dominance of the lowland area in the nation's experience of crime and criminal activity. Evidence from the *Parliamentary papers* suggests that nearly two-thirds of the crimes indicted at Scotland's supreme criminal courts were committed in lowland counties during the early nineteenth century.[10] Moreover, 63 per cent of the violent offences charged against Scottish individuals at that time were allegedly perpetrated by lowland men and women, rather than by their highland counterparts.[11]

---

10 My calculation is based on the evidence presented in *Parliamentary papers*, x, London 1812, 217–29; xi, London 1814–15, 293–309.

11 My calculation is based on the evidence presented ibid. x. 217–29; xi. 293–309. A gendered regional analysis of the parliamentary papers for 1805–14 reveals that most female criminality in Scotland at this time was charged against women from the lowland region, rather than against women from the north of the country. Interestingly, however, the

Map 1. Scotland, highlighting the lowland region.

The available evidence suggests that the lowland region was a microcosm of criminality, violence and deviance in post-Enlightenment Scotland and pre-modern Europe.

Another factor concerns the nature of social and economic change that occurred in the Lowlands during the 1750–1815 period. In Scotland as a whole at that time the rate of urban expansion was proceeding at a faster pace than anywhere else in western Europe, save Belgium, the Netherlands and England and Wales.[12] This was particularly evident in the Lowlands of Scotland (and the west of that region in particular) where population growth in the city of Glasgow, the commercial and manufacturing towns of Paisley and Kilmarnock and the port town of Greenock had at least trebled between 1750 and 1821.[13] The mid-eighteenth century was also seen as being significant for Scotland in socio-economic terms, as it was said to mark the beginning of both a major dislocation in the rural environment and Scotland's first phase of industrialisation.

As Scotland was still a predominantly rural society in the eighteenth century, the profound revolution which took place within the structure of the agrarian economy and rural society had significant ramifications for much of the country. Fundamental changes in estate management from around the mid-1770s concerned the labour structure as well as land use and distribution, and resulted in significant and widespread improvements in cultivation and a rapid growth in output. Principally owing to an increased awareness of the merits of capitalist enterprise amongst landlords, and aided by the presence of abundant labour, these changes resulted in the transformation of the rural social system throughout the Lowlands of Scotland over a short period of time.[14]

In terms of the industrial revolution that took place, in relation to lowland Scotland the scale of this change was most clearly seen in Glasgow. Described as an 'industrial powerhouse', the city of Glasgow became a focus for the expansion of specific sectors of Scotland's industrial economy from the 1750s. Textiles, coal, sugar-refining and tobacco were all industries which became synonymous with Glasgow and its conurbations and they contributed significantly to the pace and breadth of economic growth in Scotland from the

---

statistics are reversed when it comes to specifically violent crimes, where Highland women were indicted in 57% of the cases. The evidence suggests that women throughout Scotland were willing to perpetrate violent criminality. This conclusion contrasts sharply with the male experience of indicted violent behaviour, which was overwhelmingly centred in the lowlands during the first decade of the nineteenth century. Statistics derived from the parliamentary papers indicate that a study of female illegality in the Highlands of Scotland would do much to elaborate, illuminate and develop the findings of this present analysis.

[12] For further discussion see T. M. Devine, 'Urbanisation', in T. M. Devine and R. Mitchison (eds), *People and society in Scotland*, I: *1760–1830*, Edinburgh 1988, 27–52, and C. A. Whatley, *The Industrial Revolution in Scotland*, Cambridge 1997, 24.

[13] See Devine, 'Urbanisation', 35, and Whatley, *Industrial Revolution*, 65–6.

[14] For further discussion see T. M. Devine, *The transformation of rural Scotland: social change and the agrarian economy, 1660–1815*, Edinburgh 1994.

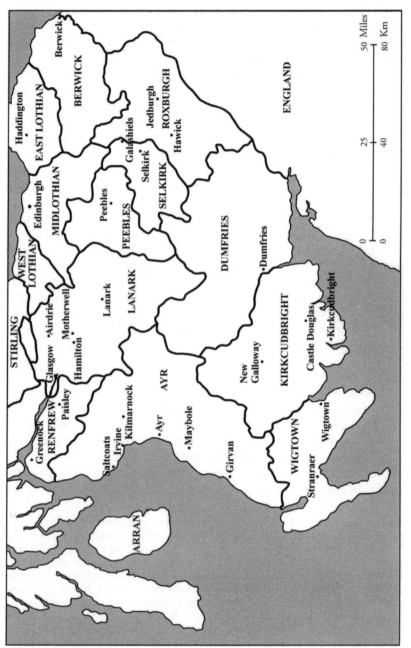

Map 2. The lowland region.

middle of the eighteenth century onwards. Other areas of lowland Scotland such as Dumfries, Haddington, Ayr, Falkirk and Hawick also had important roles to play in the industrial expansion that took place, especially in relation to manufacturing industry.[15]

As well as being significantly affected by the scale of change in agrarian society and economy, the Lowlands of Scotland can clearly be described as the heartland of Scottish urbanisation and industrialisation during the 1750-1815 period. Thus, it was considered to be both useful and interesting to examine whether the consequences of economic disruption and changes in traditional social structures had any effect on the perpetration of crime or the prosecution of illegal activity in this particular area. As women were thought to have made a substantial contribution to Scotland's industrial and agricultural transformation, it would be particularly salient to determine whether their extensive involvement in Scottish economic development meant that they were more exposed to crime and criminal behaviour during this period.[16]

This book makes a three-fold contribution to the historiography. First it adds to our knowledge of the social and cultural history of Scotland in the eighteenth and early nineteenth centuries. Second, it helps us to develop an understanding of the history of crime and criminality in the pre-modern period, and third it expands our grasp on the experience of women during this period. An investigation into the exploits of violent women during the eighteenth and early nineteenth centuries is of particular importance. Not only will such a study fill an historiographical void, it will examine the actions of aggressive women who were said to have ignored the gendered norms ascribed to them by contemporary literature, popular religion and, surprisingly, even some modern commentators. It will be interesting to determine whether Scottish women adhered to these expectations or whether they were essentially more independent than history has acknowledged. Finally, a study of crime during the Scottish Enlightenment will enable us to establish whether or not the 'peripheries' were exposed to what sociologists and subsequently historians have termed the 'civilising process'. Were contemporaries themselves aware that broad patterns of behaviour were undergoing significant change? In understanding this dimension we can assess the extent to which lowland females were exposed to the concept of the 'civilising process' and whether or not the authorities considered violent Scottish women to be a credible

---

[15] For further discussion see Whatley, *Industrial Revolution*, ch. ii; T. M. Devine, *The Scottish nation, 1700–2000*, London 1999, chs vi, viii; R. H. Campbell, *Scotland since 1707: the rise of an industrial society*, Edinburgh 1985; A. Slaven, *The development of the west of Scotland: 1750–1960*, London 1975; H. Hamilton, *An economic history of Scotland in the eighteenth century*, Oxford 1963; and S. G. E. Lythe and J. Butt, *An economic history of modern Scotland, 1100–1939*, Glasgow 1975.
[16] For women's participation in the development of the Scottish economy see C. A. Whatley, 'Women and the economic transformation of Scotland, c.1740–1830', *SESH* xiv (1994), 19–40.

threat to the moral and social order of the state during a period of rapid socio-economic, political and cultural change. Moreover the reaction of the gentry and forces of order also tell us much about how far advanced any potential 'civilising process' may have been – a process whose early phases Norbert Elias saw as a learned realisation that civilisation was a 'counterconcept to another stage of society, barbarism'.[17] This is especially pertinent since Elias argued that 'extremely gentle and comparatively considerate way(s) of correction' had proved ultimately more effective in Europe than 'insults, mockery or any threat of outward physical violence'.[18] Thus the persistence of physical violence as a means of persuading individuals to undergo moral change would indicate that a 'civilising process' was still at a comparatively early stage.

---

[17] N. Elias, *The civilizing process: the history of manners and state formation and civilization*, trans. E. Jephcott, Oxford 1994, 41.
[18] Ibid. 70.

1

Scottish Crime and Scottish Women: Undiscovered Voices and Undiscovered Vices?

'That Providence designed women for a state of dependence, and consequently of submission, I cannot doubt, when I consider their timidity of temper, their tenderness of make, the many comforts and even necessaries of life which they are unable to procure without our aid, their evident want of our protection upon a thousand occasions, their incessant study, at every age, in every state, by every means, to engage our attention, and insure our regard.'[1]

'[Women by their nature are] weake, fraile, impacient, feble and foolishe: and experience hath declared them to be vnconstant, variable, cruell and lacking in the spirit of counsel and regiment.'[2]

This chapter sets out the historiographical context for the study of Scottish female criminality between 1750 and 1815. Although research on early modern Scottish women is more advanced than is often assumed, there is an unquestionable dearth of analysis relating to the eighteenth-century period, the time-frame covered by this book. This *lacuna* has been compounded by a distinct lack of work carried out on Scottish deviance, across historical periods and regardless of gender. Clearly, by comparison, historians south of the border (and arguably those elsewhere) have gone much further in dealing with the issues of gender and crime in the pre-modern period.

By outlining the important work that has been carried out on women in early modern times in Scotland and more especially England, this commentary will provide the conceptual and contextual framework for the chapters which follow. Along the way, this section examines the research carried out on gendered deviance, and in particular analyses relating to criminal women. By doing so, the reader will appreciate why this book makes a new contribution to Scottish historiography. This section also exemplifies how this research illuminates and radically challenges much of what is already known about female deviance in the wider historiographical sphere of criminal history, both in Britain and beyond.

The historiography relating to women's history in the pre-modern period

---

[1] Dr James Fordyce, *The character and conduct of the female sex*, London 1776, 40.
[2] Extract from John Knox, 'The first blast of the trumpet against the monstrous regiment of women' (1558), taken from, E. Arber (ed.), *The English scholar's library of old and modern works*, no. ii, London 1895, 12.

has often focused on the eighteenth century and the introduction of the notion of 'separate spheres'. This concept emphasised that the experiences of men and women were starkly different. Based on their gender-defined proclivities and aptitudes, men largely participated in the public 'sphere' of work, whilst women remained in the private 'sphere' of the home.[3] Recent scholarship, however, has indicated that this ideology was not constructed during the eighteenth century, but rather its foundations can be traced back as far as late medieval times. Christine Peters, for instance, suggests that in the period after 1450 there was a general consensus about gender norms. Across Britain women were assumed to be weaker than men, both emotionally and physically. This assumption reinforced the existing patriarchy within society. As women were considered less rational than their male counterparts, it was necessary that they submitted to male authority. In turn, husbands, fathers and masters would supervise and control the irrational behaviour of women, enabling their female charges to become socially submissive and morally sound.[4]

What is significant about the eighteenth-century, however, is that historians agree that it was a time during which notions of gendered identities became sharper and more defined.[5] The perceived 'threat' of assertive women principally stemmed from the economic sector during the industrial revolution. Men feared that as women were cheaper to employ and were readily available in large numbers, they would begin to oust their male counterparts from the workplace. This led to a heightening of gender differences which is evident in contemporary literature and conduct material, such as chapbooks.[6] A particular emphasis on the anatomical and emotional disparities between men and women seemingly justified and validated commentaries which encouraged the subordination of women and their marginalisation from 'public' life.[7] As the opening quotation to this chapter illustrates, and as Hannah Barker and Elaine Chalus describe, 'With untiring regularity and varying degrees of polemic, authors reminded women of their subordinate status and attempted to mould them into a static image of idealised femininity – modest, chaste, pious, and passively domestic.'[8]

It would seem that the accelerated promotion of this 'ideology of domes-

---

[3] For further discussion see R. B. Shoemaker, *Gender in English society, 1650–1850: the emergence of separate spheres*, Harlow 1998.
[4] See C. Peters, *Women in early modern Britain, 1450–1640*, Basingstoke 2004, 1–2. See also Shoemaker, *Gender in English society*, 9–10, 308–13.
[5] See Shoemaker, *Gender in English society*, 6, 56–8.
[6] Ibid. 56–8. See also J. Eales, *Women in early modern England, 1500–1700*, London 1998, 30, and B. Hill, *Eighteenth-century women: an anthology*, London 1984, 16–24.
[7] Shoemaker, *Gender in English society*, ch. iii and pp. 85–6. See also Eales, *Women in early modern England*, 3.
[8] H. Barker and E. Chalus, 'Introduction', to H. Barker and E. Chalus (eds), *Gender in eighteenth-century England: roles, representations and responsibilities*, London–New York 1997, 2.

ticity' in the eighteenth century gave society a theoretical mechanism with which to control the actions of women. By implication, however, the perceived need for this ideology in the first place indicates that patriarchal authority felt threatened at this time by women who were becoming more assertive and autonomous and who were increasingly willing to abandon their 'domestic' duties in favour of more independent interaction with the outside world. Certainly, there is much evidence to support this hypothesis, and much of the historiography relating to the history of English women in the pre-modern period does indeed testify to women's willingness to partici-pate in 'public' life and to ignore the prescribed roles assigned to them.[9]

Despite the increasing prominence of notions of rigid gender difference and rigid gender roles in the eighteenth century, it is evident that many English women were not averse to 'active agency' either before or after 1700.[10] Research carried out on women's work in England during the pre-modern period, for instance, has indicated the substantial contribution that women made to the industrial progress of the country at that time, despite the limitations placed on their employment such as constrained status and low pay.[11] This participation was not solely limited to women from the lower orders as has often been assumed, but was spread across class boundaries as women worked in a variety of different trades and occupations, both within the home and outside it; with or without male support.[12]

Before 1800, in the legal sphere too, despite the visible and prescribed constraints on women's participation, they were still able (on occasion) to make their voices heard. This has been evidenced most clearly in the work of Laura Gowing and Amy Erickson on slander and property respectively in early modern England, but has been illustrated by other historians in more

---

9 See, for instance, the references in nn. 10–14 below.

10 For general discussion of this point see Eales, *Women in early modern England*, 14–15.

11 For a survey of much of the recent historiography on women and the urban economy see R. Sweet, 'Introduction', to R. Sweet and P. Lane (eds), *Women and urban life in eighteenth-century England: 'on the town'*, Aldershot 2003, 2, 4–6, 8–11. In the same volume see also C. Wiskin, 'Urban businesswomen in eighteenth-century England', at pp. 87–110, and H. Barker and K. Harvey, 'Women entrepreneurs and urban expansion: Manchester, 1760–1820', at pp. 111–30. See also Eales, *Women in early modern England*, 73–85; S. Mendelson and P. Crawford, *Women in early modern England, 1550–1720*, Oxford 1998, ch. v and p. 435; Shoemaker, *Gender in English society*, ch. v; K. Honeyman, *Women, gender and industrialisation in England, 1700–1870*, Basingstoke 2000, chs ii-vii and pp. 12–13, 140–2; I. Pinchbeck, *Women workers and the Industrial Revolution, 1750–1850*, London 1981; and A. Clark, *Working life of women in the seventeenth century*, 3rd edn, London 1992.

12 See, for instance, P. Sharpe, *Adapting to capitalism: working women in the English economy, 1700–1850*, Basingstoke 1996; A. Laurence, *Women in England, 1500–1760: a social history*, London 1994, esp. chs viii, ix; M. Prior, 'Women and the urban economy: Oxford, 1500–1800', in M. Prior (ed.), *Women in English society, 1500–1800*, London 1985, 93–117; B. Hill, *Women, work and sexual politics in eighteenth-century England*, Oxford 1989, chs iii–ix and pp. 259–60; M. R. Hunt, *The middling sort: commerce, gender and the family, 1680–1780*, Berkeley–London 1996; and Barker and Chalus, 'Introduction', 10–15.

13

general commentaries on the experience of women south of the border after 1600.[13] In terms of communal life in a broader sense, research has also indicated the involvement of English women in episodes where they 'overtly' promoted and defended personal interests, in debates over religious, civic and political issues, and in a wide range of other spheres of interest (ideologically at least) ascribed to men.[14]

Although we should not imagine that women in England were wholly integrated into 'public' life before 1800 or enjoyed the same status, opportunities and rewards as their male counterparts, it is clear none the less that notions of 'separate spheres' and the subordination of women into the 'private' domain of the household have been exaggerated. Certainly more work needs to be done by historians to uncover the experiences of women in early modern England, especially in the rural milieu and in relation to unmarried women. However, it seems we can conclude that just as not all men of the early modern period were necessarily power-wielding tyrants (as implied by contemporary chap-books, novels and conduct books), so not all women were shy, retiring and wholly dependent on the 'other' sex for their survival either. As Hannah Barker and Elaine Chalus point out, 'eighteenth-century women did not see notions of public and private as fixed, but fluid. Indeed, they were defined idiosyncratically, according to individual and situation, and varied even among members of the same family'.[15] Clearly, the notion of 'separate spheres' is inadequate in describing the 'public' and 'domestic' lives of women in pre-modern England.

The history of Scottish women in the period before 1850 has largely been neglected by scholars. As Sîan Reynolds points out, those writing on women's history have largely ignored Scotland. Those writing on Scottish history, moreover, have also largely ignored women.[16] Elizabeth Ewan accentuates

---

13 See L. Gowing, *Domestic dangers: women, words and sex in early modern London*, Oxford 1996, and A.L. Erickson, *Women and property in early modern England*, London 1993. See also T. Stretton, *Women waging law in Elizabethan England*, Cambridge 1998; Laurence, *Women in England*, chs xv, xvii; Shoemaker, *Gender in English society*, ch. vii; Eales, *Women in early modern England*, 14–15; M. Finn, 'Women, consumption and coveture in England', *HJ* xxxix (1996), 703–22; C. Churches, 'Women and property in early modern England: a case study', *SH* xxiii (1998), 165–80; and Sweet, 'Introduction', 3.

14 See, for instance, R. A. Houlbrooke, 'Women's social life and common action in England from the fifteenth century to the eve of civil war', *C&C* i (1986), 171–89; J. Bohstedt, 'Gender, household and community politics: women in English riots, 1790–1810', *P&P* cxx (1988), 88–122; Laurence, *Women in England*, esp. chs xiii, xvi; Eales, *Women in early modern England*, 14–15, 112; Shoemaker, *Gender in English society*, chs vi, vii; Mendelson and Crawford, *Women in early modern England*, 429; Sweet, 'Introduction', 10–12, 15–20; and E. Chalus, 'The rag plot: the politics of influence in Oxford, 1754', in Sweet and Lane, *Women and urban life*, 43–64.

15 Barker and Chalus, 'Introduction', 22. For further discussion of this see also Shoemaker, *Gender in English society*, ch. viii.

16 See S. Reynolds, 'Historiography and gender: Scottish and international dimensions', in T. Brotherstone, D. Simonton and O. Walsh (eds), *Gendering Scottish history: an inter-*

this point when she explains how Scottish history has been largely 'masculinised' by historians:

> Popular ideas about Scottish history tend to be masculine in character. Military prowess is glorified in such popular heroes as William Wallace, Robert Bruce and Rob Roy. Scotland's pride in its traditional heavy industry emphasises male muscular strength, while the radicalism of Red Clydeside is identified mainly with the skilled male workforce. Popular Scottish history has few strong female figures, resulting in the stereotyped view of women as either victims or nurturers, as passive and not active historical actors, and therefore unworthy of attention.[17]

Although Ewan may have exaggerated somewhat, it is still indisputable that Scottish historiography has been skewed towards the male experience, and that women's history has been largely marginalised or 'ghettoised'. Furthermore, of the research that has been carried out on Scottish women, much of it concentrates on either the very early experiences of women (particularly queens and notable noblewomen of the medieval period) or on the more industrialised and urban-based histories of women in the nineteenth and twentieth centuries.[18] As a result of this limited approach, the eighteenth century has suffered from a real dearth of historical enquiry where women are concerned; and one of the aims of this book is to address this gaping historiographical hole.[19]

Despite the undoubted lack of attention given to eighteenth-century

---

national approach, Glasgow 2000, 4. It is significant that the most celebrated and widely used books on Scottish history which pertain to the eighteenth-century period fail to deal with the experience of women in any substantial or meaningful way. See, for instance, Devine, *The Scottish nation*; M. Lynch, *Scotland: a new history*, London 1992; T. C. Smout, *A history of the Scottish people, 1560–1830*, London 1969; W. Ferguson, *Scotland 1689 to the present*, Edinburgh 1987; and to a lesser extent D. Allan, *Scotland in the eighteenth century: union and Enlightenment*, Harlow 2002. The exception is C. A. Whatley, *Scottish society, 1707–1820: beyond Jacobitism, towards industrialisation*, Manchester 2000.

[17] E. Ewan, 'A realm of one's own? The place of medieval and early modern women in Scottish history', in Brotherstone, Simonton and Walsh, *Gendering Scottish history*, 27.

[18] See, for example, the historiographical outlines provided by S. Reynolds, 'Historiography and gender: Scottish and international dimensions' (pp. 1–18), Ewan, 'A realm of one's own' (pp. 19–36) and J. McDermid, 'Missing persons? Women in modern Scottish history' (pp. 37–45), in Brotherstone, Simonton and Walsh, *Gendering Scottish history*. See also the historiographical commentaries provided by E. Ewan and M. M. Meikle, 'Introduction: a monstrous regiment of women', in E. Ewan and M. M. Meikle (eds), *Women in Scotland, c. 1100–c. 1750*, East Lothian 1999, pp. xix–xxx, and J. Hendry, 'Snug in the asylum of taciturnity: women's history in Scotland', in I. Donnachie and C. Whatley (eds), *The manufacture of Scottish history*, Edinburgh 1992, 125–42.

[19] One exception to the dearth of research carried out in relation to the eighteenth century is the work of Leah Leneman. See, for example, her *Alienated affections: the Scottish experience of divorce and separation, 1684–1830*, Edinburgh 1998, and R. Mitchison and L. Leneman, *Sexuality and social control: Scotland, 1660–1780*, Oxford 1989.

women by historians, enough material exists to enable general and tentative conclusions to be drawn about Scottish women's lives in the pre-1850 period. The extent to which ideological notions and gendered 'ideals' were widely produced, received and assimilated in post-Reformation Scotland is as yet difficult to ascertain, although it is clear that some individuals may well have supported the type of contention provided by John Knox in the second opening quotation to this chapter.

What is clearer still, however, is that Scottish women did not restrict their lives solely to the domestic sphere. Rather, they mirrored the experiences of their English counterparts. Work by John Finlay and Winifred Coutts, for example, shows that Scottish women regularly participated enthusiastically in the legal process in the sixteenth and seventeenth centuries.[20] In religious, political and civic affairs too, studies have shown that Scottish women were certainly not averse to demonstrations of gendered opinion via popular action, radicalism and protest in the early modern period, arguably on a scale more prolonged and intensive than their English counterparts.[21] The reasons for this will be explored in chapter 6 and in the conclusion to this volume.

It is in the world of work, however, that the most substantial research has been carried out into women's participation in 'public' life in Scotland before 1850. Elizabeth Sanderson's monograph *Women and work in eighteenth-century Edinburgh* provides a fascinating insight into how lowland women contributed to industrial progress in Scotland. As she describes it, 'far from being cocooned in a domestic world, women from all kinds of backgrounds, single, married and widowed, were actively operating in the same world as their male counterparts'.[22] Much of the evidence that Sanderson provides complements what is known about women's experience south of the border during this period. In addition, her emphasis on the significant contribution of women to the growth of the Scottish economy is verified and substantiated by the broader work of Robert Houston and Christopher Whatley, among others.[23]

---

[20] See, for instance, J. Finlay, 'Women and legal representation in early sixteenth century Scotland', and W. Coutts, 'Wife and widow: the evidence of testaments and marriage contracts c. 1600', in Ewan and Meikle, *Women in Scotland*, 165–75, 176–86.

[21] See, for instance, R. A. Houston, 'Women in the economy and society of Scotland, 1500–1800', in R. A. Houston and I. D. Whyte (eds), *Scottish society, 1500–1800*, Cambridge 1989, 118–47; M. F. Graham, 'Women and the church courts in Reformation-era Scotland', in Ewan and Meikle, *Women in Scotland*, 187–200; Logue, *Popular disturbances*, 36, 87, 106, 199–203; C. A. Whatley, 'How tame were the Scottish lowlanders during the eighteenth century?', in T. M. Devine (ed.), *Conflict and stability in Scottish society, 1700–1850*, Edinburgh 1990, 5, 8, 13, 19; and Whatley, *Scottish society*, esp. ch. v.

[22] E. C. Sanderson, *Women and work in eighteenth-century Edinburgh*, London 1996, 2.

[23] See Houston, 'Women in the economy and society of Scotland', 120–6; Whatley, 'Women and economic transformation', 19–40; and E. Ewan, '"For whatever ales ye": women as consumers and producers in late medieval Scottish towns', A. J. Mann, 'Embroidery to enterprise: the role of women in the book trade of early modern Scotland', and H. Dingwall, 'The power behind the merchant? Women and the economy in late seventeenth-century Edinburgh', in Ewan and Meikle, *Women in Scotland*, 125–36, 137–51, 152–64.

One of the most significant implications of Sanderson's work is her tenta-tive suggestion that in contrast to the experience south of the border, Scot-tish women may have encountered few barriers to entering the world of work. This suggests that in Scotland fewer restrictions were placed on women's lives. Scottish women may have enjoyed a more active and varied experience than women elsewhere. By implication, they may as a result have been more exposed to crime and criminal ventures. Sanderson's contention is largely borne out by Whatley's work on the contribution of women to Scotland's industrial revolution. He argues that between 1740 and 1830 women (and children) made a crucial contribution to the transformation of Scotland's economy. Their impact was arguably more substantial than was experienced in England and Wales at that time.[24] Whatley explains this as resulting from the technological backwardness of Scottish industry and the neces-sary requirements of cost effective production. Scottish women were quite capable of operating the basic machinery and, more important, they were cheap to employ. This was because women's wages were seen as being merely supplementary to those of their male relations.

The longstanding involvement of Scottish women in overt civic action and popular protest, coupled with the apparent ease with which they partici-pated in the economic sphere, appears to set Scottish women considerably apart from their English counterparts during the pre-modern period. These differences, yet to be fully substantiated and understood in any great detail, suggest that the experiences of women during the eighteenth-century period may have been far from uniform and homogenous, on either a local, regional or national level.

For the history of crime, the type of comparative analysis alluded to above is harder to achieve. Although the field of criminal history, and women's involvement in it, has come a long way since the publication of John Beattie's pioneering article in 1975, little of the research carried out relates to the Scot-tish experience of deviant behaviour.[25] Despite the fact that much of the work done on crime north of the border has tended to focus on female criminality, most of this has been limited to discussion of the types of crimes tradition-ally associated with women, namely witchcraft and infanticide.[26] Scholars have gone little further than this, and save for a few articles on punishment practices and general survey pieces on the potential for studying Scottish crime in the period after 1747, little has been achieved.[27] Arguably, whilst it

---

[24] Whatley, 'Women and economic transformation', 35.

[25] J. M. Beattie, 'The criminality of women in eighteenth-century England', *JSH* viii (1975), 80–116.

[26] See C. Larner, *Enemies of God: the witch-hunt in Scotland*, London 1981; Symonds, *Weep not for me*; and A.-M. Kilday, 'Maternal monsters: murdering mothers in south-west Scot-land, 1750–1815', and L. Abrams, 'From demon to victim: the infanticidal mother in Shetland, 1699–1802', in Y. G. Brown and R. Ferguson (eds), *Twisted sisters: women, crime and deviance in Scotland since 1400*, East Linton 2002, 156–79, 180–203.

[27] It is interesting to note that save for two essays on infanticide and the one on witch-

is certainly refreshing to see that the history of female criminality is receiving the attention of scholars before that of male, it is none the less remarkable that there is no historiography of male criminality, in a country traditionally associated with warfare, aggression and displays of masculine power.

As well as addressing this 'additional' gap in the historiography of Scotland and the historiography of Scottish women this book will do more. Given that Scottish women were seemingly able to participate in a wide variety of socio-economic, cultural and political activities during the pre-modern period, this volume will test whether further evidence of the seemingly more 'militant' nature of Scottish women can be gleaned from a study of their criminal behaviour.

In England (and arguably further afield), research into the history of crime has gone much further than that north of the border.[28] Despite this heightened level of interest, the conclusions that historians have derived from their research have served to marginalise and discount the activities of criminal women, and as result female deviance has been largely hidden from what is known about the broad brush history of crime.[29]

The first conclusion that historians have made regarding female criminality, is that, throughout history, English women, when compared with English men, were rarely involved in criminal activity. In all categories of offences, statistics reflect the paucity of women's participation.[30] The apparent absence

craft in the edited collection *Twisted sisters*, the other articles are more to do with general female rebelliousness and nonconformity rather than aspects of their unlawful criminality. In addition, the texts cited in n. 16 above generally fail to recognise the importance of crime in their analyses. For other work on Scottish crime see Logue, *Popular disturbances*; M. M. Stewart, '"In durance vile": crime and punishment in seventeenth- and eighteenth-century records of Dumfries', *Scottish Archives: The Journal of the Scottish Records Association* i (1995), 63–74; J. G. Harrison, 'Women and the branks in Stirling, c. 1600–c. 1730', *SESH* xviii (1998), 114–31; Donnachie, '"The darker side"', 5–24; and M.A. Crowther, 'Criminal precognitions and their value for the historian', *Scottish Archives: The Journal of the Scottish Records Association* i (1995), 75–84.

[28] For studies of pre-modern crime beyond England see, for instance, J. R. Ruff, *Violence in early modern Europe, 1500–1800*, Cambridge 2001; D. J. V. Jones, *Crime in nineteenth century Wales*, Cardiff 1992; B. Henry, *Dublin hanged: crime, law enforcement and punishment in late eighteenth-century Dublin*, Dublin 1994; U. Rublack, *The crimes of women in early modern Germany*, Oxford 1999; C. Daniels and M.V. Kennedy (eds), *Over the threshold: intimate violence in early America*, London–New York 1999; N. E. Hull, *Female felons: women and serious crime in colonial Massachusetts*, Urbana–Chicago 1987; A. Lachance, 'Women and crime in Canada in the early eighteenth century, 1712–1759', in L. A. Knafla (ed.), *Crime and criminal justice in Europe and Canada*, Ontario 1981, 157–77.

[29] For a general outline and discussion of the historiography on crime and gender in England see M. L. Arnot and C. Usborne, 'Why gender and crime? Aspects of an international debate', in M. L. Arnot and C. Usborne (eds), *Gender and crime in modern Europe*, London 1999, 1–43.

[30] See, for instance, Beattie, 'The criminality of women', 80; C. Emsley, *Crime and society in England, 1750–1900*, London 1996, 152; J. A. Sharpe, *Crime in early modern England, 1550–1750*, Harlow 1999, 154; P. Lawson, 'Patriarchy, crime and the courts: the criminality of women in late Tudor and early Stuart England', in G. T. Smith, A. N. May and

of deviant women, of course, fits in nicely with traditionally gendered notions of how women in the pre-modern period were supposed to behave. Yet as we have seen, it was not impossible for women in early modern England to step outside the boundaries of what was considered to be 'acceptable' behaviour. If a woman did breach accepted gender norms through criminality at this time, she was 'doubly damned' and was more likely to be viewed as a deviant than as a criminal, because not only was she simply breaking the law, but she was also betraying the 'notional' qualities of her sex.[31] As David Taylor explains

> Discussions of female criminality were profoundly influenced by the dominant gender ideologies of the day. Although the male criminal was a deviant figure, much of his behaviour was consistent with accepted, if not wholly acceptable, male characteristics. Men were expected to be physically strong and brave ... A female criminal was more likely to be seen as a deviant, breaching strongly held beliefs about the nature of femininity, than her male counterpart. Women were seen to have peculiar moral qualities and responsibilities that did not fall on men.[32]

Women's crimes, though rare, regularly came to be regarded as 'unnatural' rather than 'criminal', and as a result much of the research carried out on felonious women focused on offences which were considered 'abnormal' or deviant' and therefore more stereotypically female: witchcraft, scolding, infanticide and prostitution, for example.[33] Popular literature that was widely available in the pre-modern period distinguished between criminal and deviant behaviour. Criminal activity was regular law-breaking. Deviant behaviour, according to early modern pamphlets, was also unlawful, but it was additionally associated with sin and immorality. As women were not thought to have the characteristics necessary for criminal behaviour, such as assertiveness and bravado, their acts of illegality had to have an alternative

S. Devereaux (eds), *Criminal justice in the old world and the new: essays in honour of J. M. Beattie*, Toronto 1998, 21; and G. Walker and J. Kermode, 'Introduction', to J. Kermode and G. Walker (eds), *Women, crime and the courts in early modern England*, London 1994, 4.

[31] See Lawson, 'Patriarchy, crime and the courts', 18, 45–6; J. Briggs and others, *Crime and punishment in England: an introductory history*, London 1999, 183; Walker and Kermode, 'Introduction', 16; and especially S. Clark, *Women and crime in the street literature of early modern England*, Basingstoke 2003, pp. ix, 52–3, as well as L. Zedner, *Women, crime and custody in Victorian England*, Oxford 1991, 2 and ch. i.

[32] D. Taylor, *Crime, policing and punishment in England, 1750–1914*, Basingstoke 1998, 59.

[33] See Sharpe, *Crime in early modern England*, 157–9; J. A. Sharpe, *English witchcraft, 1560–1736*, London 2003; M. Ingram, '"Scolding women cucked or washed": a crisis in gender relations in early modern England?', in Kermode and Walker, *Women, crime and the courts*, 48–80; M. Jackson, *New-born child murder: women, illegitimacy and the courts in eighteenth-century England*, Manchester 1996; and T. Henderson, *Disorderly women in eighteenth-century London: prostitution and control in the metropolis, 1730–1830*, London 1999.

explanation. Men, as Taylor points out, came to be associated with crime as it emphasised the traits of masculinity. Women, on the other hand, were said to be deviant rather than criminal, as deviancy reflected characteristics such as irrationality and impressionability, thought to be key elements of the female psyche.[34]

For this reason women have been largely rejected from the analysis of more mainstream, regular or stereotypically 'masculine' offences such as homicide, assault or violent theft. As these crimes involved the use of overt aggression (which was not an accepted characteristic of the 'gentler' sex) they were assumed to be irrelevant to women's experiences of unlawful behaviour in the pre-modern period.

The belief in women's potential for innate deviance was propounded vociferously in the early modern period, especially in popular literature.[35] Social commentators regarded deviant women as threatening, but at the same time the notion that women were subordinate, timid creatures created something of a dichotomy in contemporary ideological thinking.[36] By limiting the discussion of female criminality to more deviant or 'sinful' offences, contemporaries made women more morally responsible than men, but less criminally culpable. This insinuated that for women to perpetrate crimes other than 'unnatural' offences, they must have been influenced by male superiors when doing so.[37] The subordinate position of women meant that it was believed that they could not be criminal in their own right and for their own ends, but only when coerced by men.

This gendered notion of criminal activity found in popular literature was matched in the legal sphere by the notion of *feme covert*. This convention stated that a wife could not be held responsible for her own criminal activity if she had committed the offence in the presence of her husband. This concept suggests that some women may have received more lenient treatment from the courts compared to their male counterparts.[38] However, not all indicted female criminals were married and, in any case, the extent to which the notion of *feme covert* applied in practice (either in England or elsewhere) is, as yet,

---

[34] For further discussion see Clark, *Street literature*, and J. Wiltenberg, *Disorderly women and female power in the street literature of early modern England and Germany*, Charlottesville, VA–London 1992.

[35] See Wiltenberg, *Disorderly women*, 8, 253–5.

[36] Clark, *Women and crime*, 41, 52; Arnot and Usborne, 'Why gender and crime?', 27; and Walker, *Crime, gender and social order*, 83.

[37] See, for instance, Walker and Kermode, 'Introduction', 6, and C. Z. Wiener, 'Sex roles and crime in late Elizabethan Hertfordshire', *JSH* viii (1975), 38–60.

[38] For further discussion of the notion of gendered leniency see P. King, *Crime, justice and discretion in England, 1740–1820*, Oxford 2000, 199–207; C. B. Herrup, *The common peace: participation and the criminal law in seventeenth-century England*, Cambridge 1987, 118, 150–1; P. King, 'Gender, crime and justice in late eighteenth- and early nineteenth-century England', in Arnot and Usborne, *Gender and crime*, 44–74; and M. Wiener, *Men of blood: violence, manliness and criminal justice in Victorian England*, Cambridge 2004, 124–34.

difficult to ascertain.[39] What is indisputable, however, is that the legal principle of *feme covert* has greatly contributed to the belief that female criminal activity was marginal, insignificant and unimportant. The assumption that women could not be criminally responsible has resulted in the portrayal of women either as remote, subsidiary characters in criminal activity committed by men, or, more commonly, as the victims of male wrongdoing.[40]

The assumption of women's limited criminality has meant that historians have paid scant attention to violent female behaviour. As Martin Wiener explains

> A mass of scientific study has established that from birth, males on average tend to be more aggressive, restless and risk-taking than females, and in general less amenable to socialization ... with greater physical strength combined with greater aggressiveness, men are and always have been far more seriously violent than women. ... It is in fact a cliché of criminology that violent criminals are far more likely to be male than female.[41]

Certainly, it is clear from the assorted evidence that, statistically at least, women were less often indicted for violent offences than men.[42] None the less, this scarcely renders the study of female violence anomalous and insignificant.

Recent work by scholars such as Vanessa McMahon and Garthine Walker, for instance, illustrates convincingly that women in early modern England were far from passive.[43] Just as women failed to conform to 'gendered roles'

---

[39] The principle of *feme covert* seems never to have applied in Scotland: Baron D. Hume, *Commentaries on the laws of Scotland, respecting crimes*, i, ii, Edinburgh 1797, 1844 edn, repr. 1986, ch. i at pp. 47–9. For further discussion of doubts over the applicability of this principle see also Arnot and Usborne, 'Why gender and crime?', 9, and Shoemaker, *Gender in English society*, 296–7.

[40] Historians such as Beattie and Sharpe, for instance, maintain that women commonly acted as decoys and look-outs during instances of male criminality and were rarely directly involved: Beattie, 'The criminality of women', 90; Sharpe, *Crime in early modern England*, 155. For studies on women as the victims of crime see A. Clark, *Women's silence, men's violence: sexual assault in England, 1770–1845*, London–NY 1987; S. D'Cruze, *Crimes of outrage: sex, violence and Victorian working women*, London 1998; S. D'Cruze (ed.), *Everyday violence in Britain, 1850–1950: gender and class*, Harlow 2000; E. A. Stanko, *Everyday violence: how women and men experienced sexual and physical danger*, London 1990; Briggs and others, *Crime and punishment in England*, 134–9, 183–5; Emsley, *Crime and society in England*, 158–62; and F. McLynn, *Crime and punishment in eighteenth-century England*, London 1989, ch. vi.

[41] Wiener, *Men of blood*, 1.

[42] See G. Morgan and P. Rushton, *Rogues, thieves and the rule of law: the problem of law enforcement in north-east England, 1718–1800*, London 1998, 97; King, *Crime, justice and discretion*, 196–7; McLynn, *Crime and punishment*, 128; Beattie, 'The criminality of women', 82; N. Castan, 'Criminals', in N. Z. Davis and A. Farge (eds), *A history of women in the west, III: Renaissance and Enlightenment paradoxes*, Cambridge, MA. 1993, 482, 486; Lawson, 'Patriarchy, crime and the courts', 23–4; and Wiener, 'Sex roles,' 42, 49.

[43] V. McMahon, *Murder in Shakespeare's England*, London–New York 2004; Walker, *Crime, gender and social order*.

in other aspects of their 'public' lives during this time, so women were also prepared to step outside the confines of femininity and behave in a violent, aggressive and unpredictable manner. In many instances women's violence was an act of self-defence for the protection of family interests. Of course, women were just as capable as men of being arbitrarily bad and bloodthirsty. Although much of the analysis of women's violence is its infancy and has largely been confined to episodes within the domestic sphere,[44] it is clear that the nature and effect of female violence (and attitudes to behaviour of that type) have many new things to tell us about the experiences of women in pre-modern times.

In an age when historians have given women back their autonomy in terms of socio-economic concerns, it is certainly timely for us to do the same in terms of the female criminal experience. It seems that historians have been more interested in explaining why women were largely absent from the criminal stage in the pre-modern period, rather than analysing what happened when women did break the law.[45] As a result of this bias, the history of women's criminality has been neglected and ignored, or it has been compartmental-ised to enable historians with their own agendas to mention a few types of offences stereotypically thought to represent female deviance.

Yet the evidence from this book, as well as other analyses, demonstrates that women were criminal, and that they participated in a wide range of offences, in just the same way as their male counterparts. In addition, rather than commit-ting crime solely at the behest of men, as was often believed to have been the case, women regularly behaved independently in their criminal endeavours throughout the pre-modern period. If female felons did find it necessary to participate in crime with others, it was usually with other women, and not necessarily with or at the request of male accomplices.[46] This counter-evidence shows that women cannot and should not be 'discounted' from criminal history solely on the grounds of the lower incidence of their involvement.

The dominant portrayal of women as victims in the historiography of crime is another factor which has also contributed to the marginalisation

[44] For this historiographical concentration on women's violence in the domestic sphere see the references in n. 43 above as well as Morgan and Rushton, *Rogues, thieves and the rule of law*, 112; McLynn, *Crime and punishment*, 117; and Beattie, 'The criminality of women', 83–4, 87–8.
[45] For studies explaining the lack of women's involvement in criminal activity see, for example, M. M. Feeley and D. L. Little, 'The vanishing female: the decline of women in the criminal process, 1687–1912', *Law and Society Review* xxv (1991), 719–57; M. Feeley, 'The decline of women in the criminal process: a comparative history', *Criminal Justice History: An International Annual* xv (1994), 235–74; Beattie, 'The criminality of women', esp. pp. 96–109; and Lawson, 'Patriarchy, crime and the courts', 32–57.
[46] See Beattie, 'The criminality of women', 80–96; Walker, *Crime, gender and social order*, esp. ch. iii; McLynn, *Crime and punishment*, esp. ch. vii; and M. Hunt, 'Wife beating, domesticity and women's independence in eighteenth-century London', *G&H* iv (1992), 22–3.

of female criminality in scholarly research and discussion. The suggestion of many feminist historians that the only role women played in criminal activity was as the victims of male criminals, has been largely misplaced, however.[47] For, surely, a more balanced and realistic feminist interpretation of criminal history would be to suggest that women could (on occasion) be just as empowered and thereby just as iniquitous as men. Again, evidence from the Scottish sphere, and to a lesser extent from elsewhere, suggests that this was almost certainly the case. Women habitually displayed overt aggression in perpetrating crime north of the border during the eighteenth century, as subsequent chapters will demonstrate.[48]

The evidence assessed in this volume suggests that for many women (both in Scotland and beyond), gendered notions of subordination, timidity and femininity may never have become wholly manifest. Alternatively, these concepts may simply have been interpreted differently, or perhaps they were deliberately ignored. Certainly, there was no significant difference in the penal treatment of Scottish women compared to their male counterparts. It would seem reasonable to suggest, therefore, that notions of 'gendered leniency', apparently common in England before 1850, were not so readily practised north of the Tweed at that time.[49] This evidence again points to the fact that women, and Scottish women and criminal enterprise in particular, are worthy of closer investigation.

---

[47] See the references in the latter part of n. 40 above.

[48] For further evidence of female aggression in the pre-modern period see McMahon, *Murder in Shakespeare's England*, esp. chs v, viii, ix; Walker, *Crime, gender and social order*, esp. chs iii, iv; Beattie, 'The criminality of women', 82–9; McLynn, *Crime and punishment*, 117–23; A. Finch, 'Women and violence in the later Middle Ages: the evidence of the officiality of Cerisy', *C&C* vii (1992), 29; Hunt, 'Wife beating', 22–3; Houlbrooke, 'Women's social life', 171–89; R. M. Dekker, 'Women in revolt: popular protest and its social basis in Holland in the seventeenth and eighteenth centuries', *Theory and Society* xvi (1987), 337–62; Bohstedt, 'Gender, household and community politics', 88–122; M.I. Thomas and J. Grimmett, *Women in protest, 1800–1850*, London 1982; and O. Hufton, 'Women and violence in early modern Europe', in F. Dieteren and E. Kloek (eds), *Writing women into history*, Amsterdam 1990, 76.

[49] See the references in n. 38 above. According to some English historians the more violent a female felon was, the less likely she was to attain mitigation of any sort from the legal process: King, 'Gender, crime and justice', 61–2; Morgan and Rushton, *Rogues, thieves and the rule of law*, 118–22; and Shoemaker, *Gender in English society*, 298. With the evidence of subsequent chapters showing the regular propensity for violence amongst Scottish women, this idea may go some way towards explaining why so few Scottish women managed to secure pardons or reduced forms of punishment during the eighteenth-century period: Kilday, 'Women and crime', ch. vi. It seems that if women overtly stepped outside the boundaries of acceptable behaviour, they were more likely to face the full force of the law. Whereas in England the need for mitigation was limited, due to the low incidence of violent female criminality, in Scotland a different picture emerges. As women north of the border were readily prepared to be violent, the Scottish judicial system showed female offenders little mercy. This suggests that ignorance of gendered norms and ideologies could only stretch so far. If Scottish women were unaware of convention, it did not necessarily follow that the Scottish law courts were too.

Traditional interpretations of female deviance have resulted in the ghetto-isation of women from the historiography of crime. In addition, most of the studies that have been carried out in this field have been largely metropolitan in nature, and this book suggests that a study of female criminality in the peripheries can provide new insights, conclusions and avenues for research. The evidence uncovered in this present analysis can help us to acknowledge the 'active agency' of women, and can encourage us to move away from the traditional centres of study to reveal a wholly different picture of crime and the nature of the female experience in pre-modern times.[50]

---

[50] Modern criminological studies of female deviance have gone much further than historians in reflecting the 'active agency' of criminal women, especially in relation to the twentieth century. See, for example, F. Heidensohn, *Women and crime*, Basingstoke 1996; C. Smart, *Women, crime and criminology: a feminist critique*, London–Boston 1977; P. Carlen and A. Worrall, *Gender, crime and justice*, Milton Keynes 1987; A. Morris, *Women, crime and criminal justice*, Oxford 1987; and S. K. Datesman and F. R. Scarpitti, *Women, crime and justice*, Oxford 1980.

2

Scots Law in the Age of Enlightenment

'[By the nineteenth century] the country was emerging from a state of utter lawlessness. Scotland was, at the beginning of the seventeenth century, the scene of endless crimes of violence. Murder, fireraising, theft, the maiming of cattle, rape, highway robbery, were matters of daily occurrence.'[1]

Lawlessness was perceived to be an endemic feature of early modern Scotland. As Bruce Lenman and Geoffrey Parker point out, 'The generally accepted picture of Scotland before 1707 is of a land ravaged by almost continuous political anarchy where might was right and justice was scarce.'[2] The basis for the belief that Scotland was a violent, lawless, crime-ridden society stemmed from a rudimentary understanding of the nature and provision of justice in the country during the early modern period. Historians, for instance, have illustrated how the elaborate and inherently complex court system in operation before the eighteenth century may have led 'outsiders' to perceive that private shows of force by the landed elite were more important to Scots than the distribution of even-handed justice.[3] In addition, the concept of the 'bloodfeud' (the practice by which a murderer offered 'compensation' to the family and friends of his victim), which loomed large throughout the country in the period up to 1700, may also have encouraged perceptions of the unique, unruly nature of Scottish justice as well as a belief in the 'destabilising potential' of its implementation at that time.[4]

Historical scholarship has also shown, however, that many of the 'traditional' assessments of Scotland as an ungovernable nation have been overdrawn. The nature of the court system in Scotland before the Union of 1707 was undoubtedly complex, but that did not necessarily mean that justice did not function and that the courts could not control the populace.[5] The nature of the bloodfeud, too, has been re-investigated, and found to be less violent

---

[1] G. W. T. Ormond, *The Lord Advocates of Scotland*, i, Edinburgh 1883, 89–90.
[2] Lenman and Parker, 'Crime and control', 13.
[3] See ibid; I. D. Whyte, *Scotland before the Industrial Revolution: an economic and social history*, c. 1050–c. 1750, Harlow 1995, 210–11; and especially Davies, 'The courts and the Scottish legal system', 120–3.
[4] See, for instance, J.W. Cairns, 'Historical introduction', in K. Reid and R. Zimmermann (eds), *A history of private law in Scotland*, II: *Obligations*, Oxford 2000, 47.
[5] See, for instance, Davies, 'The courts and the Scottish legal system', 120–54, and Cairns, 'Historical introduction', 14–184.

than first assumed; this was more a tool for negotiation and compromise than revenge and 'bloody' restitution.[6]

In the light of this 'revisionist' approach to the history of Scottish criminal justice, the aim of this chapter is to examine the provision of justice and the law in the pre-modern period and, more specifically, to investigate how this provision changed against the backdrop of the socio-political and socio-cultural shifts that took place in Scotland over the course of the eighteenth century. First I will look at the provision of justice in the pre-1700 period, to demonstrate the foundations for the changes that were to follow. I will then go on to determine the extent of change caused by the Union of 1707 and the Enlightenment, paying particular attention to the implementation of the Heritable Jurisdictions Act of 1747, and the implications this had for Scotland's legal provision during the next 150 years. I will then look more specifically at the justice meted out at the Court of Justiciary, the institution which has provided the bulk of the source material and primary evidence used in this work. By setting out how cases were brought to trial at the Justiciary Court, and illustrating the trial procedure that followed, this chapter provides a legal and methodological framework for the analyses contained in the five subsequent chapters, which deal with the perpetration of violent offences by Scottish women between 1750 and 1815.

Scotland hosted a fairly complex judicial system before 1700. Multiple jurisdictions (based on geographical boundaries as well as legal rights) were in operation. Specifically, south of the Forth, as in the Highlands, authority over criminal matters was largely the preserve of clan chiefs until 1747.[7] Land and kinship ties were no less important to legal authorities in the Lowlands, however, as many jurisdictions were granted on the basis of territorial ownership and others were held in perpetuity by hereditary right.[8] It is clear that in pre-modern Scotland judicial power was either inherited or bought.

Despite the 'outward' complexities of the court system and the potential for corruption that existed therein, judicial provision was still relatively coherent and commonly available in lowland Scotland during the early modern period.[9] A growing emphasis on litigation rather than retribution from the end of the sixteenth century onwards, as the bloodfeud transferred to the courtroom,

6   See J. Wormald, 'Bloodfeud, kindred and government in early modern Scotland', P&P lxxxvii (1980), 54–97; K. Brown, Bloodfeud in Scotland, 1573–1625: violence, justice and politics in early modern society, Edinburgh 1986; and Wasser, 'Violence and the central criminal courts', 4–7.
7   For further detailed discussion see Smout, A history of the Scottish people, ch. vix; Davies, 'The courts and the Scottish legal system', 120–54; Whyte, Scotland before the Industrial Revolution, 210–18; and Cairns, 'Historical introduction', 14–184.
8   See J.W. Brodie-Innes, 'Some outstanding differences between English and Scots law, III: The origins and the courts of law', JR xxvii (1915), 178, and G. Donaldson, 'The legal profession in Scottish society in the sixteenth and seventeenth centuries', JR n.s. xxi (1976), 1–2, 9–12, 16–17.
9   See n. 7 above.

resulted in the business of the Scottish courts increasing in measure from that time.[10] The Scottish legal system tended to be founded more on custom and convention than the sort of stringent statutory codification identified with its English counterpart. Consequently, when criminal matters were brought to court during this early period, they were instances of negotiation between the parties involved, rather than the kind of 'trial-based' procedure with which we are more familiar today.[11] As Bruce Lenman and Geoffrey Parker point out, in pre-Union Scotland 'keeping the peace was seen as more important than establishing guilt and disciplining offenders'.[12]

According to Stephen Davies, there were at least ten different types of court in operation in Scotland before 1747.[13] It is not necessary to elaborate upon all of these jurisdictions in any great detail, as many of them are not pertinent to the period under study in this volume. The Court of Justiciary will be dealt with in more detail later, but first it is necessary to provide a brief outline of some of the other jurisdictions that dealt with crime and deviant behaviour in pre-modern Scotland.

One of the most potentially powerful agents of discipline in Scotland during the early modern period was the Sheriff Court, which was established to represent the jurisdiction of the monarch in local areas. Sheriff Courts and their officials had a wide remit in criminal matters, but typically they could not try treason cases or the 'four pleas of the crown' (murder, rape, robbery and arson), which were reserved for higher judicial authorities. Despite its increasing ascendancy in Scottish legal affairs over the eighteenth and nineteenth centuries, before 1747 the Sheriff Court was limited in its development and control of the Scottish populace, due to the hereditary nature of its offices. By preserving the basis of its personnel in this way, the Sheriff Court remained largely independent of centralised governmental control. As a result, rather than coming to dominate the legal or judicial sphere at that time, it remained just one of a number of courts vying for business in the early modern period.[14]

Amongst these other institutions were the church courts of Scotland, and in particular the Kirk Session, which became especially influential after the Reformation period of the 1560s until around 1730.[15] In Scotland crime was not confined to the secular authorities, nor sin to the church courts, and it is clear from the remit of the Kirk Session that it could on occasion try relatively 'serious' offences such as assault. More commonly, however, the Kirk Session dealt with crimes that were 'moral' in nature such as sexual misdemeanours, slander, Sabbath-breaking and various other episodes of anti-social behaviour.

---

[10] See Whyte, *Scotland before the Industrial Revolution*, 218.
[11] See Davies, 'The courts and the Scottish legal system', 121.
[12] Lenman and Parker, 'Crime and control', 15.
[13] Davies, 'The courts and the Scottish legal system', 120.
[14] For further information see ibid. 134–8, and A. E. Whetstone, *Scottish county government in the eighteenth and nineteenth centuries*, Edinburgh 1981, ch. i.
[15] See Cairns, 'Historical introduction', 83–4.

Kirk Sessions were somewhat restricted in the forms of punishment that they could mete out. As they were ecclesiastical courts they were not permitted to impose any form of corporal punishment on the individuals convicted within their jurisdiction. As a result, shaming rituals of various sorts or fines were the most common penalties dispensed.[16]

The elders of the Kirk Session also fulfilled another important duty in the judicial process, one that is yet to be fully investigated or understood by Scottish historians of the pre-modern period. It seems that Kirk elders provided a strong moral, criminal and cultural investigative framework within Scottish society. In pursuing this, along with sheriff officers and justices of the peace, they regularly helped to interrogate suspects bound for the higher criminal courts of the country.[17] This suggests not only the widespread acceptance of the authority of the Church, but also illustrates the close collaboration between and amongst different judicial systems – a relationship that certainly merits closer attention.

One of the most complicated judicial structures relevant to the pre-1747 period in Scotland was the franchise system, which contained institutions such as the barony court and the court of regality. The jurisdictions they encompassed tended to be based around territory and land-holdings, and as a result they varied in size and could be scattered over wide and disparate areas of the country. Baron Courts could, in theory, try the same sorts of offences as the Sheriff Court, but in reality they dealt with more trivial offences such as minor thefts and assaults, and were more commonly involved in actions related to debt recovery and the execution of civil administration.[18]

The Regality Court, on the other hand, did deal with more serious crimes. As a regality it was deemed to be a 'sub-kingdom' in its own right. It was allowed to try all types of crime (except treason) as well as the 'four pleas of the crown', something even the 'superior' Sheriff Court was not permitted to do. Much of the time, however, the Regality Court tended to leave the most serious cases to the higher courts. None the less, laying claim to a few serious cases on occasion seemed to satisfy its claim to be a court of importance, whilst also avoiding unnecessary judicial violence on a large scale. Most of the court's time was spent dealing with minor acts of inter-personal violence, debt recovery, the maintenance of 'guid nichtburheid' (good neighbourhood or

---

16 For further information see Davies, 'The courts and the Scottish legal system', 123–32; M. Todd, *The culture of Protestantism in early modern Scotland*, New Haven–London 2002, 24–48 and ch. v; and Mitchison and Leneman, *Sexuality and social control*.

17 Evidence of this is in witness testimonies in a wide variety of indictments brought before the Justiciary Court between 1750 and 1815. See also Davies, 'The courts and the Scottish legal system', 130, and Whyte, *Scotland before the Industrial Revolution*, 215, who both imply that this may have been the case.

18 See Davies, 'The courts and the Scottish legal system', 141–3, and Cairns, 'Historical introduction', 55–6.

'promises to keep the peace') and various cases related to commercial legislation.[19]

In many respects Burgh Courts operated much like the franchise courts, except that they were more urban in character and jurisdiction. Although it could be argued that this description is overly-simplistic, it is true, none the less, that in many respects the Burgh Courts mirrored the activities of the franchise courts, especially barony jurisdictions. However, rather than being operated by members of the landed elite, as was the case in Baron Courts, Burgh Courts were more commonly operated by 'baillies' or magistrates selected from members of the local town council. Most of the cases brought before Burgh Courts dealt with quasi-criminal actions related to assaults, anti-social behaviour and acts of theft, as well as matters connected to commercial affairs and other general issues related to the burgh's administration.[20]

Despite the wide scope of authority evident in early modern Scotland, the complex network of courts worked together fairly proficiently. They spread the load of court business between them (through the process of 'repledging'),[21] yet the provision of justice was none the less largely 'private, local and amateur rather than central and professional'[22] during the pre-Enlightenment period. The lack of any centralised control of judicial affairs in Scotland at this time (chiefly due to the hereditary nature of many of the offices and the relative weakness of the Scottish Privy Council)[23] certainly contributed to perceptions of Scotland as a backward and lawless nation. In addition, it meant that there was little consistency in legal decisions, minimal regulation of either the legislative process or those who controlled it and broad discrepancies in the range of punishments meted out for similar offences, across different jurisdictions.

Even before the Union of 1707, however, and indeed as early as the fifteenth century, attempts had been made to centralise the provision of Scottish justice. The most notable examples of this include the founding of the Court of Session, the College of Justice and its associated Faculty of Advocates in 1532, the introduction of justices of the peace based on the English model in 1609 and the formation of the High Court of Justiciary in Edinburgh in 1672.[24] Although these courts and the Faculty of Advocates rapidly

---

[19] See n. 18 above.

[20] For further information see Davies, 'The courts and the Scottish legal system', 138–40.

[21] 'Repledging' is defined as 'withdraw[ing] (a person or cause) from the jurisdiction of another court to that of one's own, under the pledge that justice would continue to be done': M. Robinson (ed.), The concise Scots dictionary, Aberdeen 1985, 556.

[22] R. A. Houston and I. D. Whyte, 'Introduction', to Houston and Whyte, Scottish society, 26.

[23] The Privy Council was effectively the Scottish government in the early modern period. For further discussion on its functions and limitations see Davies, 'The courts and the Scottish legal system', 151–4.

[24] For further information on these changes see W. D. H. Sellar, 'A historical perspective',

became well established in Scotland, the justices of the peace did not become prominent, at least not until the mid-eighteenth century. From this period they increasingly absorbed business from the Kirk Sessions and Burgh Courts, as the restructuring of judicial provision began to take shape. Even by that time, however, justices enjoyed a more investigative or administrative role than a prosecutorial one, and certainly it was not until much later that they attained the same level of significance as they had enjoyed south of the border since the reign of Elizabeth I.[25]

Although the success of these early attempts at centralising justice was relatively limited, they were indicative of the change which would follow from 1700. It might be assumed that the breakthrough came with the union of parliaments in 1707, but this was not the case. Attempts to broker a union of laws between Scotland and England began as early as 1603, when King James VI and I assumed the crowns of both countries. However, rather than concentrate on the similarities that existed between the laws in the two kingdoms, the negotiations highlighted the perceived differences between the two, and as a result legal union foundered.

Scots law in the pre-modern period was considered to be a hybrid of many judicial elements. Brian Levack, for instance, describes it as 'consisting mainly of English law that had been imported and Scotticized during the late middle ages, Roman and canon law that had been "received" in the fifteenth and sixteenth centuries, and a large substratum of custom, which was feudal in origin'.[26] This mix of legislative origins led many to consider Scots law to be irreconcilable with its English counterpart, and it was agreed as a result that any union between the two would be ineffective and implausible.[27] Consequently, when the treaty for uniting the parliaments of the two kingdoms was devised, the eighteenth article stated that although the laws on trade, customs and excise were to follow the English example, 'all other Laws in use within the Kingdom of Scotland doe after the Union and notwithstanding

in M. C. Meston and others, *The Scottish legal tradition*, Edinburgh 1991, 43–7; N. Wilson, 'The Scottish bar: the evolution of the Faculty of Advocates in its historical setting', *Louisiana Law Review* xxviii (1968), 235–57; J. Findlay, *All manner of people: the history of the justices of the peace in Scotland*, Edinburgh 2000; Whetstone, *Scottish county government*, ch. ii; and W. Croft Dickinson, 'The High Court of Justiciary', in *An introduction to Scottish legal history* (Stair Society xx, 1958), 408–12.

[25] For further detail on the history of the justices of the peace see Findlay, *All manner of people*; G. DesBrisay, '"Menacing their persons and exacting their purses": the Aberdeen Justice Court, 1657–1700', in D. Stevenson (ed.), *From lairds to louns: country and burgh life in Aberdeen, 1600–1800*, Aberdeen 1986, 70–90; and Davies, 'The courts and the Scottish legal system', 132–4.

[26] B. P. Levack, 'Law, sovereignty and the Union', in R. A. Mason (ed.), *Scots and Britons: Scottish political thought and the Union of 1603*, Cambridge 1994, 216–17.

[27] For further discussion see J. Dove Wilson, 'Historical development of Scots law', *JR* viii (1896), 217–41, and B. P. Levack, *The formation of the British state: England, Scotland, and the Union, 1603–1707*, Oxford 1987, 68–101.

thereof remain in the same force as before ... but alterable, by the Parliament of Great Britain'.[28]

The fact that 'private' laws in Scotland were to be preserved and untouched by the Union meant that Scots law began to be used as a tool of national-istic sentiment. Scots law came to be seen as one of the key elements within Scottish society that made Scotland distinctive within the wider sphere of 'Great Britain'.[29] However, although the concessions to Scots law pleased some, in actual fact the Union did little to facilitate its further development in the longer term. If anything, the Union actually hindered Scottish legal reform as the abolition of the Privy Council in 1708 (as a result of the 'British' parliament being established in London), meant that the only real agency for centralised government control (regardless of its limitations) had been removed. As a result, Scots law remained localised, uncontrolled and largely unchecked in the decades after 1707.

Instead of being a great force for change, in relation to Scots law at least, the Union of 1707 maintained the stalemate in judicial provision which was set to continue in Scotland for a further fifty years. The real eighteenth-century watershed for Scots law came with the Heritable Jurisdictions Act of 1747.[30] This act, which was part of a more general legislative programme concerned with pacifying the Highlands in the wake of the Jacobite Rebel-lions, abolished hereditary offices and effectively made the barony and regality courts obsolete. The act also diminished the power of other local jurisdictions such as the Burgh Courts, whilst at the same time it strengthened the judi-cial reach of the more 'superior' courts. As Stephen Davies describes, the act 'brought about the final demise of a complex and distinctive legal system in favour of a formally structured order which has continued, by and large, to our own day'.[31]

As a result of legal provision becoming more centralised in Scotland at this time, there was a symbiotic growth in the strength and importance of the legal profession. The number of practising lawyers increased and, due to changes in educational provision, they were increasingly tutored in Scottish universities rather than foreign ones. In addition, their duties were put on a more 'professional' footing during this period, as they were given regular and improved payment for their services. Indeed, after 1747 lawyers came to be regarded as one of the most powerful and influential sectors of Scottish society, and were seen as indispensable in matters of political management.[32]

---

[28] *Acts of the parliaments of Scotland*, XI: (*1702–1707*), Edinburgh 1824, appendix at p. 203.

[29] For further discussion see N. T. Phillipson, 'Lawyers, landowners, and the civic lead-ership of post-union Scotland: an essay on the social role of the Faculty of Advocates, 1661–1830, in eighteenth-century Scottish society', *JR* n.s. xxi (1976), 92.

[30] 20 Geo II, c.43.

[31] Davies, 'The courts and the Scottish legal system', 120.

[32] For further discussion of these developments see Cairns, 'Historical introduction', 155–6, 159; N. T. Phillipson, 'The social structure of the Faculty of Advocates in Scotland,

Both the move to centralisation and the professionalisation of Scottish lawyers occurred during a period regarded as 'the golden age of Scottish culture',[33] and known more commonly as the Scottish Enlightenment. The distinctiveness of Scots law, which was reinforced by the Treaty of Union, made its mechanisms and procedures particularly interesting to European observers. This, in turn, encouraged much argument and debate on matters of legal thought in a Scottish context.[34]

By the mid-eighteenth century, numerous 'enlightened' legal writers had inherited the mantle of Lord Stair (1619-95) who had laid the foundations of the Scottish legal system in his work *The institutions of the law of Scotland*. The most notable of these, in relation to criminal law at least, was Baron David Hume (1756–1838), professor of Scots law at Edinburgh University. Building on Sir George Mackenzie's (1636-91) work *Law and customs in Scotland in matters criminal*, published in 1678,[35] Hume provided the classic statement of Scottish criminal law nearly a century later in his two-volume *Commentaries on the laws of Scotland respecting crimes*.[36] The end result of Hume's work, published in 1797, was not a distinctive codification of Scots law, as that was impossible, but rather a clarification and a consolidation of Scottish legal practice in criminal matters. No other legal writer had managed to achieve this before, and it was clear that the flurry of argument and debate maintained during the era of the Scottish Enlightenment had facilitated a more rational and systematic approach to the criminal law in Scotland, enabling Hume to offer precision where others had failed.[37]

Law and discipline were seen as crucial elements within Scotland's enlightenment culture, as in theory at least they enabled and encouraged the formation of a more civilised and sophisticated society.[38] In light of this thinking, and in consequence of the changes in judicial provision described above, the business of the courts started to increase after 1750. As a result of this, criminal matters came to be increasingly heard in Scotland's central judiciaries and the Sheriff Court, Justiciary Court and to a lesser extent the Justice of the Peace Court came to dominate criminal proceedings.

1661–1840', in A. Harding (ed.), *Law-making and law-makers in British history*, London 1980, 146–56; and J. Shaw, *The management of Scottish society, 1707–1764: power, nobles, lawyers, Edinburgh agents and English influence*, Edinburgh 1983.

[33] Smout, *A history of the Scottish people*, 451.

[34] See, for instance, Chitnis, *The Scottish Enlightenment*, 85–7; P. Stein, 'Legal thought in eighteenth century Scotland', in P. Stein (ed.), *The character and influence of Roman civil law: historical essays*, London 1988, 361–80; and J.W. Cairns, 'Legal theory', in A. Broadie (ed.), *The Cambridge companion to the Scottish Enlightenment*, Cambridge 2003, 222–42.

[35] G. Mackenzie, *Law and customs of Scotland in matters criminal*, Edinburgh 1678.

[36] Hume, *Commentaries*, i, ii.

[37] For further discussion see Sellar, 'A historical perspective', 52–3, and Stein, 'Law and society', 148–68.

[38] See, for instance, Phillipson, 'Lawyers, landowners, and the civic leadership', 107. For further discussion of the concept of the 'civilising process' see Elias, *The civilizing process*.

Although the Sheriff Court and the Justice of the Peace Court could in theory deal with a wide variety of offences by 1750, most of the serious criminal cases were brought before the Court of Justiciary. This seems to have been especially true when women broke the rules. Although fewer in number in terms of indictments, Scottish criminal women were seen as more despicable than their male counterparts because by their actions they had not only broken the law, but they had also betrayed a femininity that the courts wished to impose upon them. Female felonies were commonly regarded as gravely serious and inherently threatening and, as a result, women were regularly brought before the most superior court – the Justiciary Court – regardless of the actual nature of the offences charged against them.[39]

For this reason, any study of violent women in Scotland is best served by looking at the proceedings of the Justiciary Court rather than any other judiciary. Although this work largely focuses on the Justiciary Court and will inevitably exclude many indicted acts of petty violence involving women (as well as other instances which were simply not reported to the authorities), when a violent act was carried out by a woman, she was more likely to be indicted at the Justiciary Court than elsewhere, as her offence was taken so seriously on account of her gender.[40] The authorities knew that at the Justiciary Court a case would be more effectively and publicly examined, so that the woman involved could be used as an example to deter other like-minded or aggressive females.

The Justiciary Court was the supreme jurisdiction dealing with criminal matters in Scotland. Its name derived from the medieval office of 'justiciar', an official who acted on the monarch's behalf to deliver justice and discipline criminals. The first Scottish justiciar on record, one David Olifard, was exercising jurisdiction as far back as 1166, reflecting the longevity of the office and its functions.[41] Since the early period, however, the role and function of the justiciar was not fixed or regulated and, as a result, the justiciar's involvement in criminal matters was inconsistent and unpredictable. It was only after the

---

[39] This conclusion is based on my exhaustive study of the proceedings of the Justiciary Court between 1750 and 1815 relating to lowland Scotland, as well as a sampling survey of Sheriff Court and Justice of the Peace Court records over the same period. The Sheriff Courts sampled were Haddington, Hamilton, Paisley, Peebles, Selkirk, Stirling and Wigtown. The Justice of the Peace Courts sampled were Dumbarton, East Lothian, Kirkcudbright, Midlothian, Selkirk, West Lothian and Wigtown.

[40] The Justiciary Court records examined in their entirety between 1750 and 1815 in relation to this volume were: Books of adjournal, series D (JC 3); Books of adjournal, series E (JC 4); High Court minute books, series D (JC 7); High Court minute books, series E (JC 8); South Circuit minute books (JC 12); West Circuit minute books (JC 13); Register of lawburrows (JC 18); Signet minute books (JC 20); Circuit appeal registers (JC 22); Remissions (JC 24); Petitions (JC 25); Processes (JC 26); Appointments and commissions (JC 42); and Productions (JC 45).

[41] Croft Dickinson, 'The High Court of Justiciary', 408.

Cromwellian interlude that the jurisdiction was put on a much firmer footing north of the Tweed at least.[42]

In 1672 the High Court of Justiciary was formally established. It was presided over by the Lord Justice General, the Lord Justice Clerk and five Lords of Session. The High Court was to sit in Edinburgh every Monday during the session, and for the first time additional circuit courts (or ayres) were organised, with the country divided into three associated jurisdictions. The North Circuit covered courts held in Perth, Aberdeen and Inverness. The West Circuit managed the courts held in Glasgow, Stirling and Inverary, and the South Circuit dealt with the courts held in Ayr, Dumfries and Jedburgh. Initially at least, these circuit courts met once a year, presided over by two Lords. After 1747, however, the increased volume of business brought before the Justiciary Court was largely absorbed from defunct local jurisdictions. This meant that the court had to go on circuit twice a year, usually in the spring and autumn.[43]

The Justiciary Court had a wide remit when dealing with criminal offences. In the early modern period it dealt with petty crimes and moral offences from time to time, but these were increasingly assigned to the more 'inferior' jurisdictions (such as the Sheriff Court and the Justice of the Peace Court) over the course of the eighteenth century. In the main, therefore, the Justiciary Court dealt with 'serious' offences such as political and treasonous crimes, the four pleas of the crown and other felonious activities. These included counterfeiting and fraud, assault, infanticide, riot, sodomy and bestiality, theft and the sale of stolen goods (known in Scotland as resett), as well as a variety of other misdemeanours.

In the management of these crimes, the court had a wide range of punishments at its disposal. However, from the end of the seventeenth century onwards, the punishments meted out by the Justiciary Court became more fixed and prescribed.[44] Sentences of death by hanging or transportation overseas were the most common punishments received by those convicted of political crimes or serious offences, especially those which had involved the use of violence. For lesser offences heavy fines, corporal punishment and imprisonment (or even a combination of the three) were more regularly meted out by judges of the Justiciary. In any event, before 1780 at least, few of the men and women charged before the Justiciary Court were released as a result of having been found not guilty or their cases not proven,[45] and fewer still were

[42] For further discussion see Davies, 'The courts and the Scottish legal system', 147, and P. Raynor, B. Lenman and G. Parker, *Handlist of records for the study of crime in early modern Scotland (to 1747)*, London 1982, 31–2.

[43] For further discussion regarding the jurisdiction of the Justiciary Court see Hume, *Commentaries*, i, ch. i; Croft Dickinson, 'The High Court of Justiciary', 411; Cairns, 'Historical introduction', 122–3; and Raynor, Lenman and Parker, *Handlist*, 30, 32.

[44] See, for instance, Davies, 'The courts and the Scottish legal system', 149.

[45] For a brief history of the 'not proven' verdict in Scotland in relation to the Justiciary

pardoned after conviction. As Stephen Davies illustrates, 'If someone was charged with a serious crime before the Justiciary Court, then their chances of survival were slim since acquittal was rare and mercy unheard of.'[46] Although the Justiciary Court in Scotland appeared to indict fewer suspects than its counterparts south of the border, it seems it was far more likely to convict and punish the individuals brought before it than was the case in England during the pre-modern period.[47] This suggests, at least in part, that the Scottish provision of justice at the highest level was more targeted and exacting at this time when compared with the infamous 'Bloody Code'. This hypothesis needs to be properly tested through a detailed study of comparative punishment policy, and there is not enough room to do this in the present analysis.

Criminal trials heard at the Justiciary Court involved a variety of highly formalised procedures. Lists of offences carried out within the court's jurisdiction were logged in a document called 'The Porteous Roll' and, on the basis of this report, suspects were arrested and committed to jail to await trial (unless bailed) and formal charges in the form of an indictment were raised against the accused.[48] The Criminal Procedure Act of 1701 stated that a suspect's period of commitment could last no more than eighty days if an indictment had not been served, and no more than one hundred days if trial had not been commenced.[49]

By the eighteenth century the court's interests were served by the Lord Advocate or his deputy, and it was he who called indictments to be heard and who prosecuted trials on behalf of the king and the victim concerned. The prisoner was permitted a prosecutor in defence, but his involvement in the proceedings was commonly dictated by the nature of the specific offence lybelled and the weight of evidence charged against his client.

When the case or 'diet' was called before the court, the lawyers involved would initially debate on the 'relevancy' of the lybel. Trials could be abandoned or 'deserted' temporarily or permanently, depending on the circumstances of a given case, but between 1750 and 1815, such practices were not especially common.[50] Most of the cases that were indicted at the Justiciary

---

Court see J. Irvine Smith, 'Criminal procedure', in *Introduction to Scottish legal history*, 442.

[46] Davies, 'The courts and the Scottish legal system', 149.

[47] This theory has been mooted for the pre-1747 period in Scotland by S. J. Connolly, 'Albion's fatal twigs: justice and the law in the eighteenth century', in R. Mitchison and P. Roebuck (eds), *Economy and society in Scotland and Ireland, 1500–1939*, Edinburgh 1988, 121; by Lenman and Parker, 'Crime and control', 14; and by Davies in 'The courts and the Scottish legal system', 149. Work done to date on the subsequent period suggests that it may well have been the case after that time as well: Kilday, 'Women and crime', ch. vi.

[48] For further information see Hume, *Commentaries*, i, chs ii, iii, vii.

[49] For further discussion see Sellar, 'A historical perspective', 50.

[50] For further discussion see Hume, *Commentaries*, i, ch. ix, and Irvine Smith, 'Criminal procedure', 437–8.

Court during that time went through the full sequence of judicial procedure. If, however, a suspect failed to attend court to face the charges of the indictment, he was 'declared fugitate' and was 'put to the horn'. In practical terms this meant that he was identified as an outlaw, a warrant was issued for his arrest, and all his moveable goods and 'gear' were forfeited to the right and use of the crown.[51]

Providing, then, that a suspect was present at the convening of the trial proceedings, s/he would be asked to plead to the charges contained in the indictment. Further legal debate might then ensue, but eventually an assize of local landed or professional men (typically fifteen in number) was sworn in and the trial would begin in earnest.

The initial evidence presented to the court was usually that which pointed to the 'undoubted' culpability of the accused. This took the form of either a 'declaration of guilt' or a full confession to the lybel as charged. The rest of the prosecutor's evidence would then follow. Most commonly this took the form of oral witness testimony, but sometimes this was supplemented by written or artefact-based depositions. Subsequent to this proof 'evidence in exculpation' was given by the defence attorney. This type of testimony was only occasionally presented at the Justiciary Court, however, as in pre-modern Scotland more emphasis was placed on guilt being proven, than innocence being established.[52]

After all the available testimony had been heard, the assize was asked to inclose, to deliberate on the evidence they had heard, and to deliver one of three verdicts: guilty, not guilty or not proven. On the basis of the decision of the assize, the judge would either release the prisoner, or deliver sentence according to the penal provisions available for the particular offence lybelled on. Convicts could be granted 'remission' from their sentences, but during the eighteenth century at least reprieves and pardons were not that common at the Justiciary Court and sentences were usually executed in full.[53]

The transformation of the Scottish legal system after 1747 is in part evidenced by the swift and formalised nature of criminal trials held at the Justiciary Court after that date. Judicial provision in Scotland had become an organised, professional and centralised system with clear jurisdictional boundaries. Although cases could still pass through the court hierarchy, the fact that

---

51 For further information see Hume, *Commentaries*, i, ch. ix, and Irvine Smith, 'Criminal procedure', 437–8.

52 For further discussion see Hume, *Commentaries*, i, chs xii, xiii, xiv, xv. Before 1800 trial proceedings (including witness testimonies) were recorded in great detail by the clerk of the Scottish Justiciary Court. Consequently it is relatively easy for the historian to gain a thorough and intimate understanding of individual cases and the circumstances which surrounded them. After 1800, however, cases were increasingly recorded and dealt with summarily, and as a result much of this comprehensive detail was lost.

53 For further discussion see ibid. i, chs xvi, xvii, xviii, and Irvine Smith, 'Criminal procedure', 444–8.

there were fewer courts meant that the legal system was more cohesive and far easier to manage. This in turn meant that the central courts could deal with more business in a more efficient way. Whether this judicial stability resulted in a curb on violent or criminal behaviour among the Scottish populace is as yet difficult to discern, but certainly a felon was more likely to know what to expect if s/he was apprehended and indicted after 1750 than in the previous period.

Throughout the eighteenth century Scotland gradually shifted from a system of 'retributive' justice to one of 'prohibitive' justice, where keeping the peace was as important as establishing guilt and disciplining offenders. The Heritable Jurisdictions Act of 1747 had a key role to play in this transformation, but so too did Enlightenment logic, which promoted a better understanding of the Scottish legal tradition and which encouraged the distinctive traits of the nation's law and legal theory to be emphasised and celebrated on the wider European stage.[54] This growth of interest in Scots law paved the way for greater clarification of the legal process, through the writings of men like Baron David Hume. This, along with the process of centralisation, 'professionalised' the Faculty of Advocates and enabled lawyers to become one of the most powerful elements of Scottish political and intellectual society during the eighteenth century.

According to Lord Cooper, 'There is a sense in which it is true to say that Scots Law has no history; for the continuity of its growth has been repeatedly interrupted and its story is a record of false starts and rejected experiments.'[55] This chapter has shown that although this may have been an accurate description of Scottish legal provision before 1750, it cannot be applied subsequently. The Heritable Jurisdictions Act and the intellectual and socio-cultural progress of the Enlightenment period marked the end of 'interruptions' to the 'continued growth' of judicial provision in Scotland, and the system went on to develop and mature from that point onwards. The men and women indicted at the central courts after 1750 were faced with a more ordered and largely transparent trial procedure which employed clear jurisdictional sanctions. Justice became more dependent on the crime lybelled than on the character or reputation of the accused. None the less, the gender of the prisoner could influence where a trial occurred, as women were more likely to be indicted before the most 'supreme' court – the Court of Justiciary.

Establishing guilt was seemingly more important than proving innocence for all those appearing before the Justiciary Court during the eighteenth century, and this meant that chances of acquittal or reprieve diminished

---

[54] For a detailed study of the influence of the legal tradition on the formation of modern Scots law see L. Farmer, *Criminal law, tradition and legal order: crime and the genius of Scots law 1747 to the present*, Cambridge 1997.

[55] T. M. Cooper, *Select Scottish cases of the thirteenth century*, Edinburgh–London 1944, p. lxi.

the longer a trial continued. By 1750 Justiciary Court justice was largely impersonal and determined and this seems to have been truer for the women brought to court at this time than the men, especially if the felony involved aggressive or violent behaviour. In such instances women were seemingly doubly damned: not only had they committed a crime, but they had also rejected the 'norms' of feminine behaviour and behaved in a masculine and unseemly manner. As the following chapters illustrate, Scottish women seem to have been quite willing to break these legal and ideological rules during the pre-modern period, even within the confines of the more regulated and meticulous legal system which had been established by 1750.

3

Homicide

'Women of this stamp are generally so bold and unblushing in crime, so indifferent to right and wrong, so lost to all sense of shame, so destitute of the instincts of womanhood, that they may be more justly compared to wild beasts than to women.'[1]

The writing of women into criminal history has certainly not been neglected by scholars of the subject, especially in relation to the pre-modern period.[2] However, as chapter 1 has shown, studies in the main have either looked at women as the common victims of illegal activity, or have placed greater emphasis on the understanding of non-violent criminal women and their actions.[3] This preoccupation stems back to the long-held view that women rarely participated in violent activity, and that when they did so, they behaved in a covert, non-aggressive, non-confrontational manner, in line with prescribed gender norms and ideologies.[4] As Peter Spierenburg has argued, violence was a male culture in which women did not participate.[5] This view has led historians to ignore the history of violent female offenders. Their behaviour has been dismissed as uncommon, limited and uncharac-teristic, and as a result violent women have been deemed unworthy of more detailed investigation.

Yet the suggestion of a gender disparity in violent crime makes women worthy of attention. To what extent and why were women less likely than men to engage in unlawful violent behaviour? Did the method, motivation

---

[1]   M. E. Owen, 'Criminal women', *Cornhill Magazine* xiv (1866), 153.
[2]   Aside from a variety of crime-specific studies see also the material relating to criminal women in more general works on the history of crime such as J. M. Beattie, *Crime and the courts in England, 1660–1800*, Oxford 1986; Kermode and Walker, *Women, crime and the courts*; Emsley, *Crime and society*; R. B. Shoemaker, *Prosecution and punishment: petty crime and the law in London and rural Middlesex, c. 1660–1725*, Cambridge 1991; Morgan and Rushton, *Rogues, thieves and the rule of law*; and McLynn, *Crime and punishment*.
[3]   See the references in n. 2 above and especially Hufton, 'Women and violence', 75–95. An exception to this general trend in the historiography of women's criminality is Walker, *Crime, gender and social order*, although Walker's work tends to concentrate on perceptions of criminal women in seventeenth-century Cheshire rather than providing a detailed analysis of the nature of women's criminality during this period.
[4]   See especially Beattie, 'The criminality of women', 82; McLynn, *Crime and punish-ment*, 129; P. Spierenburg, 'How violent were women? Court cases in Amsterdam, 1650–1810', *Crime, History and Societies* i (1997), 9–28; and B. Hanawalt, 'The female felon in fourteenth-century England', *Viator: Medieval and Renaissance Studies* v (1974), 254–6.
[5]   Spierenburg, 'How violent were women?', 27.

and type of violent activity that women carried out differ from that of their male counterparts? What was the reaction of the legal authorities and society in general to women who had stepped outside the boundaries of 'appropriate' behaviour and used violence in the perpetration of crime?

Violent crimes brought before the Justiciary Court generally fall into the category of 'crimes against the person'. As the term suggests, crimes against the person consist of homicide, infanticide, assault (both verbal and physical), popular disturbances and robbery. There are three key reasons why a study of homicide is valuable in understanding violent criminal activity and attitudes towards its perpetration. Firstly, as it was considered the most violent form of behaviour, homicide is usually the best recorded crime amongst criminal statistics. Certainly it was the most detectable. From the limited work that has been done on this subject, it seems that homicide did not contribute substantially to unrecorded crime levels, known as the 'dark figure' of criminal statistics.[6] The extremely serious nature of the offence would encourage reporting of the crime and would render the authorities more anxious to investigate it and thereafter to make an arrest. Furthermore the nature of the material evidence relating to a homicidal act (with perhaps the important exception of poisoning cases) was exceedingly difficult to conceal and this must have aided detection enormously. Despite the absence of advanced forensic knowledge, it can be supposed that the number of indictments for homicide was a reasonably accurate reflection of the number of non-poisoning cases that actually took place.[7]

The second reason for studying homicide is that because it has been well recorded, it is the one violent offence that has received a lot of attention from criminal historians. Consequently, there is more comparative evidence at hand to facilitate a more nuanced understanding of the offence, the individuals who committed it and the public's reaction to it.

Finally, as homicide was considered the most violent form of crime, it provides the criminal historian and criminologist with representations and behaviour related to the ultimate example of aggressive criminality. This is all the more compelling if we are looking at the actions of women in this respect, as it allows the analysis of an activity thought to be completely alien to women. Women were said to participate rarely in violent criminal activity, so an examination of their involvement in the most serious type of

---

6 See, for instance, idem, 'Long-term trends in homicide: theoretical reflections and Dutch evidence, fifteenth to twentieth centuries', in E. Johnson and E. Monkkonen (eds), *The civilization of crime: violence in town and country since the Middle Ages*, Urbana, ILL. 1996, 63–105; J. S. Cockburn, 'Patterns of violence in English society: homicide in Kent, 1560–1985', *P&P* cxxx (1991), 70–106; and especially M. Eisner, 'Modernisation, self-control and violence: the long-term dynamics of European homicide rates in theoretical perspective', *British Journal of Criminology* xli (2001), 618–38.
7 For further information on the detection and prosecution of homicide in the early modern period see M. Gaskill, *Crime and mentalities in early modern England*, Cambridge 2000, ch. vii.

violent crime would offer a substantial insight into female deviancy and its portrayal.

The aim of this chapter, then, is to look first at the legal context of homicide in Scotland to establish how the crime was regarded by the legal establishment of the eighteenth century. The nature and incidence of murder and how it was carried out by Scottish women will then be examined in order to see how female behaviour in this respect compared to male. I will then attempt to establish an 'offender profile' for the women accused of homicide, in order to understand the motives behind their murderous activities. Finally, by looking at reactions to the behaviour of homicidal women via an analysis of the punishments they received, the study hopes to illustrate how murdering women were regarded by eighteenth-century Scottish society and how this compared to attitudes elsewhere. Overall, this chapter seeks to test the hypothesis that women were less violent and aggressive than their male counterparts in the light of the evidence from homicide indictments brought before the Scottish Justiciary Court.

The legal context

Baron David Hume, writing in the late eighteenth century, defined homicide as a crime 'by which life is taken away, and the person of a human creature is destroyed'.[8] In this definition, he makes no reference to 'forethocht felony' or its English equivalent, 'malice aforethought', with which his contemporaries south of the border were so concerned. Premeditation was a key issue in English courts throughout the early modern period for two reasons. First, the degree of 'malice aforethought' determined which of the various categories of homicide the defendant was to be charged with. Second, the level of culpability attributed to the accused was determined by the degree of premeditation employed in the offence. Establishing the extent of culpability had significant implications during the sentencing process and could mean the difference between life and death for a convicted killer. Making such determinations was all part of the trial procedure in England. However, due to the varied nature of homicide indictments, trying to distinguish between cases on the basis of premeditation made English law appear highly complex in this respect.[9] The Scottish courts, on the other hand, were more concerned with trying to prove that a given homicide had taken place rather than whether or not it was a 'forethocht felony'. In addition, the principle in English law of *feme covert*, whereby a married woman was not deemed responsible for criminal activity if her husband was present when she was carrying out the offence, did not apply in Scots law. Married women were just as culpable

---

[8]   Hume, *Commentaries*, i, ch. vi, p. 179.
[9]   For further discussion of this see Beattie, *Crime and the courts*, 79–80, and McLynn, *Crime and punishment*, 36–41.

as single women in Scotland and the circumstances surrounding their illegality, in terms of the rationale behind their actions, was rarely an issue.[10] Consequently, therefore, the relatively uncomplicated nature of Scots law enabled Hume to go a stage further and, unlike his English contemporaries, he provided a clear and precise categorisation of homicide. Hume recognised four kinds of homicide: aggravated murder, murder, culpable homicide and murder 'free from all blame'.[11] This last section included casual and justifiable homicide.[12]

Generally, in Scotland, the punishments meted out by the courts were graduated according to the severity of the offence. In Scottish murder cases a conviction would result in a sentence of execution with little chance of remission. Here the practical application of Scots law with respect to homicides stands in stark contrast to what we know of the function of the English 'Bloody Code'. South of the Tweed guilty verdicts did not commonly result in execution, since the extensive application of 'mercy' by the judicial authorities was a widespread instrument of penal policy.[13]

There were only two conditions that had to be met in Scots law for a homicide charge to apply to a given case. First, and somewhat obviously, someone had to have been killed. This qualification separates homicide from attempted killing, which is a different offence altogether. The second condition was that it had to be shown that the victim died from the direct and specific actions of the accused. To put it another way, the cause of death had to be certain. If the victim died sometime after he or she had been attacked, their death may have been caused by something other than the initial assault allegedly inflicted on them by the accused.[14] Once these conditions had been met, the pannel (or accused individual) was indicted on a charge of homicide and then it was left to the court's discretion to decide what type of homicide the lybel would contain.

---

10 For further discussion of *feme covert* and its applicability in England see Shoemaker, *Gender in English society*, 297, and King, 'Gender, crime and justice', 64.

11 For further discussion see Hume, *Commentaries*, i, ch. vi, pp. 191–291.

12 Casual homicide occurred when an individual was killed by accident. Justifiable homicide occurred when an individual was killed by an 'officer' executing his duty. For further discussion see W. D. H. Sellar, 'Forethocht felony, malice aforethought and the classification of homicide', in W. M. Gordon and T. D. Fergus (eds), *Legal history in the making: proceedings of the Scottish legal history conference, Glasgow, 1989*, London 1991, 55–6.

13 For further discussion see, for instance, J. H. Langbein, 'Albion's fatal flaws', *P&P* xcviii (1983), 96–120.

14 See Hume, *Commentaries*, i, ch. vi, pp. 179, 181–2.

The incidence of homicide

Of the homicide charges brought before the Justiciary Court relating to south-west Scotland between 1750 and 1815,[15] 216 related to murder (unspecified as to whether aggravated or otherwise), fifty-three related to culpable homicide and there was one case of justifiable homicide.[16] If all these cases are taken together to show the overall incidence of homicide indictments pertaining to south-west Scotland during the late eighteenth- and early nineteenth-century period, the gender disparity in this respect is significant. Seventy-nine per cent of the cases (or 213 out of 270 indictments) were brought against men and 21 per cent (or fifty-seven cases out of 270 indictments) were brought against women. Although not directly comparable, due to variations in legal context and in the types of criminal records researched, it is interesting to note that the findings of this study with respect to the incidence of homicide indictments appear relatively similar to those uncovered elsewhere. Men predominate in this kind of criminal activity.[17] John Beattie, for instance, in his sampling of the Surrey judicial records between 1663 and 1802, noted that of 284 charges for murder and manslaughter, 87 per cent were against men and 13 per cent were against women.[18] James Sharpe, in his study of the Essex assizes between 1620 and 1680 found that of 310 homicide suspects, 84 per cent were male and only 16 per cent were female.[19] Likewise, Peter

[15] For the purposes of this study the 'south-west' is taken to be the area as far north as Glasgow, stretching east to the far corner of the shire of Dumfries and as far south as Kirkcudbright. This area makes up three-quarters of the region of Scotland known as the Lowlands. The study also includes material from the High Court of Justiciary based in Edinburgh. Given the geographical spread of the evidence uncovered, I consider the findings of this study to be representative of lowland Scotland as a whole.

[16] When the charge against the pannel was murder or culpable homicide, I have counted the offence as that for which he or she was eventually convicted. If the pannel was acquitted, I have used the witness testimony, the Advocate Depute's declaration and/or the judge's interlocutor on the relevancy of the lybel, to arrive at the type of homicide implied in the indictment: this was the case in only a negligible number of the indictments.

[17] It should be noted that this qualification holds true for any of the comparisons made in this chapter, and indeed the rest of the book. Rather than evidence from studies elsewhere being used as direct comparisons to the south-west Scottish experience, they are merely included as points of interest.

[18] See Beattie, 'The criminality of women', 85.

[19] My calculations on the evidence presented: see J. A. Sharpe, *Crime in seventeenth-century England: a county study*, Cambridge 1983, 124. Most studies do not offer specific data on the gender breakdown in cases of alleged homicide and indeed other offences, preferring instead to provide statistics on the lack of women's involvement in crimes against the person in general. See, for example, Henry, *Dublin hanged*, 77–99, and J. R. Ruff, *Crime, justice and public order: the sénéchaussées of Libourne and Bazas, 1696–1789*, London–Dover, NH 1984, 68–105. The issue of homicide incidence is further complicated by the tendency among historians to combine statistics for female homicide with those of infanticide, the latter being an entirely different offence: see Morgan and Rushton, *Rogues, thieves and the rule of law*, 112.

Spierenburg, in his study of the court cases in Amsterdam between 1650 and 1810, found that only twelve murder charges out of 144 were levelled against women, such that females there accounted for a mere 8 per cent of all homicide indictments.[20] The general trend that emerges, then, is that, with respect to homicide, female criminality is conspicuously uncommon.

This consensus, that women were rarely fatally violent, should not lead us to conclude that women were rarely violent at all, however. As subsequent chapters will show, this hypothesis can be discounted by the evidence of Scottish women's involvement in other (non-fatal) violent activities. Yet from indictment evidence at least, it seems clear and incontrovertible that women rarely resorted to murder in the eighteenth century. What is more difficult to determine, however, is whether the incidence of their participation in this type of criminality changed over time.

The question of whether society is more violent nowadays when compared to an earlier period has caused intense debate in the historiography of crime.[21] Homicide rates are regularly used as a gauge to measure the violent nature of a particular society, nation or populace. With regard to female homicidal activity however, this task is troublesome, due to the paucity of data available. Certainly, the evidence related to Scotland does not show any statistical bias towards either a growth or a decline in homicide incidence over the sixty-five year period between 1750 and 1815 for either males or females. The rate over time remains fairly static, with no overall trend discernible. Clearly, there are not enough cases to warrant an in-depth statistical analysis of homicide trends like that carried out by Malcolm Feeley and Deborah Little, James Cockburn or Lawrence Stone for England in the early modern period.[22] In any case, perhaps this type of analysis is best carried out in relation to property offences and other non-violent crimes where the data is more voluminous and the variables involved are more consistent. Trends in theft, for instance, might be explained by economic indicators which are easy to measure and can be effectively analysed in relation to a geographical area or a group of people. Murder, on the other hand, is often based on specific emotional prompts or personal reactions. As a result, homicide indictments collectively tell us less about the nature and circumstances of crime over time as they are individualistic and unpredictable.

---

[20] See Spierenburg, 'How violent were women?', 17.

[21] For a summary of the debate see Cockburn, 'Patterns of violence', 70–106.

[22] See, for instance, Feeley and Little, 'The vanishing female', 719–57; Cockburn, 'Patterns of violence', 70–106; and L. Stone, 'Interpersonal violence in English society, 1300–1980', *P&P* ci (1983), 22–33.

Modus operandi

Running parallel to the argument that women committed far fewer offences than men is the contention by some that when women did participate in crime, their offences were usually committed without violence.[23] The modern criminologist Carol Smart explains that in general 'Violent offences ... do not appear to be easily reconciled with the traditional conceptualisation of feminine behaviour. Murder and other violent acts against the person appear to be the complete antithesis of the gentle, retiring, caring role of the female sex.' [24] It would appear to follow from this that if a woman were to commit an act of homicide, she would favour doing so in a manner that did not involve overt violence.[25] Poisoning fits well with this description. Indeed, of the *modus operandi* used by women in murder cases brought before the Justiciary Court between 1750 and 1815, poisoning was by far the most favoured approach. It accounted for twenty of the forty-eight cases, the next most popular being strangulation, with a count of six.[26] However, women did not necessarily turn to poisoning due to revulsion at being involved in a violent crime, nor did they do so to offset a lack of physical strength. It is much more likely that women mainly chose poisoning as it was easier to conceal, both in administration and effect. It was, for example, a lot less conspicuous and simpler for a woman to go to an apothecary to acquire rat poison than to go to purchase a firearm. It was also relatively easy for a woman, in the role of nursemaid or food-preparer, to administer the poison to the intended victim. Additionally, as Otto Pollak infers, because the symptoms of poisoning are not unlike those of other diseases such as cholera, the actual act of murder was often hidden, unless there was any suggestion of foul play such as an unexpectedly rapid death.[27] Of course, it could be argued that men could also resort to such tactics to commit homicide. However, they were less likely to be in a position that enabled them to administer the poison in the first instance without raising suspicion and indeed of the 168 murder cases from south-west Scotland brought against men, only six involved the use of poisoning. The evidence suggests that poisoning was a gendered crime.

---

[23] See the references cited in n. 2 above for further discussion.

[24] C. Smart, *Women, crime and criminology: a feminist critique*, London–Boston 1977, 16.

[25] For further discussion see Wiener, 'Sex roles', 49. For further general discussion of women's involvement in homicide see Walker, *Crime, gender and social order* (esp. ch. iv) and J. Knelman, *Twisting in the wind: the murderess and the English press*, Toronto–London 1998. It should be noted that Walker's evidence relates to early seventeenth-century Cheshire and Knelman's examples and evidence relate to England in the nineteenth century.

[26] The remaining nine cases were instances of culpable homicide and will be analysed later on in this chapter.

[27] See O. Pollak, *The criminality of women*, Philadelphia 1950, 17–18. For further detailed discussion of this offence see also K. Watson, *Poisoned lives: English poisoners and their victims*, London 2003.

Certainly, poisoning showed a clear degree of premeditation, and in the English courts in the early modern period it was 'detested because it tapped a profound male fear of female deviousness; it was the ultimate horror even to conceive of the possibility that the polite yet secretive female might harbour dark homicidal urges under the mask of gentility'.[28] In Scotland in the eighteenth century poisoning, perhaps in the context of the relatively recent 'witch hunt', was also regarded as abhorrent. Men and women alike brought before the Justiciary Court at this time for an alleged homicide involving poisoning were always charged with murder and never the lesser offence of culpable homicide. Having said this, however, not one of the twenty-six pannels (accused) involved in such cases was convicted. This was because the cause of death had to be clearly proven in poisoning cases.[29] Although this prerequisite did not deter prosecutors from doing their utmost to gain a conviction, cases were difficult to prove conclusively.

A good illustration of this is the case of Jean Semple, accused of the murder by poisoning of her husband, David Baird. This was heard at the West Circuit Court in 1773.[30] Witnesses testified to a long history of abuse of the husband by his spouse, even quoting her as saying that she would eventually 'ding the life out of him'. It was then testified by an apothecary that Jean Semple had bought some rat poison from him, which surprised the apothecary as he knew David Baird well and knew that he 'kept four or five cats'. Next a neighbour, whose barn was rat-infested, testified that he had asked the deceased if he had similar problems with his out-houses and David Baird had 'replied in the negative'. Then the deceased's eldest son, William Baird, swore on oath that after eating porridge and milk his father complained of 'a dry boke ... a great drouth [drought] and a pain in his belly'. William then testified that despite these ailments his mother did not send for a doctor for three days, and thereafter David Baird died on the third of December 1772.

In addition to this, one Alexander Taylor, a surgeon in Glasgow, performed an autopsy on the victim and discovered the 'inner surface of the stomach spotted in different places and discovered a white gritty powder in its contents'. After many experiments trying to determine whether the cause of death was arsenic or corrosive sublimate he 'concluded it was arsenick'. The surgeon and his assistants even went as far as taking a sample of the said 'gritty powder', making it 'up into peels with wheat bread' and feeding it to a chicken which they had locked in a room. The chicken died seven hours later. Even after all this evidence, the pannel was not convicted. The case turned on the evidence of Beana Cumming, a witness for the defence, who overheard a conversation between a Doctor Graham and the deceased, in which the former said to the latter 'I gave you the poison to be given to the rats but not to be taken by yourself. Go home to your wife and drink a quan-

28 McLynn, *Crime and punishment*, 119. See also Emsley, *Crime and society*, 156.
29 For further discussion see Hume, *Commentaries*, i, ch. vi, pp. 288–90.
30 NAS, JC 13/18.

tity of milk.' Cumming's testimony implied either that the victim had accidentally consumed some poison, or he had attempted suicide. This evidence was enough to convince the jury to find Jean Semple not guilty. She was released from the bar and set at liberty.

Even though poison was the most popular *modus operandi* in murder cases, accounting for twenty of the forty-eight case, of the remaining twenty-eight cases, twenty-six involved the use of overt violence.[31] These women, far from committing crimes in a manner befitting the 'fairer' sex, were more often than not 'tigerish in their ferocity'[32] in terms of their homicidal instincts. Strangulations, drownings, batteries, slashings with razors, stabbings with knives, 'dashing brains out' with pokers and cudgels and stonings all appear in these twenty-six cases. Certainly the aggressive nature of these women cannot be doubted. Two examples further illustrate this.

The first case was brought before the West Circuit Court in 1767. It alleged that

Agnes Dougall carried Joanna Finlay (her daughter begot upon her in fornication by one Robert Finlay), along with her from her house then at Anderston, towards the River Clyde. At the side of a hedge on the lands of Lancefield, the said Agnes Dougall did murder the said Joanna Finlay her daughter by cutting the throat of the child with a table knife. The cutt [cut] given by the said Agnes Dougall with the said knife being across the throat of the said Joanna Finlay and the windpipe or great vessels of the neck being divided causing a great effusion of blood, the immediate death of the said Joanna Finlay was occasioned.[33]

In testimony heard at the West Circuit Court later that year, the surgeon who had performed the autopsy on the girl estimated her to be eight or nine years old and explained that 'The throat of the child was cutt [cut] almost from ear to ear by a sharp instrument in such a manner as behoved to be the cause of immediate death.' He also observed 'a wound across the fingers of the child' which he apprehended 'must have been occasioned by the child's grasping at the sharp instrument in her defence'. Another witness for the prosecution testified that soon after the pannel's apprehension, he asked her how she could do such a thing to her own child, to which she replied that 'they gard [made] her do it, for that the Elders had threatened to put her into

---

[31] In two cases the method used in the murder was unspecified as the pannels had been declared fugitate. This means that they had not appeared in court to face the indictments against them. As a result, a warrant was issued for their arrest, and all their moveable goods and 'gear' were forfeited to the right and use of the crown.

[32] McLynn, *Crime and punishment*, 118. For corroboration that women could behave as aggressively as men in committing violence see Finch, 'Women and violence', 29, and Hufton, 'Women and violence', 76.

[33] JC 26/180.

the Correction House for fornication and upon that account she had taken revenge upon her own child'.[34]

Another case which illustrates the typical ferocity of Scottish murderesses was brought against Isobel McLean at the West Circuit Court in 1787. The indictment charged that

> Upon the thirtieth day of July ... you the said Isobel McLean, did wickedly and maliciously assault the deceased Henry Small your husband within his own house in Glasgow, and did give him repeated and violent blows and bruises upon the belly and other parts of his body. You did tread and trample upon him with your feet and did likewise cutt off his private member to the great effusion of his blood, with a knife, or some other Sharp instrument which you aimed at the trunk of his body, and which struck his member in consequence of his stooping down to elude the blow, you at the time threatening instantly to put him to death therewith. And thereafter, when the said Henry Small was laid on his bed in a wounded and languishing condition by reason of the cruel treatment he had received, you the said Isobel McLean in prosecution of your wicked and unnatural purpose of depriving your husband of his life did take the opportunity of the absence of several persons who had come to render assistance to the said Henry Small, and did with your own hands drag him out of bed by the hair of the head, and throw him down with violence on the floor, at the same time biting and tearing at him with your teeth. In consequence of these wounds and bruises so wickedly and unnaturally inflicted by you the said Isobel McLean on your own husband, he the said Henry Small soon thereafter died in a matter of hours.[35]

The propensity for brutality amongst the Scottish women indicted for murder was also evident in indictments for the other 'species' of homicide that was brought before the Scottish courts during the eighteenth century. Culpable homicide is a crime defined as 'a killing caused by fault which falls short of the evil intention required to constitute murder'.[36] Even in the nine charges of this nature brought against women in relation to south-west Scotland during the period in question, six involved brutal attacks on the victim, the methods in the remaining three cases being unspecified. Take, for example, the case of culpable homicide brought against Jean Inglis at the South Circuit Court in 1755.[37] This case was a private prosecution brought by the victim's husband who described the pannel as a midwife and formerly close companion of the now deceased Margaret Sutherland, his wife. Jean Inglis was called for after the said Margaret Sutherland went into labour. After 'having got access to the room ... the said Jean Inglis bolted the door, rushed furiously upon the

---

[34] The relationship between church discipline, illegitimacy and female criminality is explored in chapter 4 below.

[35] JC 26/243.

[36] Robertson, *Concise Scots dictionary*, 127.

[37] JC 26/156.

deceased and used her most barbarously and inhumanely'. After having delivered the child, the victim suffered 'a most extraordinary flooding' and was
'in a most miserable condition'. Margaret Sutherland thereafter survived for
exactly four weeks and four days 'in great agony but in sound mind' claiming
that 'the furious woman with the use of a broken bottle had effectually done
her business. ... That she could not live having no bowells [bowels], these
having been torn out by the midwife, and she was now left with her death
upon her'. The other culpable homicide cases contain similar evidence. It is
clear that the line between whether or not a crime involved a high degree
of 'evil intention' was obviously a very fine one. In any event, the degree of
violence shown by Scottish women killers during the eighteenth century is
both startling and unexpected. Scottish women murdered with open force
rather than with concealed deviousness and they could be quite as violent to
men as to women. These findings clearly challenge and undermine many of
the stereotypical notions of fatal female criminality written about elsewhere.
But what can be said about the murderesses themselves? Who were these
women and in what circumstances did they resort to killing?

Defendant characteristics

A variety of common defendant characteristics is identifiable from indictment
evidence. The first of these is linked to the methods employed in killing. In
77 per cent of cases women acted alone. Men also predominantly murdered
alone, but the incidence of them doing so was proportionately less than that of
their female counterparts (62 per cent of the cases brought against them at the
Justiciary Court). The exceptions to homicidal felons acting alone occurred
when murders were committed in the furtherance of another offence. These
crimes were seen as being the 'grossest' of all violent activity by the authorities of the day, and certainly they were the most feared.[38] Rather than a
conscious attempt to destroy all evidence linking a perpetrator or perpetrators
to a given crime scene, these offences were most common when the victim
offered resistance to being robbed or having their property stolen. However,
it does not necessarily follow that just because an individual is motivated to
commit a robbery (through want or greed) that they will be thereby inclined
to commit murder. This is true even in situations when it might have been
prudent for them to do so.[39] It would seem, therefore, that rather than being
seen as a means to an end, murder during the committal of another crime was
only resorted to in the most desperate of situations.

There were obvious exceptions to this, one being the case of the Adam
sisters, Margaret and Agnes, which was brought before the West Circuit
Court in 1774. The indictment charged that on the 29 October 1773

---

[38] See, for instance, Beattie, *Crime and the courts*, 78.
[39] See McLynn, *Crime and punishment*, 43.

you both did go into the shop of the deceased Janet McIntyre shop-keeper in the City of Glasgow. After drinking some spirits there in company with the said Janet McIntyre, you and each of you after having shut and bolted the door of the said Janet McIntyre's shop did wickedly and feloniously seize upon, bruise and strangle her until she was dead. You then robbed her of the sum of ten shillings and six pence sterling or thereby. Upon the neighbours, being alarmed at the noise and knocking at the door to get in, one or other of you, answered by desiring those who knocked to let alone, for that Janet McIntyre was drunk and in her bed. But the neighbours on the outside of the door not being satisfyed [satisfied] with the answer, broke open the door, and found the said Janet McIntyre lying dead on the floor and both of you concealed in or under a bed. The above mentioned ten shillings and six pence sterling of which you robbed the said Janet McIntyre, by taking it from her or out of her cash box or drawer, was found concealed in the bosom or breast of you the said Agnes Adam.[40]

Scottish women were clearly not averse to committing murder in the furtherance of another offence. The commonly brutal nature of Scottish women's participation in offences against property will be examined in more detail in chapter 7.

A further characteristic among the female defendants charged with homicide is that, like the Adams sisters, they overwhelmingly perpetrated their offences in 'urban' areas.[41] Some 68 per cent of those accused (or thirty-nine cases out of fifty-seven) had allegedly killed in the town, whereas 32 per cent (or eighteen cases out of fifty-seven) had allegedly killed in the country. This trait merely serves to confirm the work of the Scottish criminal historian Ian Donnachie, who claims that in the first half of the nineteenth century law-breaking was more prevalent in Scottish towns than in the countryside.[42] Whilst Donnachie's comment is strongly supported by the evidence of this present analysis, in part this characteristic is a reflection of the imbalance in population distribution during the pre-modern period. Whether the prevalence of urban criminality is also evident amongst the other offences against the person dealt with in this study will be examined in due course. For now

---

40 JC 26/198.

41 The reference works used to determine which of the *locus operandi* (crime scenes) were urban and which were rural were M.W. Flinn (ed.), *Scottish population history: from the seventeenth century to the 1930s*, Cambridge 1977; J. Bartholomew (ed.), *The gazetteer of the British Isles: statistical and topographical*, Edinburgh 1887; *Place names and population in Scotland: an alphabetical list of populated places derived from the census of Scotland*, Edinburgh 1967; and S. Lewis, *A topographical dictionary of Scotland comprising the several counties, islands, cities, burgh and market towns, parishes and principal villages with historical and statistical descriptions; embellished with engravings of the seals and arms of the different burghs and universities*, i, ii, London 1846. These works were used throughout the book, and not only in this specific chapter.

42 See Donnachie, '"The darker side"', 5, and 'Profiling criminal offences: the evidence of the Lord Advocate's papers during the first half of the nineteenth century in Scotland', *Scottish Archives: The Journal of the Scottish Records Association* i (1995), 85–92.

it is enough to say that the favoured *locus operandi* for homicide amongst the indicted Scottish lowland women was urban rather than rural in nature.

At any rate, the predominance of female homicidal activity in urban areas is not merely a Scottish phenomenon. Malcolm Feeley and Deborah Little, for instance, as well as John Beattie, argue that as women's lives were more restricted, scrutinised and controlled in rural areas, they had less opportunity to commit crimes there.[43] However, the comparative freedom that city life afforded women must have facilitated opportunities for criminality, both violent and otherwise, that were not open to them in rural areas. Women's lives were still restricted in the urban environment in terms of their access to certain social spheres, as we will see, but that restriction was less explicit in towns than in the countryside.

There is one further identifiable feature that links almost all the primary source evidence relating to the incidence of indicted female homicidal activity in lowland Scotland. In the overwhelming majority of cases the victim and the offender were either related or acquainted. This seems to be a fairly common feature of this type of violent crime. John Beattie, Julius Ruff and Frank McLynn (for the eighteenth century) and James Sharpe (for the seventeenth century) all agree that the majority of women brought to court upon a charge of homicide were accused of killing someone known to them.[44] Indeed, between 1750 and 1815 some 58 per cent (or thirty-seven cases out of sixty-four) of all family homicides were charged against south-west Scottish women. Furthermore, if the number of cases in which the victim was simply acquainted with his or her aggressor is added to this, the figures are even more startling. Eighty-eight per cent (or fifty cases out of fifty-seven) of all homicides charged against females were allegedly committed against relations or acquaintances compared with 27 per cent (or fifty-eight cases out of 213) of the cases charged against males.

Some explanations for this gender disparity concern the apparently limited social activity of women.[45] Women were clearly less likely than men to become involved in disputes with strangers that might result in homicidal violence. It seems that women rarely accepted challenges to duels and brawls and, as a result, they were less likely to be placed in a situation where a murder or culpable homicide could result.[46] However, little evidence exists from the Justiciary Court material to confirm these arguments, aside from the fact that

[43] For further discussion with respect to violent crimes see Feeley and Little, 'The vanishing female', 719–57, and Beattie, 'The criminality of women', 96–109.
[44] See Beattie, 'The criminality of women', 83; Ruff, *Crime, justice and public order*, 80; McLynn, *Crime and punishment*, 46, 117; and J. A. Sharpe, 'Domestic homicide in early modern England', *HJ* xxiv (1981), 29–48.
[45] For further discussion see Beattie, 'The criminality of women', 84; McLynn, *Crime and punishment*, 122–3; Finch, 'Women and violence', 28–30; Spierenburg, 'How violent were women?', 24–5; and Shoemaker, *Gender in English society*, 299–300.
[46] For further discussion of duelling see D. T. Andrew, 'The code of honour and its critics: the opposition to duelling in England, 1750–1850', *SH* v (1980), 401–13.

only twelve of the women accused of homicide were deemed by the court to be in employment. This suggests that for the majority of these women (nearly 80 per cent of those accused) everyday experiences were restricted to home and family life, rather than the more multi-faceted or versatile life offered by the world of work. In the context of female homicides it seems that these restrictions had a particular resonance in rural areas. Whatever the case, it is clear that Ian Donnachie's comment that there was 'an almost equal mix of intra-family and extra-family murder'[47] in early nineteenth-century Scotland, cannot readily be applied here. Certainly it is logical to assume that if women's lives were more or less restricted to the domestic sphere, then they would be more liable to participate in criminal activity within that environment, explaining why statistics relating to domestic or family homicides are so biased towards female offenders.

Motives

The motivations for homicides both within the domestic sphere and beyond are hard to determine from the indictments of the Justiciary Court due to the relative lack of importance which the Scottish courts attached to the issue of premeditation. Where motives can be discerned from the evidence, they are very much case-specific and exceedingly variable, making it virtually impossible to draw any meaningful conclusions about the background to this type of violent crime – indeed, there were rarely witnesses to homicidal acts. Nevertheless, there are some pointers. It is clear that in the Lowlands between 1750 and 1815 the most common victim in domestic homicides was the husband. More than three-quarters of the cases of domestic homicide charged against females were mariticides (the killing of a husband by his wife).[48] James Sharpe suggests that as domestic enmity was a common phenomenon, it is not surprising that tensions exploded into acts of ferocity on a regular basis.[49] Although Sharpe is writing about seventeenth-century England, his comments are readily applicable to late eighteenth- and early nineteenth-century Scotland and even to the present day. The criminolo-

---

[47] Donnachie, '"The darker side"', 14. See also Stone, 'Interpersonal violence in English society', 32, for a similar conclusion.

[48] Twenty-eight cases out of thirty-seven, or 76% of the homicide indictments charged against these women, referred to the murder of their husbands. This detail is further established by the fact that in terms of marital status the largest category of those accused of homicide comprised widows or relicts. Thirty-two women (or 56%) were widows, seventeen (or 30%) were married and only eight (or 14%) were single. These findings appear to be at odds with those of Peter Spierenburg who found that women rarely killed men in early modern Amsterdam: 'How violent were women?', 25. For a detailed analysis of women's involvement in domestic homicide in the early modern period see Sharpe, 'Domestic homicide', 36–45.

[49] Sharpe, 'Domestic homicide', 31.

gist Carol Smart describes most domestic homicides as being 'victim precipi-tated', that is 'the eventual victim was the original aggressor'.[50] It must often have been the case that women on the receiving end of years of physical and mental abuse (with divorce not an option in economic terms or other-wise), built up tensions, jealousies and hatred over that time which would eventually result in a sudden outburst of spontaneous violence. This could either take the form of a 'hot-blooded' act of homicide or a simple act of self-defence. The evidence of instruments used in the committal of these offences by the indicted women of lowland Scotland seems to lend weight to this argument. With the exception of poison and two cases involving stones, the assaults were carried out using implements which would have been near at hand when tempers frayed: household objects such as razors, kitchen knives, pokers and cudgels.

Indeed, it is perhaps surprising that more wives did not kill their husbands in light of the dictatorial and abusive relationships that are suspected to have existed at this time.[51] However, for many women, living as economic depend-ants in already impoverished conditions, the removal of the bread-winner from the household, no matter how beneficial and attractive a prospect in the short-term, might well on reflection seem likely only to worsen the long-term situation for her and the mouths she had to feed.

It is harder to determine the motives for the killing of other family members and also of neighbours and acquaintances, although monetary disputes were often the initial source of tension in these instances. Of course, in some cases no motive existed at all as the pannel was clearly insane, but only in the most severe cases was this brought to the attention of the court.[52] What is inter-esting, or unusual, about the Scottish evidence is that although women over-whelmingly killed in the domestic sphere, the victims of their violence were usually their husbands. Other studies have flagged up a significant proportion of women killing children and servants, but these were not evident in any substantial numbers in eighteenth-century Scotland.[53] Clearly, as we will see, although Scottish women regularly assaulted children and domestic servants, their actions were rarely fatal. Husbands were the prime target for the female murderesses of lowland Scotland, and perhaps this factor alone explains

[50] Smart, *Women, crime and criminology*, 17. See also Walker, *Crime, gender and social order*, 135.
[51] For further discussion of domestic violence in the pre-modern period see chapter 5 below.
[52] Three males and only one female were declared insane by the court out of all the alleged offences committed in south-west Scotland and indicted at the Justiciary Court between 1750 and 1815. As the individuals concerned were deemed unfit for trial, their cases were dismissed and they were set at liberty.
[53] See, for instance, Sharpe, 'Domestic homicide', 29–48; Hufton, 'Women and violence', 82–4; Beattie, 'The criminality of women', 83–4; and Cockburn, 'Patterns of violence', 95.

the 'brutal' nature of the treatment they received from court officials upon conviction.

The treatment of female killers

It is clear from the historiography of 'general' female criminality in the early modern period that women could expect to receive more lenient treatment from the courts than men.[54] According to the historian Geoffrey Elton, this widespread tendency can be explained, at least in part, by what he calls 'an often instinctive chivalry, or if you like embarrassment, which was a common reaction of that day when confronted with women who broke the rules'.[55] Moreover, and in respect of capital convictions, female convicts were not regarded as effective examples of the value of hanging as a deterrent to crime. As John Beattie points out, 'It was plainly more advisable to execute those whose death would confirm the wisdom and justice of the law rather than those whose suffering might excite pity, and perhaps even hostility.'[56] This principle seems to have been especially pertinent to female convicts, and as a consequence women were less likely to be convicted by the courts than men, and thereafter less likely to receive the ultimate punishment. This gendered 'leniency' only applied to female offenders who were found guilty of petty or non-violent offences. Women who stepped outside the boundaries of female respectability could expect harsher treatment from the authorities.[57] Women convicted of violent offences were considered abnormal, unnatural, animalistic (as the comment at the outset of this chapter illustrates) and certainly unfeminine, and therefore they must receive exemplary punishments to answer their exemplary behaviour.[58]

In practical terms, in an English context, attempts to make examples of violent women were most evident in the treatment of women who had killed their husbands. The maintenance of the expected relationship between

[54] See, for example, King, 'Gender, crime and justice', 44–74; Morgan and Rushton, *Rogues, thieves and the rule of law*, 118; and Shoemaker, *Gender in English society*, 297. For further discussion of attitudes towards convict women and their treatment (in relation to the nineteenth century) see Zedner, *Women, crime and custody*, and 'Women, crime and penal responses: a historical account', in M. Tonry (ed.), *Crime and justice: a review of research*, xiv, Chicago–London 1991, 307–62.

[55] G. R. Elton, 'Introduction: crime and the historian', to J. S. Cockburn (ed.), *Crime in England, 1550–1800*, London 1977, 13. For further discussion see also E. A. Anderson, 'The "chivalrous" treatment of the female offender in the arms of the criminal justice system: a review of the literature', *Social Problems* xxiii (1976), 350–7.

[56] Beattie, *Crime and the courts*, 436.

[57] For similar conclusions see King, 'Gender, crime and justice', 61–2; Morgan and Rushton, *Rogues, thieves and the rule of law*, 118–22; and Shoemaker, *Gender in English society*, 298.

[58] For further discussion of the perceptions of female killers in the early modern period see Walker, *Crime, gender and social order*, 140.

husband and wife in respect of male domination and female subservience was held to be of immense importance to the fabric of society. Consequently, any English woman who had inverted the gender order by killing her spouse was charged with petty treason and burned at the stake.[59] It would seem that 'chivalric instincts' only extended so far. Male convicts found guilty of killing their wives were simply hanged. Although this type of gendered punishment for petty treason was practised in England until the 1790s, in Scotland the practice had all but died out by 1720.[60]

Despite this concession to gender, the legal authorities in Scotland did not shy away from the punishment of women, especially those who had been accused of murder. Even taking into account the notion that exceptionally violent women had to be treated harshly since they were traitors to the so-called 'gentler sex', the treatment of the women indicted for murder in eighteenth-century Scotland appears harsh. Not only is this so in comparison with their Scottish male counterparts, but also with women similarly accused elsewhere at this time. Evidence from Lancashire, the Old Bailey and Surrey, for instance, suggests that women were rarely convicted of murder, and proportionately far less likely to be hanged than men.[61] Clearly, only a scant number of women were used as 'examples' to deter the English populace from criminal or deviant behaviour.

In Scotland during the eighteenth century, 60 per cent of the women accused of murder were convicted and, more significantly, nearly two-thirds of that number were hanged.[62] This contrasts with the treatment of men similarly accused: 53 per cent of defendants were convicted and only 37 per cent of them subsequently sentenced to death.[63] Although women in general make up only a small fraction of the total number of individuals hanged in Scotland between 1750 and 1815, with reference to murder indictments their treatment was proportionately far harsher than that of men, and far more unsympathetic than that experienced by English women. Women murderesses in Scotland were also far less likely to be granted a post-sentence pardon than men. In addition, after the 1752 Murder Act, when attempts were made to make executions more shocking and intimidating to the spectator, Scottish women were almost as likely as Scottish men to receive an aggravated

[59] See R. Campbell, 'Sentence of death by burning for women', *Journal of Legal History* v (1984), 44–59.
[60] See Hume, *Commentaries*, ii, ch. xvii, p. 482. One explanation for the early removal of petty treason in Scotland could be that it recalled public executions during the witch-hunt centuries before: Larner, *Enemies of God*.
[61] See King, 'Gender, crime and justice', 55, and Beattie, *Crime and the courts*, 97.
[62] Thirty-four women were convicted of murder out of fifty-seven accused (60%). If we take poisoners out of the equation (bearing in mind that poisoners were rarely convicted due to the nature of the evidence in their indictments, and indeed none of the women accused of poisoning here were convicted), the conviction rate reaches 92% of those accused. Twenty-one (or 62%) of the women convicted of murder were hanged.
[63] 113 men were convicted of murder out of 213 accused (53%). Forty-two (or 37%) of the men convicted of murder were hanged.

execution, usually the public dissection and anatomisation of the convict's body after its removal from the gallows.[64]

Scotland during the eighteenth century is described as having 'an inno-cence of the noose'[65] due to the rarity with which capital convictions were carried out. However, in extreme cases of bad behaviour, the full force of the law could be brought to bear on an individual for his or her actions. Certainly, women murderesses were deemed worthy of the hangman's attention in Scot-land during this period, and it is clear that definite steps were taken to make examples of violent females of this type. But how can this seemingly strin-gent and ruthless attitude be explained? Given that so many of the women accused of murder in Scotland had been charged with mariticide, and in the absence of the provision for petty treason which existed south of the border, perhaps the legal authorities in Scotland felt that these women were abnor-mally deviant and unnatural and had to be punished accordingly. Perhaps the authorities felt that the population had to be reminded of the expected roles of wife and husband in the context of strict Scottish religiosity, and that by making 'bloody' examples of female killers the populace would be shown what could happen to those who upset the balance. In general, it would seem that fatally violent women in Scotland were not to be forgiven, understood or sympathised with, as was regularly the case with men. Rather, and on account of their overt rejection of gender norms, they had to be ruthlessly, and visibly, punished.

It has been a commonly held assumption amongst scholars that women did not commit crime, and especially violent crime, as frequently as men. Furthermore, it is believed that when women did perpetrate a violent offence, they behaved less aggressively than their male counterparts. This chapter has tested this hypothesis in relation to the evidence of homicide indictments brought before the Justiciary Court between 1750 and 1815.

Homicide, for obvious reasons, was deemed to be the most serious offence of all those indicted at the Justiciary Court. Although some interesting patterns develop from a close analysis of female homicidal activity, the incidence of such activity is relatively rare, in comparison with the male involvement in murder and culpable homicide. Certainly lowland Scotland in the late eight-eenth and early nineteenth centuries did not have the same incidence of homicidal activity as Dublin at this time. There, as Brian Henry describes, a contemporary citizen observed that 'murder in this city has become so

---

64 All but one of the males sentenced to death received punishments of aggravated execu-tion. This was the case for all but four of the women similarly sentenced. For further discussion of the implications of the Murder Act see Hume, *Commentaries*, ii, ch. xvii, pp. 481–2; McLynn, *Crime and punishment*, 272–3; and P. Linebaugh, 'The Tyburn riot against the surgeons', in D. Hay, P. Linebaugh, J. G. Rule, E. P. Thompson and C. Winslow (eds), *Albion's fatal tree: crime and society in eighteenth-century England*, London 1975, 65–118.
65 V. A. C. Gatrell, *The hanging tree: execution and the English people, 1770–1868*, Oxford 1994, 9.

common, that it has lost all its horrors; every day teems with new instances of the most horrid barbarity'.[66] Significantly, however, the feature common to both Dublin and lowland Scotland between 1750 and 1815 with respect to homicide was the lack of female involvement.

In total, fifty-seven south-west Scottish women, compared to 213 south-west Scottish men were brought to the Justiciary Court in the sixty-five year period, charged with murder or culpable homicide.[67] The rarity of female participation in fatal killing seems to validate the assumption that women were rarely involved in violent criminality. Most of the fifty-seven women indicted for homicide were unmarried, a significant proportion being widows. This reflects the fact that a substantial number of these women were accused of mariticide. In the vast majority of cases the women had committed their alleged offences alone, and had done so in an urban rather than a rural area. In only a few cases was the victim a stranger to the accused, as predominantly a woman was charged with killing a member of her immediate domestic circle, most commonly her spouse. Most of Scottish men, on the other hand, were indicted for killing someone who was a stranger to them.

Explanations as to why this was the case appear to revolve around the perceived restricted role of women in eighteenth-century society. Julius Ruff suggests that the incidence of female crime is lowest in societies where women have little independence and highest in those where they have greater freedom.[68] He quotes Leon Radinowicz who stated that 'Any member of a society who starts to take an increasing role in the economic and social life of that society will be more exposed to crime and will have more opportunities and therefore will become more vulnerable and more prone to criminal risk.'[69] It is apparent from the evidence that rather than being involved in random brawls with strangers at hostelries or gaming-houses which resulted in an act of homicide being perpetrated (as was so often the case with men), Scottish women's actions were regularly targeted at people they knew and commonly occurred within the home.

It seems plausible to argue, then, that the scope of women's violent behaviour was more restricted than that of their male counterparts. However, the fact that more than half the Scottish women indicted had used extreme violence in their homicidal activities suggests that although fewer in number, and more limited in scope, they could regularly behave just as aggressively in the committal of this type of criminal activity as men, if sufficiently motivated to do so.

The violence that these women employed was not typically at the behest of others, nor was it some sort of imitation of the behaviour of men, as Peter

---

[66] Henry, *Dublin hanged*, 77–8.

[67] One of the 213 men was indicted for justifiable homicide.

[68] See Ruff, *Crime, justice and public order*, 89.

[69] Leon Radinowitz, cited in S. Titus Reid, *Crime and criminology*, Hinsdale, ILL. 1976, 58, and quoted in Ruff, *Crime, justice and public order*, 89.

Spierenburg argues was the case.[70] Although women killers in Scotland may have had logical reasons for their murderous activities, they were evidently violent in their own right and for their own sake. Clearly, aggressive women existed in eighteenth-century Scotland just as aggressive men did. The nature of this fatal violence and the authorities' reaction to it, however, resulted in women being punished in a more exemplary way than their male counterparts as they had too visibly stepped outside the boundaries of 'expected' feminine behaviour. Scottish women's treatment in this respect seems to have been harsher than that experienced by women killers elsewhere during this period, perhaps due to the greater proportion of mariticide cases brought to court.

What this chapter has shown is that attempts by historians to dismiss female criminal activity and violent female criminal activity in particular, can no longer be justified. The lesser incidence of fatal female violence does not necessarily imply that women were less belligerent in the committal of offences than men. The lowland women of eighteenth-century Scotland were just as aggressive as men in their murderous activities. The reaction of the Scottish courts to women killers not only reflects this, but also reflects just how hazardous it was for Scottish women to abandon 'gendered' notions of womanhood to meet their desired ends.

[70] See Spierenburg, 'How violent were women', 26.

4

Infanticide

'The Miscreant kills the Fruit of her own Womb,
To make Damnation her eternal Doom.'[1]

Infanticide and child murder are exceptionally emotive crimes. Not only is this due to the innocence of the victims concerned, but also because this type of criminality inverts the expected protectionist relationship (based on maternal instinct) between a mother and her child. Society has long debated whether women who kill their offspring should be pitied or punished, and this debate looms just as large today as it did some 300 years ago. The reason infanticide merits closer attention in this book relates to its distinctive categorisation as a gender-specific 'violent' crime. Unlike the other violent offences investigated, in the case of child murder there is an almost complete absence of male protagonists. Consequently infanticide can be used as a touchstone to test the legitimacy of gendered or feminist readings of crime (such as those outlined in chapter 1), in the context of a criminal environment dominated by women. In addition, far from being seen as an obscure or atypical branch of criminal legitimacy, infanticide has much to tell us about the psyche of women criminals in general and violent women criminals in particular. Consequently much of the analysis presented has parallels and resonances with the conclusions presented in the other offence-based chapters of this study.

Some historians have counted infanticide as a 'species' of homicide and have made no statistical distinction between the two offences in terms of indictment incidence. However, in any study which explores the nature of female crime in the pre-modern period, this crime, arguably more than any other, merits special attention in its own right.[2] This is because infanticide (which in this book is taken to mean the murder of a newborn child)[3] is a rare example of a gender specific crime: men were seldom involved. This crime, by its very nature, offers a unique insight into the world of women rarely illuminated at other times. Apart from the criminal evidence itself, midwives and local women offered their 'expertise' in the court-room and descriptions of

---

[1] Extract taken from *A warning to the wicked or Margaret Dickson's welcome to the gibbet*, Edinburgh 1724.

[2] For studies which treat infanticide as a 'species' of homicide see Walker, *Crime, gender and social order*, esp. ch. iv, and Morgan and Rushton, *Rogues, thieves and the rule of law*, ch. v.

[3] For further discussion on the definitional aspects of this crime see Jackson, *New-born child murder*, 6–7.

pregnancy, birth and maternity (a world most of the time hidden from men) were debated in the traditionally male-dominated sphere of legal practice. In addition, infanticide is also a vital tool of analysis since it reflects the fluctuating nature of legal and societal attitudes towards criminal women and their victims during a period of intense legal reform and judicial review. Finally, as a great deal of interest and concern was voiced about this type of crime, especially during the eighteenth century, there is a wealth of material and opinions upon which to base an analysis of the crime and its circumstances.[4] Indeed, compared to all other crimes brought before the Scottish Justiciary Court during the 1750–1815 period, it is infanticide indictments which provide the richest and most detailed court documentation. Consequently, the study of infanticide in this peripheral area can provide a more nuanced picture of violent crime.

The aim of this chapter is to provide a detailed study of Scottish women indicted for infanticide. Initially, the chapter will investigate how infanticidal mothers were regarded and treated by the law courts and the 'authorities' of the day. I will then focus on the nature and incidence of infanticide and the typical characteristics of the women indicted. Lastly, an attempt will be made to explain women's involvement in this type of emotionally-charged crime, especially given the shocking and unusually bloodthirsty measures that Scottish women regularly employed in killing their newborns, in comparison to infanticidal mothers elsewhere.

Attitudes to infanticide

Although encouraged in some eastern societies as a method of controlling population size and gender makeup, by the late sixteenth century most European states had singled out the crime of infanticide for particularly severe punishment. The instigation of a Europe-wide moral and legislative opposition to child murder evolved as a result of the confluence of three contemporary concerns amongst the authorities of the day. The first was a determination to protect infant life. Throughout Europe, by the eighteenth century, there was widespread concern that little was being done to eradicate violence against foetal or newborn life. Religious and legal institutions were thus encouraged to be more proscriptive in their defence of 'innocent blood'

---

[4]   These factors explain the wealth of writing on the subject of infanticide especially in recent years. See, for example, the references to major studies in nn. 2, 3 above and also P. C. Hoffer and N. E. C. Hull, *Murdering mothers: infanticide in England and New England, 1558–1803*, New York 1984, and L. Rose, *The massacre of the innocents: infanticide in Britain, 1800–1939*, London 1986. For Scotland see Symonds, *Weep not for me*. (It should be noted that the analysis and conclusions provided in this chapter advance the work of Symonds who used a sampling survey of the Justiciary material as part of her study of Scottish infanticide, rather than looking at all the available records.)

at this time, by becoming more hostile to interference with the natural course of human generation.[5]

The second key concern with the nature of infanticide voiced in the pre-modern period was the crime's obvious link with maternal deviance. The killing of a newborn child by its mother openly contradicted normally under-stood and expected maternal feelings and was regarded as a wholly unnatural transgression. Infanticide was clearly seen as a crime against womanhood, and more importantly a crime against perceptions of how women, and mothers in particular, were expected to behave. Women who contravened this norm and killed their newborns had turned their backs on civil society, humanity and their gender. During the eighteenth century in particular, these women were commonly given the appellation 'monster' or 'demon' in court indictments as a reflection of the abhorrence provoked by their crimes.[6] Clearly, and in order to protect notions of maternity and gendered normality, infanticide could not be tolerated in a more 'enlightened' society.

The third aspect of contemporary thinking, and indeed the one which was the real concern of the moralists of the day, was the apparent need to control the sexual morality of the populace. A growth in vagrancy across Europe from the seventeenth century onwards resulted in the authorities becoming increasingly anxious about how sexual immorality and criminal behaviour could be effectively managed.[7] Such a concern was also manifest in the Scottish Church of the period, as increasing numbers of defendants were brought before the Kirk Session to answer charges of fornication. As Rosalind Mitchison and Leah Leneman argue 'The Scottish Church in the pre-modern period displayed extreme distaste for physical intimacy between the sexes: it usually labelled any such demonstration "scandalous carriage" and penalized it.'[8] Over time however, this 'distaste' and 'concern' was transferred from the actual act of fornication itself to the frequent end product of such activity: illegitimacy.[9] The increasing condemnation of illegitimacy in Scotland (as elsewhere in Europe during the eighteenth century) was not based solely on fears of the spread of immorality, however. Economic factors also played a part. The Church and the authorities of pre-modern Europe did not want

---

[5] For further discussion see R.W. Malcolmson, 'Infanticide in the eighteenth century', in Cockburn, *Crime in England*, 208.
[6] See, for instance, ibid. 189–90, and especially M. Francus, 'Monstrous mothers, monstrous societies: infanticide and the rule of law in Restoration and eighteenth-century England', *Eighteenth-Century Life* xxi (1997), 133–56.
[7] Hoffer and Hull, *Murdering mothers*, 12.
[8] Mitchison and Leneman, *Sexuality and social control*, 9. For further discussion see K. M. Boyd, *Scottish church attitudes to sex, marriage and the family, 1850–1914*, Edinburgh 1980.
[9] For an exploration of the increasing concern with illegitimacy in Scotland see Mitchison and Leneman, *Sexuality and social control*, chs iv–vii. For further discussion of the idea that Europe during the early modern period was characterised by sin, fear and shame see J. Delumeau, *Sin and fear: the emergence of a western guilt culture 13th–18th centuries*, trans. E. Nicholson, New York 1990.

the financial burden of additional mouths to feed in a regularly strained and unpredictable economic climate, especially when this 'burden' had been 'conceived' in sinful fornication. Indeed, several historians have argued that the cost of illegitimacy rather than its incidence ultimately resulted in the statutory legal changes at the end of the seventeenth century.[10] It was this 'new' legislation which formed the basis for the indictments of the women accused of infanticide before the Justiciary Court between 1750 and 1815.

The twenty-first act of the second session of the first parliament of King William and Mary entitled 'An Act anent the Murdering of Children' directed juries to capitally convict women accused of infanticide regardless of whether there was any direct evidence of murder. According to Baron Hume, 'The circumstances selected for this purpose are, that the woman have concealed her pregnancy during the whole period thereof, and have not called for help to her delivery, and that the child is found dead or is missing.'[11] The wording of the statute clearly illustrates the presumption that if a woman had concealed her pregnancy, by implication, she must have killed her child.

Despite the stern legal provision available to convict and punish infanticidal women, the statute was not fully enforced on a regular basis during the eighteenth century. Deficiencies in the evidence presented to the courts, and uncertainties amongst the legal authorities about how to deal with infanticidal women, were the most significant factors in this. Forms of 'judicial leniency' such as granting petitions for banishment to avoid trial, and allowing (what amounted to) dubious defence pleas to mitigate individual cases, culminated in a moderation of the statute at the beginning of the nineteenth century.[12] The wider unwillingness of the courts to deal with infanticide cases according to the statute is reflected in a low conviction rate in eighteenth-century England and the fact that more than a third of the indicted southwest Scottish women successfully petitioned for banishment and were never brought to trial.[13]

Exceptions to this judicial leniency occurred, however, when there was incontrovertible evidence of violence having been inflicted on the child. As this was far more common in lowland Scotland than elsewhere, it follows that the conviction rate in Scotland was far higher than in other countries at this time. Almost 60 per cent of the women indicted for infanticide who had not petitioned for banishment were capitally convicted. This is a remarkable figure, and although some of the women would be pardoned at a later stage, it still reflects the courts' determination to punish those women who had

10 For further discussion see Jackson, *New-born child murder*, 15 and ch. ii, esp. pp. 37–47, and Ruff, *Violence in early modern Europe*, 151.
11 Hume, *Commentaries*, ii, ch. vi, p. 291.
12 See Jackson, *New-born child murder*, chs v–vi. For more on the changing nature of Scottish judicial opinion regarding infanticide see Kilday, 'Maternal monsters', 156–61.
13 See Jackson, *New-born child murder*, 3. Of the 140 women indicted from south-west Scotland 37% petitioned for banishment to avoid trial and all were successful with their petitions.

blatantly stepped outside the boundaries of 'respectable' behaviour. Further-more, women convicted of infanticide after 1752 could expect to receive the aggravated punishments usually reserved for perpetrators of particularly vicious homicides, and they were regularly sentenced to public dissection and anatomisation, another reflection of how seriously the authorities regarded violent women and violent mothers in particular.[14]

The extent to which these legal statutes and provisions for punishment were actually necessary in relation to the Scottish experience of infanticide deserves further detailed exploration. By examining the incidence of indict-ments that fall into this unique category of crimes against the person, we can enrich and nuance our understanding of violence in a periphery.

Incidence and methods

Incidence of indictments

The so-called 'dark figure' of enigmatic statistics is considered by historians and criminologists alike to be more a problem for the crime of child murder than for any other offence.[15] Clearly, the highly masked nature of this offence, coupled with the obvious lack of testimony from the subsequent victim, makes infanticide one of the most secretive and invisible crimes. Indeed, the very statute charged against those accused of infanticide, as has been shown, emphasised the act of 'concealment'. The number of women who were successful in hiding their pregnancy, the actual act of infanticide itself and the related incriminating evidence can therefore never fully be known.

The deficiency of statistics related to infanticide is compounded by the fact that in the cases that were brought to court, the degrees of proof neces-sary to charge a suspect in the first place were somewhat derisory. It is clear that many indictments were founded on little more than circumstantial neighbourhood gossip or unsubstantiated rumour rather than on firm 'mate-rial' evidence of wrong-doing.[16] In this way infanticide looks like a close cousin of witchcraft.[17] Clearly sometimes those accused of child murder were

---

[14] Aggravated punishments for violent infanticide were also prevalent elsewhere in Europe in the pre-modern period. For example, infant killers were ordered to be drowned, impaled, beheaded or burned in various European courts from the late sixteenth century onwards: Ruff, *Violence in early modern Europe*, 153.

[15] See, for example, Malcolmson 'Infanticide in the eighteenth century', 191, and J. R. Dickinson and J. A. Sharpe, 'Infanticide in early modern England: the court of great sessions at Chester, 1650–1800', in M. Jackson (ed.), *Infanticide: historical perspectives on child murder and concealment, 1550–2000*, Aldershot 2002, 43.

[16] See Beattie, *Crime and the courts*, 117.

[17] For an interesting discussion of the links between infanticide and witchcraft see M. Tausiet, 'Witchcraft as metaphor: infanticide and its translations in Aragón in the sixteenth and seventeenth centuries', in S. Clark (ed.), *Languages of witchcraft: narrative, ideology and meaning in early modern culture*, Basingstoke 2001, 179–96.

the victims of false or mistaken identification. The evidence and testimony of midwives and doctors which led to and influenced indictments was also flawed according to contemporary commentators such as the surgeon Christopher Johnson, especially when a conviction was craved by the majority against a given suspect.[18]

Despite the inadequacies of the evidence, it is still possible to offer substantive conclusions about the nature of infanticide in pre-modern Europe. The work done by historians of infanticide in England in the seventeenth and eighteenth centuries suggests that criminal indictments for infanticide were not common. James Sharpe calculates that between 1620 and 1680, eighty-three women were accused of child murder at the Essex assizes and Robert Malcolmson shows that sixty-one cases were tried at the Old Bailey between 1730 and 1774.[19] John Beattie claims that a ninety-five-year sampling survey of the Surrey assizes between 1660 and 1800 reveals that sixty-two women were indicted for the murder of their newborn children during that entire period.[20] Considering the rigorous legislative measures that were in place in an attempt to eradicate this crime it is perhaps surprising that not more women were indicted, especially in the period of Sharpe's study, during which, in 1624, the English equivalent of the later Scottish statute concerning infanticide was passed. Yet none of these three historians attempts to explain the relatively low incidence of infanticide apparent from their data, preferring to concentrate on the lack of male involvement in the perpetration of this crime as being its most important characteristic.[21] But can the incidence of infanticide elsewhere in Europe shed further light on this conundrum?

The evidence from eighteenth-century France on the subject of child murder is somewhat more confusing than that from England during the same period. There, by an edict of Henri II in 1556 (which was not abolished until 1791) if a woman failed to register her pregnancy and her newborn child died without baptism or proper burial, she would be regarded as a murderess.[22] Maria Piers vividly describes eighteenth-century France as 'the scene of infanticide of unprecedented magnitude' where, as a result of massive over-population, mothers 'disposed of human beings, as an exterminator might dispose of rodents'.[23] However, she gives no statistical evidence to reinforce

---

[18] C. Johnson, 'An essay on the signs of murder in new born children', *Edinburgh Medical and Surgical Journal* x (1814), 394.

[19] See Sharpe, *Crime in seventeenth-century England*, 135, and Malcolmson, 'Infanticide in the eighteenth century', 191.

[20] Beattie, *Crime and the courts*, 114–15.

[21] Other studies of infanticide in early modern England have revealed higher indictment levels than the three illustrated here, but the overall incidence of infanticide in the areas examined was still rare in comparison with other types of crime. See, in particular, Dickinson and Sharpe, 'Infanticide in early modern England', 38, and Jackson, *New-born child murder*, 39.

[22] See Ruff, *Crime, justice and public order*, 169–70.

[23] M. W. Piers, *Infanticide*, New York 1978, 56, 79.

these conclusions and her findings contrast sharply with the work of Julius Ruff in his study of the *sénéchaussées* of Libourne and Bazas between 1696 and 1789. Ruff came across only three indictments for infanticide during that entire period. He explains the lack of incidence as being due to the readiness of contemporary unmarried French women to go through their pregnancies, give birth and then pursue the father of their bastard offspring through the civil courts for substantial maintenance awards.[24] It is unclear which of the two commentators provides the most accurate account of infanticidal behaviour since both constitute such extremes of opinion.[25] So, before coming to the Scottish experience, the frequency of child murder in one other European country which is much more closely related to Scotland in terms of its legal and religious context must be considered, namely Ireland.

The Irish parliament did not officially ratify the infanticide act passed in England in 1624 and in Scotland in 1690 until 1707, but it would appear from the evidence available that such legislation was definitely required by that time. James Kelly, in his study of eighteenth-century Irish infanticide, claims that there were exactly 235 instances of infanticide recorded in the predominantly Dublin-based Irish newspapers between 1721 and 1800.[26] This relatively high incidence of infanticide in Ireland, certainly in comparison with England and Ruff's analysis of the French experience, is substantiated by Brian Henry who claims that over a mere fifteen-year period in the eighteenth century between 1780 and 1795, some thirty-four infanticides were committed in Dublin city alone.[27] Both Kelly and Henry contend that the strict sexual and moral code prevalent in Ireland at this time forced many unmarried women into acts of child murder and concealment of pregnancy in order to avoid the ignominy and public condemnation that was a consequence of illegitimacy for both the mother and her child. Indeed, it would seem to be clear that certainly in relation to England and France, this 'code' was more influential in Ireland than elsewhere in Europe.

The English, French and Irish experiences of infanticide in the premodern period, and the eighteenth century in particular, appear far from homogeneous. Where, though, does the Scottish lowland experience fit into the pattern?

---

[24] See Ruff, *Crime, justice and public order*, 170.

[25] Similar conflicting evidence appears in relation to early modern Germany. Ulinka Rublack, for instance, found seventy-six women indicted for infanticide in seventeenth-century Württemberg whereas Ulbricht's study of Schleswig-Holstein between 1700 and 1810 revealed 340 cases of infanticide. No tangible explanation for these 'regional' discrepancies is apparent from the evidence provided. These are my calculations on the material presented in Rublack, *The crimes of women*, 163, and O. Ulbricht, 'Infanticide in eighteenth-century Germany', in R. J. Evans (ed.), *The German underworld: deviants and outcasts in German history*, London 1988, 110.

[26] J. Kelly, 'Infanticide in eighteenth-century Ireland', *Irish Economic and Social History* xix (1992), 6.

[27] Henry, *Dublin hanged*, 37.

Between 1750 and 1815, 140 women were brought before the Justiciary Court charged with child murder and concealment of pregnancy said to have been committed in the south-west of Scotland.[28] These indictments accounted for nearly a quarter of charges of crimes against the person; indeed in terms of frequency of indictment in that category infanticide was second only to assault of authority. Furthermore, if the total number of indictments for infanticide brought against Scottish lowland women during this period is added to the total number of indictments for homicide, accusations of women causing wilful death increase triple-fold to a level almost as great as that charged against men.[29] Also, bearing in mind the the 'dark figure' in statistics for this offence in particular, it appears logical to consider the 'true' extent of infanticide in lowland Scotland as being considerably more substantial than the Justiciary Court evidence suggests.

Even considering the limitations of comparing the findings of one criminological study to another outlined in the previous chapter on homicide, the available evidence for Scotland clearly adds another dimension to the European trends of infanticidal evidence. Although not as prolific as in Ireland or the wilder estimates for France (if we are to agree with Piers), accusations of child murder levelled against women in lowland Scotland were certainly more prevalent than those in some southern English counties or in the *sénéchaussées* of Libourne and Bazas during the pre-modern period. Just how this criminal act was carried out should now be examined for us to gain an impression of the 'type' of Scottish woman charged with infanticide before the Justiciary Court in the mid eighteenth- and early nineteenth-century period. Was she passive or fundamentally aggressive? To what extent were the stereotypical norms of womanhood and motherhood confirmed or refuted by the actions of these women?

Methodology

As fifty-three of the 140 women brought before the Justiciary Court during the period covered by this study were either declared fugitate or had petitioned for banishment, specific details of their alleged offences were not provided in their indictments.[30] This was almost certainly because they would not be facing trial and therefore evidence and witness testimony became unnecessary. Of the remaining eighty-seven women accused there was often

---

[28] In terms of the incidence of infanticide in south-west Scotland over time, there is no real discernible trend in evidence. There appears to have been a relatively steady indictment rate during the period. Little work has been carried out on infanticide trends over time by other scholars, although Mark Jackson makes a similar conclusion regarding a steady rate of cases being brought to the northern circuit courts in England between 1720 and 1800: *New-born child murder*, 3.

[29] As fifty-seven south-west Scottish women were indicted for homicide, and 140 were accused of infanticide, the total number of women who were charged with committing a crime where the death of the victim resulted was 197. The corresponding figure for south-west Scottish men was 213, a difference between the two sexes of only sixteen.

[30] A full definition of the process of fugitation can be found at p. 36 above.

no substantive, or direct, evidence of any kind linking them to the actual crime itself. Frequently the evidence used to indict in the first instance was flimsy and insubstantial. For instance, in less than 10 per cent of cases was the victim's body found in the living quarters or immediate surroundings occupied by the accused. Whether falsely charged or otherwise, however, if the cause of death of the victim and the *modus operandi* employed in the original act was in any way brutal, a conviction would be imminent regardless of pleas of mitigation.

According to Samuel X. Radbill's early generalisation, 'The methods used in infanticide have not changed much throughout history. Blood is rarely shed.'[31] Radbill's comments appeared to be confirmed by other initial studies of the means employed by women in carrying out infanticide. Richard Helmholz, in his study of the province of Canterbury during the fifteenth century, concluded that 'overlaying' was the most common method used in episodes of infanticide.[32] Keith Wrightson, Robert Malcolmson and James Kelly also maintain that in the seventeenth and eighteenth centuries rather than adopting more overt forms of violence, asphyxia was the principal means of child murder.[33] As Laura Gowing observes during the pre-modern period, infanticide was 'understood to be a crime not of violent activity but of passivity or neglect'.[34]

Yet the profile of those accused of infanticide in lowland Scotland between 1750 and 1815 provides a profoundly different picture. One Justice of the Peace for Dumfries in 1778 described such women as 'Monsters of the vilest kind'.[35] In only 19 per cent of the cases were no discernible 'marks of violence' discovered on the body of the victim.[36] Approximately 6 per cent of the fatalities were suffocated, 7 per cent were strangled, 5 per cent were drowned, but in a highly significant 63 per cent of the indictments brought to trial blood was shed; 48 per cent of the infants had been killed by means of attacks with a sharp instrument and 51 per cent battered to death. This evidence suggests, therefore, that the women accused of infanticide in lowland Scotland appear to have committed this crime in a much more 'violent' manner than other studies of this offence would have predicted.[37]

---

[31] S. X. Radbill, 'A history of child abuse and infanticide', in R. E. Helfer and C. H. Kempe (eds), *The battered child*, Chicago 1968, 9.

[32] R. H. Helmholz, 'Infanticide in the province of Canterbury during the fifteenth century', in R. H. Helmholz (ed.), *Canon law and the law of England*, London 1987, 160.

[33] See K. Wrightson, 'Infanticide in earlier seventeenth-century England', *Local Population Studies* xv (1975), 15; Malcolmson, 'Infanticide in the eighteenth century', 195; and Kelly, 'Infanticide in eighteenth century Ireland', 18.

[34] L. Gowing, 'Secret births and infanticide in seventeenth-century England', *P&P* clvi (1997), 106.

[35] JC 26/216: Archibald Malcolm in Duncow of Kirkmahoe.

[36] This figure includes five women who had allegedly committed the crime of infanticide through exposure. For further discussion see pp. 73–4 below.

[37] Work done by Lynn Abrams on infanticide in Shetland suggests that there may well

It is clear, for example, even in the less aggressive *modus operandi*, that the women involved were not averse to substantial degrees of violence. For instance, Janet McGuffog was indicted before the South Circuit Court in 1787 accused of having given birth to a fully developed son whom she 'did immediately strangle with such ferocity that it did turn blae [blue] and by which means the neck bones of the said child became but splinters'.[38] Similarly, Mary Thomson, also indicted at the South Circuit Court in 1802, was charged with giving birth to a fully developed female child in a field near Irvine in Ayrshire whom she 'did then and there strangle with the aid of its own umbilical cord ... the pressure of which caused the child's windpipe to separate'. The child was found later by a farmer who testified in court that 'one of its eyes was out and a piece cut off its tongue, as he thought, picked out by birds of prey'. [39] Also, Mary Spier (*alias* Fellow) was indicted at the West Circuit Court in 1804 charged with having 'stopped' her newly-born daughter's mouth with 'earth, grass roots and corn roots'. The said mixture 'had been thrust into the throat and was so hard stoped [stopped] there that it had kept open the child's mouth'.[40] Similar 'violent' methods of asphyxiation were employed by Janet Gardener (West Circuit Court, 1751), Agnes Marshall (West Circuit Court, 1770), Grizel Ninian (*alias* McLean) (South Circuit Court, 1772) and others.[41]

Even though the violence of their ultimate intentions could never be doubted, there were, of course, women accused of infanticide who adopted less aggressive methods of asphyxiation. However, their incidence before the Justiciary Court was relatively rare. An example of such behaviour was that displayed by Elizabeth Frazer who was indicted at the West Circuit Court in 1804 charged with 'being delivered of a male child come to the full time... in a house in Bridgetoun in the Barony of Glasgow and county of Lanark'. The court heard that the accused 'did then and there wickedly and feloniously bereave of life and murder her said child by tying it up in a linen bag... alongst with a smoothing iron for the purpose of making it sink, and afterwards throwing it into a well'.[42]

By far the most common method used by lowland women accused of infanticide was attacking the child with a sharp instrument, usually a knife or

be a regional dimension to the nature of Scottish infanticide. She found only two cases of violent infanticide in her study of child murder on the islands between 1699 and 1800: 'From demon to victim', 202 n. 64. Moreover, a preliminary survey of infanticide in the Highlands, which I am currently undertaking, has not yet revealed the degree and frequency of violence evident in the indictments brought to the Justiciary Court in the south-west lowland region of the country. The regional disparity seemingly in evidence in pre-modern Scotland requires more in-depth and detailed investigation than is possible in this present analysis.

[38] JC 26/246.
[39] JC 26/314.
[40] JC 26/322.
[41] See in order of appearance JC 26/144, nos 2650–78; JC 26/191; JC 26/196.
[42] JC 26/322.

razor. Thirty women were indicted for cutting the throats of their children, including Sarah Quarrier (South Circuit Court, 1752), Jean Stewart (South Circuit Court, 1755), Christian Kerr (South Circuit Court, 1767), Janet Hislop (West Circuit Court, 1777), Elizabeth Buntine (West Circuit Court, 1788) and Isobel Perston (West Circuit Court, 1798).[43] Indeed, Jean Allison's indictment at the West Circuit Court in 1805 was typical in this respect. After she had given birth to her daughter, it was alleged that she 'barbarously, wickedly and inhumanely cutt [cut] the child's throat from ear to ear with a razor in a gret [great] effusion of blood, with such force as causing the windpipe thereof to sever in two'.[44] Stabbings made up the remaining attacks on newborn children with sharp instruments. Pitch-forks, pen-knives, lances and nails were most commonly used in this type of offence.

Numerous Scottish women were also accused of battery between 1750 and 1815. Janet Cooper (South Circuit Court, 1768) and Lilias Miligan (South Circuit Court, 1774) were indicted for 'dashing' their infants' skulls off the ground, Elizabeth Swinton (West Circuit Court, 1791) was accused of 'dashing' her child on a tree trunk, Hannah Main (West Circuit Court, 1793) allegedly killed her newborn son with a hammer and Catherine MacDonald (West Circuit Court, 1797) after using a 'spead [spade]' to attack her child in which its 'left leg above the knee was torn off … its right leg was disjointed and its nose flatted [flattened]', fed the child's remains to a neighbourhood dog.[45]

The evidence in the Justiciary records emphasises the readiness of Scottish lowland women to resort to violent means when committing infanticide. Of course it might be argued that these crimes only came to court in the first instance and to the Justiciary Court in particular, due to their exceptionally violent nature. There may have been many more 'less violent' crimes of infanticidal 'overlaying' and suffocation which went undetected by the authorities. Across the social scale, the nature of contemporary dress (aprons, shifts or the 'hoop skirt') and the frequency of female maladies (other than pregnancy), which were treated more often as personal 'embarrassments' to be dealt with in private, meant that concealment of pregnancy was relatively easy for some women to achieve during this period.[46]

Despite this caveat, it is clear that Scottish lowland women brought before the Justiciary Court were atypically brutal in the committal of infanticide. They regularly used levels of violence only rarely used elsewhere in Europe at this time, and, crucially, bloodshed was the norm, rather than the exception. Before we suggest possible reasons for infanticide, bearing these excessive levels of violence in mind, it is important to understand something about

---

43 See in order of appearance JC 26/146, nos 2722–41; JC 26/155; JC 26/183; JC 26/212; JC 26/251; JC 26/294.
44 JC 26/326.
45 See in order of appearance JC 26/186; JC 26/201; JC 26/263; JC 26/270; JC 26/290.
46 For further discussion see Gowing, 'Secret births and infanticide', 87–115.

the profile or background of the offenders involved. Even though there is a significant difference between the nature of infanticide in Scotland and in other European countries, the key characteristics of the defendants themselves are very similar both over time and geography.

Defendant characteristics

The first common characteristic of women accused of child murder was that they had committed the crime on their own newborn infants and had done so acting alone. Only five of the 140 cases brought before the Justiciary Court relating to south-west Scotland between 1750 and 1815 involved the use of an accomplice. Two of these were women and three were men. There was indeed no instance of a man being the sole defendant in an infanticide case throughout the entire period. Of the five accomplices, three were declared fugitate by the court, along with their co-accused principals, for not appearing to answer to the charges against them and little is subsequently known of the circumstances of their cases. Of the two remaining cases, Jean Baillie was indicted with her 'master' Alexander Baird at the West Circuit Court in 1777 and Sarah McDougall was charged with her mother Mary McPherson at the South Circuit in 1792.[47] There is clearly not enough evidence of complicity in the records to warrant any in-depth analysis of these types of infanticidal anomalies; instead it is more pertinent to conclude that when Scottish women committed infanticide, they usually did so unaided.

The second common characteristic of women accused of infanticide is that they were unmarried. As Peter Hoffer and Natalie Hull explain, 'Unwed infanticide suspects played a role, not just as targets for frustration and anger, but as a living definition of the boundary of unacceptable deviance'; they 'had ignored social norms and official pronouncements too flagrantly'.[48] Up to 133 or some 95 per cent of the women indicted before the Justiciary Court for south-west Scotland between 1750 and 1815 for this offence were spinsters, five were relicts (widows) and only two were married. That so few married women faced charges of infanticide is probably not an accurate reflection of their involvement in this type of offence. Child murder was no doubt easier to conceal within marriage through the deliberate neglect of an infant. Overt infanticide, on the other hand, was more commonly the preserve of the unmarried mother, anxious to get rid of the source of her shame and inconvenience in a period when pregnancy outside marriage was considered sinful and dishonourable.[49]

The evidence uncovered for south-west Scotland in this respect suggests a relatively high level of illegitimacy in that area. The work of Rosalind

---

[47] See in order of appearance JC 26/212; JC 26/266.
[48] Hoffer and Hull, *Murdering mothers*, 31.
[49] See Sharpe, *Crime in seventeenth-century England*, 136.

Mitchison and Leah Leneman appears to confirm this hypothesis.[50] The figures for illegitimacy levels for Scotland as a whole show a downward trend from the 1660s through to the 1720s after which they fluctuate. There is no obvious subsequent pattern, in stark contrast to the pronounced rise in corresponding eighteenth-century English statistics for illegitimacy.[51] The one significant exception, when the general trends are broken down, is south-west Scotland which shows a markedly upward trend in illegitimacy levels from the 1750s.[52] The distinctiveness of the south-west of Scotland in relation to bastard-bearing was still significant by the time of civil registration in 1855: while, during the early 1860s the illegitimacy ratio for the whole of Scotland was just over 9 per cent, and for England as a whole was between 6 and 7 per cent, the figure for the south-west of Scotland was more than 13 per cent.[53]

Christopher Smout explains high illegitimacy levels in Scottish rural areas in the nineteenth century by asserting that unmarried pregnancy conferred little disgrace upon the mother or child since such areas were characterised by an absence of the social 'restraints' present elsewhere in the country.[54] Furthermore, there was no need for a woman pregnant with an illegitimate child in rural lowland Scotland to resort to infanticide to conceal her shame. The rural community placed no pressure upon her, and would rather support her both emotionally and financially.[55] Smout's explanation, however, does not seem to correspond with the evidence of infanticide indictments at the Justiciary Court, almost three-quarters of which derived from rural crimes.[56] If, as Smout argues, there was absolutely no social stigma attached to illegitimacy, why were so many women accused of and tried for infanticide in rural areas?

In addition, Smout's claim of there being fewer 'social restraints' in Scottish rural areas seems to be at odds with what we know about the nature of crime in that type of locale. As we have seen in relation to homicide, killing was more common in towns where individuals had greater freedom and opportunity to be engaged in the type of situation where murder could

---

[50] It must be borne in mind that Mitchison and Leneman's study does not extend over the same geographical area as that examined in the Justiciary records: it does not consider parishes in the Lanarkshire, Renfrewshire or Dunbartonshire regions. For further discussion see L. Leneman and R. Mitchison, 'Scottish illegitimacy ratios in the early modern period', *Economic History Review* 2nd ser. xl (1987), 61–3, and Mitchison and Leneman, *Sexuality and social control*, 244–5.

[51] Mitchison and Leneman, *Sexuality and social control*, 146.

[52] Ibid. 147.

[53] Ibid. 9–10. See also idem, *Girls in trouble: sexuality and social control in rural Scotland, 1660–1780*, Edinburgh 1998, 2, 75.

[54] T. C. Smout, 'Aspects of sexual behaviour in nineteenth-century Scotland', in A. A. MacLaren (ed.), *Social class in Scotland: past and present*, Edinburgh 1976, 80.

[55] Ibid. 71.

[56] For a predominance of infanticide in rural areas elsewhere see Jackson, *New-born child murder*, 42, and Morgan and Rushton, *Rogues, thieves and the rule of law*, 112.

result. Killing was far less common in rural areas, on the other hand, because of the closeness of the community and the level of supervision that existed as a result of this. So how can we explain the high incidence of infanticide in lowland rural areas?

Perhaps the more intensive supervision of women in the countryside meant that it was far harder for them to conceal their pregnancies and to dispose of their unwanted offspring than it was for women in urban areas. Consequently, as rural women were more likely to be caught, they were more likely to be indicted, and the incidence of them being brought before the Justiciary Court is a relatively accurate indication of the incidence of this type of crime in country areas. In contrast, infanticide in urban areas was no doubt far easier to conceal, so that the incidence of indictment probably significantly under-estimates the real propensity for child murder in towns.[57]

Mitchison and Leneman offer a slightly different explanation for the levels of significant illegitimacy in south-west Scotland. They state that in various instances throughout history the area displayed a characteristic resist-ance to 'authority'. Citing episodes such as the Covenanting rebellion of the mid-seventeenth century and the Levellers' revolt of 1724, Mitchison and Leneman argue that dissent was endemic in the south-west of Scotland.[58] They go on to claim that this 'dissent' was not only directed towards the government or landowners, but also towards the Church.[59] The high level of resistance to church discipline prevalent in the south-west of Scotland might suggest that women from that area would be less likely than women elsewhere to subscribe to the moral guidelines prescribed by the Church authorities in their sexual behaviour. Men, too, appeared to have played a part in reac-tion against church authority. For instance, men from the south-west were more reluctant than men elsewhere to confess illegitimate parenthood before the Kirk Session between 1660 and 1780.[60] The contention of Mitchison and Leneman therefore is that illegitimacy levels were higher in south-west Scotland due to a more truculent attitude there to the moral doctrines of the Church. However the extent to which such an attitude was harboured among the women indicted for infanticide before the Justiciary Court is not apparent from the evidence.

Another reason for the unusual levels of illegitimacy and infanticide in south-west Scotland may have been the persistent presence of large numbers of soldiers.[61] The itinerant nature of military service could have meant that

---

[57] The indictment rate for homicide in urban areas, although greater than in the coun-tryside, was probably also under-estimated. However, as the murder of an adult was harder to conceal than the murder of a newborn baby, the incidence of murder indictments in relation to towns was probably a closer reflection of the incidence of that type of killing than the evidence for infanticide in the same locale.

[58] Mitchison and Leneman, *Sexuality and social control*, 146, 243.

[59] Ibid. 145.

[60] Ibid. 145, 205. See also idem, *Girls in trouble*, 83, 108.

[61] See Stewart, '"In durance vile", 72. M. W. Piers argues that similar circumstances

many young women were abandoned by their suitors and perhaps the fathers of their illegitimate offspring when it was time for the battalion to move on. This hypothesis is only speculation, however, as the Justiciary records rarely reveal who was responsible for the defendants' initial 'condition' in infanticide indictments.

What is more readily apparent is the third and final common characteristic of the women brought to court under such charges: they were predominantly employed as domestic servants. In south-west Scotland between 1750 and 1815, 74 per cent of the 140 females indicted for child murder were in employment and of these some 90 per cent were employed in domestic service. The high incidence of participation in this type of offence by these women in contemporary England has led one commentator to contend that the servant-girl was 'very vulnerable to unmarried motherhood, from which it might be inferred that she was correspondingly prone to infanticide'.[62] It is probably not that surprising that so many of the women accused of child murder were domestic servants. Most servant-girls were of child-bearing age and they worked in close proximity to men. In addition, illegitimate pregnancy would be disastrous for domestic servants as they were usually only employed on the basis that they remained single and childless. The loss of reputation to a household employing an unmarried pregnant servant would rarely be tolerated; she would inevitably be dismissed without a reference. The pressure on such women to conceal their pregnancies and thereafter rid themselves of the cause of ruin to their character and economic livelihood in the form of their bastard offspring can easily be understood.[63]

Motives

The first area of motivation to be examined is why women in Scotland during the mid-eighteenth and early nineteenth centuries predominantly chose infanticide as the means of ridding themselves of their unwanted newborn offspring rather than the other options open to them at this time. Provisions for a nationwide adoption service and improvements in abortive techniques to reduce the risk of fatal complications in the procedure for the mother did not exist until the mid-nineteenth century.[64] Nevertheless, it is perhaps surprising

---

caused an increase in both illegitimacy and the spread of sexually transmitted diseases throughout eighteenth-century France: *Infanticide*, 59–61. For further discussion of the association between soldiers and infanticide see Rublack, *The crimes of women*, 183.

[62] Sharpe, *Crime in seventeenth-century England*, 137. See also Gowing, 'Secret births and infanticide', 92, and Jackson, *New-born child murder*, 49.

[63] For further discussion see Beattie, 'The criminality of women', 84; Malcolmson, 'Infanticide in the eighteenth century', 192–3, 203; and R. Sauer, 'Infanticide and abortion in nineteenth-century Britain', *Population Studies: A Journal of Demography* xxxii (1978), 85.

[64] See Malcolmson, 'Infanticide in the eighteenth century', 187, 207–8.

that Scottish lowland women rarely resorted to the relatively simple act of 'exposure' as a means of infanticide.

Exposure, or 'dropping', as it was commonly called, involved the abandoning of a newborn infant in a relatively public place such as the steps of a church, in a market place or in the doorway of an affluent household, presumably so that it would be found and cared for. Although it was believed to be a fairly common occurrence in eighteenth-century England,[65] only five southwest Scottish women were indicted for exposure between 1750 and 1815. The lesser incidence of this form of infanticide is possibly explained by the high risk of detection involved in carrying out the offence. It was no doubt difficult to abandon a baby and escape from the scene without being noticed.

One of the five women charged with exposure before the Justiciary Court was Ann Parker (alias Ann Hepple), a midwife from Glasgow. She was charged at the West Circuit in 1806 with 'the crime of exposing an infant child, *not her own*, by laying it down in a common or public stair'.[66] The nature of the offence charged seems to suggest a relationship to the practice common in Glasgow and Edinburgh by the late nineteenth century: baby-farming, also known as 'wet-nursing'.[67]

According to Otto Pollak:

> Baby farmers were women to whom unmarried mothers turned over their newly born infants, ostensibly to have the children cared for and brought up against the payment of a lump sum. Actually there was a quiet understanding that the children should be made to die inconspicuously. Neglect and insufficient food soon weakened the children so that they succumbed easily to diseases, and the overburdened practitioners in the urban and rural districts, where these baby farms were ... located, seldom had time enough to probe carefully into the death causes of the children.[68]

The fact that monetary payment was involved in this kind of arrangement may have prevented many contemporary mothers from using such measures. However, it may well also have been the case that, although baby-farming was relatively widespread, it was largely concealed during the 1750 to 1815 period.

Motivation for infanticide usually originated after conception, when efforts to conceal the pregnancy were first attempted. Although it must be accepted that in some cases failure to disclose pregnancy was not a deliberate decision made with criminal intentions, it would seem to be the case that for

---

65 See McLynn, *Crime and punishment*, 112, and Malcolmson, 'Infanticide in the eighteenth century', 188.

66 JC 13/34: my emphasis added.

67 For further discussion of this type of 'employment' see Rose, *Massacre of the innocents*, 82–4, and Sanderson, *Women and work*, 49–53.

68 Pollak, *The criminality of women*, 19–20.

the women indicted for child murder before the Justiciary Court the motives for concealment of pregnancy were similar to those for infanticide.

One of the principal suggested motives for infanticide amongst the majority of unmarried women was the need to avoid the social stigma of being considered 'of easy virtue' and of having produced an illegitimate child. The contemporary opprobrium associated with an illegitimate pregnancy, substantiated by moralistic and religious commentators alike, would seemingly not only tarnish the reputation of the woman directly involved and damage her prospects of a 'good' marriage, but would almost certainly affect the status of the rest of her family amongst the wider community in which she lived. This disgrace became manifest if a woman was brought before the Kirk Session suspected of an illegitimate pregnancy. She was charged to account for her condition, name the man responsible and if found guilty would be fined and ordered to make 'appearances' before the entire congregation.[69] Bearing this in mind, therefore, it is perhaps not surprising that the guilt and shame involved in an unmarried pregnancy are suggested as key incentives for women to terminate the life of the cause of such derogation. Some historians have even gone so far as to say that the nature of pre-modern church discipline was a direct cause of infanticide at that time, as women simply could not face the embarrassment of appearing before the church authorities.[70] However, this argument must be treated with some caution, judging from the evidence discussed here. Given the high rate of illegitimacy prevalent in the region under discussion, can it be argued that the failure of church discipline caused women to commit infanticide in the south-west? Illegitimate pregnancies were clearly more acceptable there and the strength of the Church and its attitudes was seemingly not as influential as elsewhere in the country at this time.

As has also been shown, economic factors provide potent incentives for the committal of infanticide. Falling pregnant during employment (especially as a domestic servant) meant dismissal and a loss of livelihood and means of support. This forfeiture of income was then compounded by the spectre of financial hardship caused by the additional mouth to feed, clothe and care for. As Martin Daly and Margo Wilson comment, 'If the history of infanticide reveals anything ... it is surely that acts of desperation are principally the products of desperate circumstances.'[71] In the south-west of Scotland, however, the provision for illegitimate children from the poor law was more generous and comprehensive than in many other parts of the country.[72] This

---

[69] For further discussion see Mitchison and Leneman, *Sexuality and social control*, 136, and *Girls in trouble*, 17.

[70] See, for instance, idem, *Girls in trouble*, 34, and Ulbricht, 'Infanticide in eighteenth-century Germany', 108.

[71] M. Daly and M. Wilson, *Homicide*, New York 1988, 69.

[72] See R. A. Cage, *The Scottish poor law, 1745–1845*, Edinburgh 1981, especially the maps between pp. 35–6 and pp. 38–9.

suggests more than a concern with specifically providing for their unborn children. Scottish women who were eager to maintain their independence and security through the earning of a wage may well have considered concealment of pregnancy and child murder as the only viable options open to them if they wanted to ensure their personal economic survival.

Lionel Rose suggests another possible economic motive for women to commit infanticide. A pregnant woman would pay a few pennies a week into a fund set up in case anything happened to her child during labour and delivery in order to enable her to pay for its funeral. Rose contends that women were deliberately killing their infants after birth, claiming the money (plus interest accrued) from the burial insurers, giving the child an inexpensive funeral and reaping the profits made. However, although Rose suggests such practices were common in Glasgow during the nineteenth century, linking this to the historical reality of infanticide is problematic. Surely in order successfully to claim the money due to them, the women concerned would have to make the death of the child appear natural to the insurers or the premium would not be paid out.[73] Yet, as the evidence for this study has already indicated, there were relatively few apparent 'natural' deaths in comparison with obviously violent ones, suggesting that this type of motivation was probably not as common as Rose insists, at least in relation to the earlier 1750–1815 period. Furthermore, as the women involved in this type of practice would necessarily have had to reveal themselves to be pregnant, it may have been more common amongst married women, who, like 'natural' deaths, accounted for relatively few indictments in the present investigation.

Another possible reason for committing infanticide, one that appears more plausible given the violent nature of child murder in the cases brought before the Justiciary Court between 1750 and 1815, turns upon the attitude of the accused towards her victim. Many instances must have occurred of women who had accepted a proposal of marriage on the acknowledged custom of pre-nuptial sex with their suitors, but on discovering themselves to be pregnant were readily abandoned by their 'betrothed' and as a result the women wrought their revenge upon what they perceived to be the reason for their abandonment and isolation – their newborn infant.[74]

This inducement to the act of infanticide involves a considerable degree of psychological dissociation. The evidence of the brutality involved in the committal of that crime in Scotland between the mid-eighteenth and early nineteenth centuries does indeed suggest that types of temporary insanity (perhaps induced by alcohol consumption), whether in the form of psychogenic infanticide or paranoid delusional hallucinations, may well have been 'unconscious' incitements for women to murder their newborn offspring.[75] In

---

73 For further discussion see Rose, *Massacre of the innocents*, chs xv, xvi.
74 For further discussion see ibid., 24; Malcolmson, 'Infanticide in the eighteenth century', 204; and Symonds, *Weep not for me*, 165.
75 For further discussion of this see Hoffer and Hull, *Murdering mothers*, 145–58.

terms of evidence brought before the courts, however, these types of defence pleas did not play any significant role in infanticide cases until the nineteenth century.[76] Nevertheless they may well have been applicable to some of the indicted Scottish lowland women one hundred years earlier, even though not enough was known about the nature and implications of such conditions at that time.

It is clearly difficult to discern a particular reason for the behaviour of infanticidal mothers. It is even more difficult to explain why the women of lowland Scotland were seemingly so much more violent in the perpetration of this kind of murderous activity than their counterparts elsewhere during the pre-modern period. Shame must have been a significant factor, even bearing in mind the more 'indifferent' attitude to the Kirk that seems to have existed in the south-west region at the time. Economic factors, revenge, jealousy, feelings of abandonment and loneliness as well as manifestations of mental incapacity may well also have had a part to play. Could it also be argued, however, that if lowland women behaved more violently than expected in other crimes against the person, such as homicide, then this tendency would also extend itself to their behaviour in the committal of infanticide? Is it possible that these women were simply more aggressive in personality than women elsewhere? Were Scottish lowland women who committed brutal infanticides simply conforming to the violence that existed in the society around them and which they had internalised as normal? Had these women committed this crime in a manner that they deemed acceptable and familiar, unable to identify with their more genteel and 'civilised' female counterparts elsewhere? This conjecture needs to be examined more thoroughly and in relation to other violent offences before any definitive conclusions can be drawn.

The only statement that can be made with relative conviction regarding the reasoning behind women's participation in this type of offence, as with their participation in other crimes against the person, is that no single common or simple explanation is discernible from the evidence. As Peter Hoffer and Natalie Hull conclude:

Motivation for the crime of infanticide was as varied as the personalities … of the women who attempted it and the situations in which they found themselves. External pressures like social ostracism, shame, loss of employment and reputation, and forcible intercourse, were certainly motives for the crimes, but before any individual would undertake it, these influences had to pass through the filter of individual character and perception.

[76] For more on medical defences relating to infanticide cases see D. Rabin, 'Bodies of evidence, states of mind: infanticide, emotion and sensibility in eighteenth-century England' (pp. 73–92), H. Marland, 'Getting away with murder? Puerperal insanity, infanticide and the defence plea' (pp. 168–92), and C. Quinn, 'Images and impulses: representations of puerperal insanity and infanticide in late Victorian England' (pp. 193–215), in Jackson, *Infanticide*.

Outside forces created stress, but response to stress was not uniform. When fear and anger were overwhelming enough to cause the perpetrator to view the child as a thing, a cancer or a foreign object, or to make the perpetrator believe that such injustices as led to conception and would follow from successful birth were unsupportable, the crime might follow ... Infanticidal mothers ... frustrated at their own lives and unable to reach back into their own childhoods for resources to nurture the growth of the new lives entrusted to them, ... struck out at the cause of their misery.[77]

The statutory provision concerned with infanticide (Act 1690 c.21) was unique in Scots law as it automatically presumed a woman to be guilty of child murder if she concealed the pregnancy or if the baby was subsequently found dead or was missing. Even though the severity of the statute made it increasingly difficult to enforce as a capital offence during the post-Enlightenment period of more 'compassionate' societal attitudes, the rate of prosecutions brought before the Justiciary Court still remained substantial. Up to 140 women were indicted for concealment of pregnancy and child murder between 1750 and 1815. Although less than in contemporary Ireland, the incidence of infanticide in lowland Scotland was greater than that described in studies of eighteenth-century southern English counties or Julius Ruff's account of pre-revolutionary France. However, although variations in infanticidal frequency exist, there are certain key characteristics related to the defendants involved which are common to all studies of this crime. Predominantly the evidence shows that those accused were unmarried rural women acting alone who, if in employment, were domestic servants. Aside from these bonds of association, however, the evidence for lowland Scotland differs from that described elsewhere in one further crucial respect – modus operandi. Whereas women in other areas were preponderantly indicted for the crime of child murder through suffocation or 'overlaying', Scottish lowland women appeared to employ far more violent methods in their murderous activities, throat-slitting being the most popular. The Justiciary Court records are not very forthcoming about the motives behind the crimes of concealment of pregnancy and child murder, although it can be supposed that the shame and guilt of an illegitimate pregnancy, the economic consequences of that pregnancy and perhaps to a lesser extent temporary insanity were the chief factors involved.

The findings of this chapter have profound implications for criminal and gender history. Infanticide in lowland Scotland was far more shocking, brutal and bloodthirsty than is evidenced in any other currently available analysis of the offence. Women in that region were thus not only ignoring the norms of acceptable gendered behaviour but were also abandoning what was considered to be appropriate maternal behaviour as well. The relatively high conviction rate of these women and the aggravated punishments regularly meted out to

77 Hoffer and Hull, *Murdering mothers*, 157–8.

them are a reflection of the various authorities' attempts to 're-gender' or femi-nise women whom they considered to be 'abnormal' and to warn potentially criminal women against stepping outside the norms of 'respectable' female conduct. The reasons why Scottish lowland women behaved so aggressively in the perpetration of infanticide remain partially opaque, but their actions shatter traditional conceptions of infanticidal women as pitiable, desperate 'victims' who killed with a conscience.

5

Assault

'Ye see a woman in Gallawa kens her place in the hoose, an keeps't. She's no the meeserable non-entity a woman turns in Englan' efter she's mairry't; there's nae "Love, honour, and obey" in her mairriage promises; she's joost as deservin o' love, honour, and obedience as him, an she's a fule if she disna hae her share o't; she promises tae tak him, that's a'. Catch a Gallawa woman ca'in her man "my master" the wey the puir ignorant English yins dis! No likely! He's nae maister o' her's.'[1]

Apart from a few notable exceptions, the crime of assault has received scant attention from historians of the pre-modern period.[2] This is perhaps surprising, as assault arguably more than any other crime can tell us about the nature of 'ordinary' or 'regular' violence – the type that occurred on a day-to-day basis. Although often less spectacular than murder or child-killing, instances of assault can reveal much about how men and women reacted to the situations they faced in their everyday lives, and are thus a useful mechanism for investigating the forms and causes of 'usual' violence. Yet many historians have found the analysis of pre-modern assault charges to be overly complex and largely unfruitful. This is because in England, Ireland and France assault was very much a non-specific 'umbrella-term' for every offence from a life-threatening incident down to a petty squabble. As a result, coherent analysis of the English experience of assault seems to have been difficult to achieve.[3]

In Scotland, even though the definition of assault in the eighteenth and nineteenth centuries was 'an intentional physical attack upon the person,

1 Extract from 'Gallawa wifes', in R. de Bruce Trotter, *Galloway gossip 80 years ago* (The Stewartry Edition), Dumfries 1901, 103–4.
2 The exceptions to the paucity of material on assault are Hunt, 'Wife beating', 10–33; J. Warner and A. Lunny, 'Marital violence in a martial town: husbands and wives in early modern Portsmouth, 1653–1781', *Journal of Family History* xxviii (2003), 258–76; J. Hurl-Eamon, 'Domestic violence prosecuted: women binding over their husbands for assault at Westminster quarter sessions, 1685–1720', *Journal of Family History* xxvi (2001), 435–54; J. Bailey, *Unquiet lives: marriage and marriage breakdown in England, 1660–1800*, Cambridge 2003; P. King, 'Punishing assault: the transformation of attitudes in the English courts', *Journal of Interdisciplinary History* xxvii (1996), 43–74; and Walker, *Crime, gender and social order*, chs ii, iii. It should be noted that with the exception of the last title, all the other works concentrate almost exclusively on assaults committed by men.
3 See, for instance, Beattie, *Crime and the courts*, 75–6; Sharpe, *Crime in seventeenth-century England*, 117–19; R. Gillespie, 'Women and crime in seventeenth-century Ireland', in M. MacCurtain and M. O'Dowd (eds), *Women in early modern Ireland*, Edinburgh 1991, 43–51; and Ruff, *Crime, justice and public order*, 70–105.

either seriously threatened or actually accomplished',[4] when a given case came to court, the categories of offence were much more specific. Attempted murder, 'common' aggravated assault,[5] aggravated assault of authority, hame-sucken (the assault of an individual within his or her own dwelling place), rape and sexual assault[6] and a series of minor offences such as gross insult and abuse, violent threatenings and writing incendiary letters, were all charged in the indictments and warrants of the Justiciary Court. The clear distinction made between crimes of this nature makes a detailed analysis of the offence more practical for lowland Scotland between 1750 and 1815. In any case, as assault in general terms was the most common single crime against the person that was brought before the Justiciary Court in relation to lowland Scotland, a closer scrutiny of this type of offence is surely vital for any understanding of indicted violent criminality during the period under review.

Although comparisons between other studies can be imperfect, it is still interesting to note that the apparent *lacuna* in the evidence for assault has not prevented criminal historians from constructing the fundamentals of a gendered analysis of this crime for the pre-modern period – however flawed. More often than not, this has been born out of an attempt to emphasise the lack of women's participation in offences involving violence, rather than to investigate and analyse female behaviour *per se*. James Sharpe, for instance, calculates that women committed just over 8 per cent of the total number of indicted assault cases in seventeenth-century Essex.[7] In eighteenth-century Surrey, on the other hand, John Beattie found that nearly 20 per cent of the indictments for assault were levelled against women.[8]

The relatively low incidence of female assault indictments fits in well with the traditional notion that violent behaviour was almost exclusively a male phenomenon. The supposed protection offered to wives by their husbands has, in particular, been used to explain women's reluctance to take part in crimes of assault. For, even when women wanted to get involved in a 'physical' dispute with another individual, it was expected that her husband would take her place in any episode which necessitated the use of levels of violent aggression. The principle of coverture has meant that women have commonly been associated with verbal violence in disputes, rather than physical attacks, and

---

[4] A. M. Anderson, *The criminal law of Scotland*, 2nd edn, Edinburgh 1904, pt II, 158.
[5] I have used the word 'common' to distinguish this type of assault from assault against authority.
[6] As no women were charged with being art and part or even accessory to this offence between 1750 and 1815, it does not warrant close attention in this study.
[7] My calculation based on the evidence presented in Sharpe, *Crime in seventeenth century England*, 117.
[8] This figure is given in relation to the general category Beattie denotes as 'assault and wounding': 'The criminality of women', 85.

this has led to the belief that women preferred to fight 'with tongues rather than fists' in their attempts to assert authority or opinion.[9]

Assaults by women have thus long been seen solely in relation to their apparent dependency on men. Coverture, however, was extremely limited and inconsistent in its application and certainly had no relevance to single women or widows.[10] In addition, and as has been shown elsewhere in this volume, Scottish women were regularly prepared to behave violently and forcefully in their own right, regardless of the concerns and prescribed gender roles of men. This seems to have been no less the case when the crime of assault is considered. In lowland Scotland between 1750 and 1815 women were indicted in 37 per cent, or 292 out of 791 cases of assault brought before the Justiciary Court.[11] The participation of Scottish women, at over a third of all indictments for this type of offence, appears to be significantly higher than in evidence found elsewhere in Britain in the sixteenth, seventeenth and eighteenth centuries and warrants further investigation. Furthermore, if an analysis of individual types of assault is undertaken, the evidence of the Justiciary Court suggests that in some instances women participated just as often if not more frequently than men in certain types of non-fatal violence against the person.

The purpose of this chapter is to look at the nature of interpersonal violence in lowland Scotland during the pre-modern period and to examine why lowland Scottish women were willing to resort to violent assault to resolve disputes. First the legal context of the offence is examined to determine the extent to which assault was viewed as a serious offence by the authorities of the day. The chapter then falls into three sections, which deal with the principal forms of assault in which lowland women were involved: domestic assault, communal assault and the assault of authority. Each section investigates the offenders, the methods they used to carry out the offence and the rationale behind the violence involved. By analysing women's actions in this respect, this chapter identifies why evidence from the Justiciary Court suggests that Scottish women were more commonly indicted for acts of physical aggression than their English counterparts. Were lowland women more comfortable with violent behaviour than women south of the Tweed, or were violent Scottish women more likely to be detected by the authorities? By illuminating the nature of assault in pre-modern Scotland, this chapter will contribute much to our understanding of the place of violence in the everyday lives of Scottish women during the eighteenth and nineteenth centuries.

---

[9]   For example, Richard Allestree commented in the seventeenth century that 'a woman ordinarily [has] only that weapon of the tongue to offend with': *The whole duty of man, laid down in a plain and familiar way for the use of all but especially the meanest reader*, London 1716, 276–7.

[10] For further discussion of the relationship between coverture and crime see Walker, *Gender, crime and social order*, 76–7, 111.

[11] This figure rises to 40% if comparisons between men and women are made in only the crimes for which women were indicted i.e. discounting rape and hamesucken.

The legal context and attitudes towards assault

In Scotland, in general terms, assault was a non-capital, common law crime which was punished according to the discretion of the court and depending on the circumstances of the given case.[12] In cases of attempted murder or 'common' aggravated assault there was only one central condition to be met for a charge to result. This was that regardless of the instrument used to facilitate the assault, the attack itself had to be 'attended with immediate pain and distress, as by bringing the person to the ground, effusion of blood, or contusion of body'.[13] Apart from this, the law concerning attempted murder or 'common' aggravated assault was only concerned with the degree of violence involved and whether the attack had been provoked.[14]

Clearly Scottish courts were interested in hearing explanations for outbursts of aggression, as well as determining the degree of violence offered in the particular assault in question. Cases brought to the Justiciary Court, the supreme criminal court of the country, would therefore only deal with the most serious assault cases, instances where the violence offered was brutal and difficult to excuse. For this chapter to conclude successfully its investigation of the nature and levels of everyday violence in Enlightenment Scotland, it needs to scrutinise other evidence beyond that presented at the court of Justiciary.

Unlike the other serious violent offences examined in this book, indictments for assault were not the sole province of the Justiciary Court. Other Scottish courts (which dealt with matters at a more local level) could hear cases of assault or could register warrants of arrest for those individuals suspected of the offence. Consequently, an in-depth survey was conducted of pertinent material from a wide variety of Justice of the Peace Courts and Sheriff Courts for lowland Scotland between 1750 and 1815.[15] Although the evidence uncovered from these additional sources is incorporated throughout this chapter, it is important to note from the outset that, unlike the experience of the Justiciary Court, the involvement of women in assault cases in the Justice of the Peace Court and, more significantly, the Sheriff Court was almost negligible compared to that of men.

---

[12] There were some exceptions to this general rule as some specific statutes did exist for the crime of assault. These are outlined in Hume, *Commentaries*, i, ch. ix. None of these statutes were cited in the indictments of the lowland Scottish women charged with assault at the Justiciary Court between 1750 and 1815.

[13] Hume, *Commentaries*, i, ch. ix, p. 331.

[14] Ibid.

[15] For information on the provenance and jurisdiction of these courts see chapter 2 above. For both courts, material was sampled at five-year intervals between 1750 and 1815. The records for each year sampled were studied in their entirety. The Justice of the Peace Courts examined were East Lothian, Midlothian, West Lothian, Kirkcudbright, Selkirk and Wigtown. The Sheriff Courts examined were Paisley, Haddington, Stirling, Wigtown, Selkirk, Hamilton and Peebles. These geographical regions were closely comparable with the jurisdictional areas covered by the High Court of Justiciary and its circuit courts.

As outlined in chapter 2, the Justice of the Peace Court rarely heard assault cases and more commonly dealt with petitions connected to theft and communal disturbances as well as non-criminal matters such as land development, enclosure, provision for the poor and highway repair. The sampling survey revealed that only four cases of 'common' assault were heard before the justices in lowland Scotland; two of these involved female defendants. In the Sheriff Court, on the other hand, indictments for assault were a regular occurrence, with 287 cases of 'common' assault being heard between 1750 and 1815 in the lowland shires. However, the proportion of female accused was less than 2 per cent of the total, with only five cases of assault being charged against women during the period under review.

Explanations for the low incidence of women in indictments for assault in these courts of lower jurisdiction are difficult to ascertain, but a few suggestions can be made. It is possible that women were more commonly involved in more serious assaults, and that is why they are more prevalent in indictments at the Court of Justiciary. This, though, seems unlikely. Alternatively, and more plausibly, perhaps there actually were very few women who committed assault, but because when they did so, they stepped outside what was considered to be normal or appropriate 'feminine' behaviour, they were more likely to be sent to the Justiciary Court, where an example could better be made of them. The proportionately high level of female involvement in assault at the Justiciary Court could therefore be explained not as evidence of lowland women being more willing than women elsewhere to employ non-fatal violence, but of violent lowland women simply being more likely to be indicted at a higher court than their European counterparts during the pre-modern period. For instance, if all the assault indictments charged at the Sheriff and Justiciary Courts in Scotland during the period from 1750 to 1815 are calculated, the proportional participation of lowland women drops from 37 per cent to around 14 per cent.[16] This figure is much more in line with estimates of women's participation in assault in other studies of the pre-modern period.[17] It seems plausible to suggest, then, that Scottish men were accused of assault within a variety of different jurisdictions within the Scottish legal system; this accounts for their figuring less prominently, in proportional terms, in Justiciary Court evidence. Scottish lowland women, on the other hand, seem to have been indicted more or less exclusively at the supreme court in the country. This suggests that the Scottish authorities regarded female criminality as extremely serious, even if it was non-fatal in nature. Certainly, in the earlier part of the period, Scottish women were more likely than men

---

16 Through linear extrapolation it can be calculated that approximately 1,435 cases of assault were heard at the Sheriff Courts of lowland Scotland between 1750 and 1815, and around 25 of these cases were levelled against women. When adding these figures to the evidence from the Justiciary Court, it can be estimated that around 317 assault indictments were levelled against lowland women out of an approximate total of 2,226 cases. This represents a proportional total of 14%.

17 See, for instance, the evidence presented in nn. 7, 8 above.

to receive an 'exemplary' punishment for assault. They were more likely to be whipped when found guilty of 'common' assault before 1775, whereas men were more likely to be fined or incarcerated.[18]

A third reason for the absence of women accused of assault from courts other than the Court of Justiciary might be that authorities and communities either ignored violent women or dealt with them in an 'extra-legal' way if the offence committed was not considered to be overtly serious. These hypotheses will be examined in more detail in relation to the 'types' of assault that lowland women actively participated in during the eighteenth- and early nineteenth-century period.

The legal context of the offence of assault of authority was somewhat more complicated than that of attempted murder or 'common' assault. Although still only an offence at common law, the courts dealt with those convicted of this type of offence far more harshly than those found guilty of the other varieties of assault. This was because, to legal minds at least, assault of authority was closely associated with treason and seditious practices. This type of crime was not only seen as a threat to the social order in the area where it was alleged to have been committed, but also to the wider authority of the state throughout the country. Those convicted, regardless of gender, had to be made examples of in order to deter others from behaving in a similar manner, and as a result the courts applied the most severe forms of punishment open to them within the boundaries of non-capital discipline.[19] The weighty consideration given to this type of offence by the legal authorities is probably the main reason why indictments for assault of authority were far more prevalent in the Court of Justiciary than in either the Sheriff Court or the Justice of the Peace Court between 1750 and 1815.[20]

There were several conditions in Scots law which had to be met in order for a charge of the assault of authority to result. First, as Baron Hume described, 'The person deforced must be a lawful officer; one of the regular and proper executors of that sort of diligence or warrant which is hindered.'[21] The officer must have notified the accused that he was acting in an official capacity and must have proceeded to do so in a lawful manner. Finally, the degree of violence offered was unimportant; an offence was committed as long as

---

[18] For further discussion see Kilday, 'Women and crime', ch. vi. This conclusion seems to be at odds with the Essex experience of assault convictions between 1748 and 1821 where similar punishments were given out regardless of gender. See King, 'Punishing assault', 54–5.

[19] For further discussion of the attitude and response towards the crime of assault of authority in Scots law see Hume, *Commentaries*, i, ch. xiii.

[20] The sample survey of the Justice of the Peace Courts revealed only two cases of assault of authority, both of which were levelled at men. At the Sheriff Court forty-seven cases of this type were indicted, with seven involving female defendants. The paucity of evidence from these two courts of lesser jurisdiction stands in contrast with the Court of Justiciary where 361 cases of assault of authority were heard over the same period (1750–1815).

[21] Hume, *Commentaries*, i, ch. xiii, p. 386.

the officer was hindered from doing his duty.[22] As can be seen, nearly all the conditions which have to be met in order to validate a charge of the assault of authority are concerned with the behaviour of the assaulted officer rather than his assailant. This makes this type of offence rather unusual in Scots law but it demonstrates a determination on the part of the legal authorities that indictments for the assault of authority should be obvious and transparent in order to maximise convictions and to enable the courts to use whatever punishments they deemed appropriate.

Attitudes towards the crime of assault on the part of the Scottish authorities appear not have altered very much over the course of the eighteenth century. The incidence of assault indictments for men, and especially for women, fluctuates to such an extent that no discernible trends are evident. This suggests that the individuals who resorted to assault were reacting to specific personal circumstances rather than to national grievances or other socio-economic trends. Certainly the trend in evidence in eighteenth-century Essex, where juries were becoming tougher on assault over time (seen in an increase in indictments and a greater willingness to use harsher punishments) was not apparent in lowland Scotland.[23] North of the border there was no real increase in indictments between 1750 and 1815 for either male or female defendants, and furthermore, towards the end of the period, judges were moving away from exemplary punishments for women. They became more inclined to use imprisonment which was increasingly regarded as a more measured and effective sanction, and one which was already in operation for male convicts.

'Common' assaults seem to have been largely tolerated by the Scottish authorities at this time, unless the attack was particularly vicious or unwarranted. Making examples of a few felons was deemed enough to control the populace and prevent widespread violence and unrest. For some, however, the Scottish authorities were too lenient in their attitudes to assault. A petition to the Justice of the Peace Court in West Lothian in the early decades of the nineteenth century, for instance, asked that the 'progress' of assault in the county be monitored as the public were concerned that the authorities were being too relaxed and that violent crime was getting out of control in that area.[24] Although the petition enabled the community to voice its concerns, there was no discernible response from the courts, either in that specific locale or in the lowland region in general at that time.

The comparatively 'moderate' attitude of the Scottish authorities in the 1750–1815 period appears to have been mirrored elsewhere by the middle decades of the nineteenth century, when, although violence was still consid-

22 See ibid. 390–5.
23 See King, 'Punishing assault', 52–74.
24 See JP 15/2/4. The petition was contained in a minute book from the quarter sessions of the Justice of the Peace Court held in West Lothian and dates between 1813 and 1823.

ered unacceptable, it was also becoming 'privatised'.[25] The introduction of policing at this time made assault gradually become more covertly domestic, whilst less overtly communal in nature. Increasingly, as a result, it came to be regarded as outside the domain of legal sanction and reproach. Back in eighteenth-century Scotland, however, the tolerant attitude of the authorities only went so far, as indictments for domestic assault, communal assault and the assault of authority reveal. If an incident were particularly cruel, violent, bloody or anti-authoritarian, the individuals concerned had a case to answer – regardless of whether the defendant in question was male or female.

Domestic assault

Historians of the seventeenth, eighteenth and nineteenth centuries consider domestic violence to be a male activity.[26] Primarily this is because during that time men could lawfully chastise their wives in order to maintain an expected level of obedience and 'proper' moral conduct from them.[27] Despite the fact that this correction was supposed to be limited in its application, there were no regulations or directives in place to curb the behaviour of an especially authoritative husband. Consequently, when instances of domestic violence were brought to the public's attention, on the whole these were episodes when a husband's 'chastisement' had exceeded reasonable bounds and the woman concerned had been seriously injured. The nature of the available evidence then has led historians and social commentators alike to view domestic violence as a gender-specific crime in which, in general, men primarily were the aggressors and women were the victims.

The evidence of the Justiciary Court in relation to lowland Scotland between 1750 and 1815 does seem to confirm that women did not commonly perpetrate domestic violence. Only twenty-eight of the 109 indictments for 'common' assault charged against Scottish women related to assaults carried out within the home. Furthermore, the sample survey of Justice of the Peace

---

[25] See, for instance, Ruff, *Violence in early modern Europe*, 140, and Tomes, 'A "torrent of abuse"', 328–45.

[26] See the conclusions in Gowing, *Domestic dangers*, esp. ch. vi; Bailey, *Unquiet lives*, esp. ch. vi; Warner and Lunny, 'Marital violence in a martial town', 258–76; Hurl-Eamon, 'Domestic violence prosecuted', 435–54; Hunt, 'Wife beating', 10–33; L. Leneman, '"A tyrant and a tormentor": violence against wives in eighteenth- and nineteenth-century Scotland', *C&C* xii (1997), 31–54; and E. Ross; '"Fierce questions and taunts": married life in working-class London', *Feminist Studies* viii (1982), 575–602.

[27] See the analysis in R. Phillips, *Putting asunder: a history of divorce in western society*, Cambridge 1988, 323–44; S. D. Amussen, '"Being stirred to much unquietness: violence and domestic violence in early modern England', *Journal of Women's History* vi (1994), 70–89; A. Clark, 'Humanity or justice? Wifebeating and the law in the eighteenth and nineteenth centuries', in C. Smart (ed.), *Regulating womanhood: historical essays on marriage, motherhood and sexuality*, London–New York 1992, 187–206; and R. B. Siegel, '"The rule of love": wife beating as prerogative and privacy', *Yale Law Journal* cv (1996), 2117–207.

Courts and the Sheriff Courts in the lowland region failed to reveal any instances of domestic violence where women were the defendants. Certainly the 'right to chastise' did not apply to wives in the same way it did to husbands; women were not supposed to upset the traditional authoritative hierarchy of the home. However, if we consider that women in lowland Scotland some-times resorted to killing in the domestic sphere, it is clear that the rules of patriarchal authority were scarcely unchallenged in the Scottish household. It is perhaps surprising, then, that so few lowland women were indicted for non-fatal domestic assault between 1750 and 1815.

It is possible that very few Scottish lowland women were driven to perpetrate domestic violence in the eighteenth and nineteenth centuries. However, as there is abundant evidence of their enthusiasm for committing other forms of 'common' assault and especially the assault of authority, this seems unlikely. There are two possible explanations for the apparent lack of domestic violence. The first of these is a basic lack of reporting of this kind of offence to the authorities.

Whether or not an assault was reported to the authorities depended on both the severity of the offence committed and the victim involved. Minor 'one-off' assaults, unlike repeated or life-threatening attacks, might be considered by those involved unworthy of the time and cost of a prosecution. This may have been especially true if the victim and the aggressor were related or lived under the same roof. The incidence of domestic assaults committed by female assailants might also be under-reported if their victims were members of the opposite sex. Certainly it is reasonable to suggest that a husband assaulted by his wife would incur considerable derision from his friends and the commu-nity at large if he was to indict his spouse for the offence. Women were clearly accepted as being subordinate to their male counterparts, especially inside the marital relationship. Consequently, any reversal of these 'roles' would result in the victim being subjected to domestic and community ridicule and this would foster an unwillingness on the part of the husband to report the offence to the authorities.[28] Of course, it could also be argued that women, who were perhaps more often the victim than the aggressor in this type of offence, were also less likely to report crimes of this nature to the authorities for fear of public contempt, but more commonly because they had accepted assault as intrinsic to their marital life and as the right of their husband. They may also have baulked at the cost of a private prosecution against their attacker, or because a notably low level of conviction meant that it was very likely that the accused would return to the household to abuse her more intensely and more frequently than before.[29]

---

[28] For further discussion see Beattie, 'The criminality of women', 87; Warner and Lunny, 'Marital violence in a martial town', 268; L. Stone, *The family, sex and marriage, 1500–1800*, London 1977, esp. pp. 136–42; and R. K. Marshall, *Virgins and viragoes: a history of women in Scotland from 1080 to 1908*, London 1983, esp. ch. ix.

[29] For low conviction rates related to assault in Scotland see Kilday, 'Women and crime',

This form of what we could term 'licensed violence' was not just restricted to the relationship between husband and wife. Parents and employers were also permitted to commit a considerable degree of domestic chastisement upon their children and workers, especially domestic servants.[30] Violent actions against these members of the domestic circle were seen as the unquestionable right of those in authority in order to control the morals and behaviour of their inferiors. These crimes were most probably also under-reported, and this may well have been especially true if the victim was male and his attacker was female.

Aside from a general unwillingness to report episodes of domestic violence, particularly those carried out by women, there may be another explanation for the absence of female defendants appearing in Scottish courts on charges of domestic assault. There is some evidence to suggest that in certain areas of the lowlands of Scotland, particularly during the eighteenth century, domestic violence was 'controlled' and 'punished' by communities, without any recourse to the law courts or the legal authorities of the day. 'Riding the stang' was a form of ritualised community satire prevalent in the north of England and the lowlands of Scotland from roughly the sixteenth to the early nineteenth centuries.[31] Commonly reserved for wife beaters, women could also be called upon by a community to 'ride the stang' if they had assaulted their husbands or had been overly-domineering in the household. The person 'popularly convicted' was placed astride a rough tree trunk which was then elevated on the shoulders of a few men or women and then carried round the village or town so that the community could jeer at the scene and if necessary could prevent the culprit from trying to get off the 'stang'. As is described in an episode involving a wife beater from Galloway dated from the end of the eighteenth century, the men of the village

ch. vi. The unwillingness of Scottish women to accuse their husbands of assault is borne out by the fact that less than 10% of the men indicted at the Justiciary Court between 1750 and 1815 for 'common' assault were accused of domestic violence against their wives. For further discussion of women's reluctance to report domestic violence see the references cited in nn. 26, 27 above as well as Clark, *Women's silence*, and S. D'Cruze, *Crimes of outrage: sex, violence and Victorian working women*, London 1998.

[30] For further discussion of this version of domestic violence see Daniels and Kennedy, *Over the threshold*, esp. ch. ii; P. Rushton, 'The matter in variance: adolescents and domestic conflict in the pre-industrial economy of northeast England, 1600–1800', *JSH* xxxv (1991), 89–107; M. May, 'Violence in the family: an historical perspective', in J. P. Martin (ed.), *Violence and the family*, Chichester–New York 1978, 150–8; E. A. Foyster, 'Silent witnesses? Children and the breakdown of domestic and social order in early modern England', in A. Fletcher and S. Hussey (eds), *Childhood in question: children, parents and the state*, Manchester 1999, 57–73.

[31] See, for instance, Whatley, 'How tame were the Scottish lowlanders', 18; F. P. Cobbe, 'Wife-torture in England', *Contemporary Review* (Apr. 1878), 56–7; and E. P. Thompson, *Customs in common*, London 1993 edn, 471–2.

tie't his hans ahint his back, an they set him on the stang an tie't his legs thegither at the knees, yt he couldna wun aff. A woman gaed tae every side tae haud him on, an heaps o' wullin wifes got haud o' the stang an liftit it up. The wecht wus naething amang sae mony o' them, an aff they mairch't richt up tae the heid o' the toon ... singan 'Ocht yt's richt 'll no be wrang, Lick the wife an ride the Stange.' At the words 'wife' and 'stang' they liftit it as heich as they could, an than loot it suddently fa' again; an he cam doon wi a thud every time on some o' the ens o' the brenches yt had been left stickin oot for his benefit, an the scraiches o' him wus fearful. The stang wus through atween his legs, ye ken.[32]

In other parts of Britain, variations on the practice of 'riding the stang' took place and were commonly referred to as 'charivari', 'rough music' or 'riding the skimmington'.[33] Regardless of the methods undertaken, and whether the experience was brutal or otherwise, the ritual involved an overwhelming degree of shame and humiliation for the individual or individuals involved. In episodes where women were the primary targets of community contempt, their husbands were also shamed in the ritual to emphasise the fact that it was the failure of male authority which had resulted in the wife forgetting her place in the domestic hierarchy. Any violence or aggression the wife had displayed was not at issue and not what was being punished. Rather it was her readiness to step outside normal patriarchal authority that had to be curbed and could not be tolerated.

Episodes of 'rough music' and 'riding the stang' show the extent to which 'outsiders' were prepared to intervene in domestic matters.[34] They also reflect the fact that certain communities were determined to ensure that normalised forms of household and patriarchal order were maintained over time. Although there is not enough evidence yet to suggest that these forms of community ritual were sufficiently common to account for the almost total absence of women from indictments for domestic assault in the lowland region, it is conceivable that they provide part of the explanation for their absence.

Of the cases of domestic assault that did make it as far as the Justiciary Court, it was very rare for a case to reach the verdict stage of a trial, as all too often the charges were dropped by the victim soon after proceedings had been initiated. This means that in the twenty-eight cases brought against lowland women, there are only a few instances where testimonial evidence is

32 Extract from 'Ridin the stang', in de Bruce Trotter, Galloway gossip, 441–2.
33 For further discussion see Thompson, Customs in common, esp. ch. viii; D. E. Underdown, 'The taming of the scold: the enforcement of patriarchal authority in early modern England', in A. Fletcher and J. Stevenson (eds), Order and disorder in early modern England, Cambridge 1987, 116–36; and M. Ingram, 'Ridings, rough music and the "reform of popular culture" in early modern England', P&P cv (1984), 79–113, and '"Scolding women"', 48–80.
34 See R. Phillips, 'Women, neighbourhood, and family in the late eighteenth century', French Historical Studies xviii (1993), 1–12; Hurl-Eamon, 'Domestic violence prosecuted', 445–7; and Hunt, 'Wife beating', 23–4.

presented to the court regarding the nature of the assault alleged to have been committed. Nevertheless, what the assault evidence does reflect, in line with what has been shown in relation to other offences against the person, is that lowland Scottish women were not averse to using violence when committing criminal acts.

Mary McFarlane and her daughters Mary and Elizabeth, for instance, were indicted at the High Court of Justiciary in Edinburgh in 1750 charged with the 'common' aggravated assault of their former servant Elizabeth Algie. McFarlane and her daughters claimed that they gave Elizabeth Algie 'charge of attending certain parcels of their cloaths [clothes] which were washed' and from which she did 'either carelessly lose, or wilfully secrete or spirit away several valuable pieces'. When the women interrogated their servant about the missing clothes, Elizabeth Algie could not provide an adequate explanation for why the clothes had gone missing. Consequently, Mrs MacFarlane said that 'some of us chided her for being so careless ... as we though we had good reason to do with our own servant, whom we thought we had right and authority to command'. Elizabeth Algie's description of the 'chiding' was that the trio 'beat her with their fists and otherways upon her face and other parts of her body to the effusion of her blood and tore her cloaths [clothes] from her body and shut and bolted the door of their house upon her [in the late of night] with intention to have murdered her'.[35]

Another case was indicted at the South Circuit Justiciary Court in 1766 against Agnes Keir. The court heard how Agnes had 'conceived a groundless malice and ill will' against her husband Alexander Colquhoun who was a merchant in Wigtown. Witnesses had testified that Agnes had expressed to them her desire that her husband should be 'put out of the way' and that she had begged several men in the town to help her achieve this. On Saturday 28 September 1765, Agnes began to abuse and maltreat her husband. She 'dragged him out of bed by the hair of the head and seized a chopping knife' which she then used to attack him, slicing off a portion of his 'private member' and stabbing him repeatedly in the shin which resulted in 'the large bone of the leg [being] fractured and shattered, with two splinters being separated from the broken extremities of the bone from which a large effusion of blood issued'. Although Alexander Colquhoun survived his wife's brutal attack, 'he was confined to his bed in the greatest pain and agony for several weeks'.[36]

Although the comparative paucity of the evidence regarding domestic assault makes it difficult for any substantive conclusions to be drawn about the types of women involved and their motives for behaving in this manner, a few trends are apparent from the evidence. First, the overwhelming majority of the women indicted were married. Second, most of the women had used 'weapons' of some kind, usually household objects such as pokers and smoothing irons. Third, almost all the female defendants had committed domestic assaults in

[35] JC 3/27. My notes in parenthesis.
[36] JC 26/177. My note in parenthesis.

urban areas rather than the countryside. Whether these factors were common characteristics in domestic violence in lowland Scotland or whether they are simply a reflection of the few cases that were reported, is difficult to determine from the evidence at hand.

Motives for domestic assault could stem from the mere refusal to do a prescribed task, accusations of impropriety in other relationships or criminal activity, self-defence or even the accidental breakage of crockery. Violence could ensue from the most trivial of disagreements. Typically, however, all of these motives were very much related to the environment in which the eventual act of aggression was to occur. Arguably, as the quote at the opening of the chapter suggests, married women in lowland Scotland seem to have been more 'forward' or 'aggressive' in the domestic sphere than their counterparts elsewhere in Britain during the period from 1750 to 1815. Evidence from Castle Douglas in Dumfries and Galloway in the late eighteenth century, for instance, indicates the existence of a Henpeck't Husband's Emancipation Society.[37] This suggests that some lowland Scottish women did manage to upset the patriarchal order that so many community leaders, social commentators and legal officials had tried to promote and maintain since the early modern period. In all probability then, lowland Scottish women were more commonly involved in domestic disputes than the court evidence suggests. This seems likely, especially when we consider just how forceful and willing lowland women were when participating in arguments outside the home.

Communal assault

According to Margaret Hunt

> Women may not have assaulted their husbands in large numbers, but they seem to have had little compunction about assaulting anyone else. The records show mother and daughter teams, adult sisters, groups of female work-mates, and wives egged on by their husbands assaulting women and men (though usually other women) in the fields, in the church-yard, in alehouses, on the highway and at the market.[38]

Similarly, in lowland Scotland, the overwhelming majority (some 76 per cent) of 'common' assault cases allegedly perpetrated by women between 1750 and 1815 were committed outside the domestic sphere. An atmosphere of antagonism seems also to have been quite generally prevalent in lowland Scotland in the eighteenth century. As Marion Stewart describes for Dumfries at that time, 'There was a great deal of brawling and violence, drunkenness and assault' and what she terms a 'general rumbustiousness'.[39]

---

37 See 'The henpeckit husbands', in de Bruce Trotter, *Galloway gossip*, 60–2.
38 Hunt, 'Wife beating', 22–3.
39 Stewart, '"In durance vile"', 71.

Although violent behaviour was recognised as a regular feature of life in the seventeenth and eighteenth centuries throughout Europe, this does not mean it was condoned or ignored. Communities did their best to maintain law and order, using informal sanctions like episodes of 'rough music' or more formal methods of reproach when the violence was more public than this. Litigation was used not only as a means of enacting punishment, but it could also be used as a measured form of social mediation to resolve tensions between different groups within a given locale.[40]

The high number of prosecutions for communal 'common' assault in lowland Scotland, in comparison to those for domestic violence, suggests that individuals were much more inclined to report this sort of offence to the authorities.[41] The common explanation for this, both in lowland Scotland and elsewhere during the seventeenth and eighteenth centuries, was the fact that individual or family honour had been slighted as a result of the 'assault' and reputations were now at stake.[42]

Communal assault in eighteenth-century Scotland could take a variety of forms. As this volume concentrates on women's violence, defamation and the writing of 'incendiary' letters do not warrant significant attention. Such activities could act as precursors to violence, although they were rarely mentioned in the charges lybelled.[43] Far more common were charges of ordinary aggravated assault and hamesucken. Respectively, these offences constituted 81 per cent and 17 per cent of the total number of communal 'common' assault charges levelled at lowland Scottish women between 1750 and 1815.

Before investigating the nature of these assaults in more detail, it is important to point out that as well as the formal indictment, there was an alternative method of litigation that helped victims of violence deal with their attackers. Letters of Lawburrows were 'the legal security required from or given by a person that he will not injure another'.[44] Commonly, these 'letters' were applied for after a prolonged period of harassment, threatening or aggression by one party against another. The accused individuals charged that from the date of the 'letter' the petitioner and his or her family would be 'kept harmless and skaithless [unharmed] in their persons and possessions and shall no

[40] For further discussion see J. A. Sharpe, '"Such disagreement betwyx neighbours": litigation and human relations in early modern England', in J. Bossy (ed.), *Disputes and settlements: law and human relations in the west*, Cambridge 1983, 167–87.
[41] Nearly three times as many communal assaults as domestic attacks were indicted at the Justiciary Court between 1750 and 1815. If we add in the indictments derived from the sample survey of the Sheriff Courts and Justice of the Peace Courts, the ratio of communal assaults heard by the lowland Scottish courts compared to domestic ones remains at three to one.
[42] For further discussion see Hufton, 'Women and violence', 93, and Ruff, *Violence in early modern Europe*, 117, 121–3.
[43] For further discussion of these 'modes' of assault see Gowing, *Domestic dangers*, and Walker, *Crime, gender and social order*, esp. ch. iii.
[44] Robertson, *Concise Scots dictionary*, 361. See also *APS*, iii. 222.

way be troubled or molested therein'.[45] Letters of Lawburrows were strongly favoured by victims, especially in instances of minor communal assault, as they required no evidence in order to be granted, just the say-so of the petitioner and therefore they negated any need for a prolonged and costly trial. In addition, as the defendants were bound to pay a fixed penalty of four hundred merks Scots if they broke the conditions of the 'Letter of Lawburrows',[46] the petitioners involved could feel reassured that if the defendants wanted to harangue them in the future, they would have to pay for the privilege.

In lowland Scotland between 1750 and 1815 in the Justiciary Court alone there were 2,396 such 'Letters of Lawburrows' admitted to the processes of court. Of these 1,415 (or 59 per cent) were brought and granted against men, and 981 (or 41 per cent) against women. Similar bonds of caution to keep the peace or for good behaviour were also in evidence at courts south of the border during the early modern period, but the proportion of Scottish women accused via this method in the eighteenth century is more significant than that seen elsewhere.[47] This suggests that, in Scotland, 'Letters of Lawburrows' were more regularly preferred by those seeking redress for minor communal assaults than by plaintiffs elsewhere, especially when the assailant concerned was a woman. Perhaps the more common use of lawburrows against lowland women reflects an awareness of how pragmatic the Scottish legal authorities were with females indicted for violent offences and a willingness to avoid the harsh realities of a Justiciary Court trial for the parties concerned. The courts also welcomed the use of lawburrows as letters could be swiftly expedited, reflecting the efficiency and effectiveness of the judicial system to the parties involved.

Of the cases that were indicted at the courts in lowland Scotland, some general observations can be made which relate to the characteristics of the defendants involved. Firstly, most of the women charged with communal assault were married and in the main they had committed the offence in a rural area rather than an urban one. More significantly, perhaps, is the fact that unlike homicides (including infanticides) and domestic assaults, lowland women rarely acted alone when perpetrating assault beyond the home. Rather than being involved in face-to-face confrontations as individuals, women were more likely to join others (both male and female), not necessarily to compensate for a lack of physical prowess, but more likely

---

45 Letters of Lawburrows were also found amongst the Sheriff Court and Justice of the Peace Court material sampled, although not in significant numbers. For examples of the details contained in Letters of Lawburrows where women were accused see, for instance, NAS, SC 67/46/1, dated at Stirling, 21 June 1751; JC 26/248, dated at Lochmaben, Dumfriesshire, 8 May 1788; JC 26/351, dated at Glasgow, 26 June 1811.
46 One merk was the equivalent of 13s. 4d. Scots or 1s 1½d sterling: Robertson, *Concise Scots dictionary*, 817.
47 Garthine Walker for instance found that 21% of the individuals charged to find caution to keep the peace in early modern Cheshire were women: *Crime, gender and social order*, 25.

because of a common interest or motive. Perhaps this was often in the face of a perceived threat to personal safety or in defence of family livelihoods. One woman wielding a stick and throwing stones might not be taken as seriously as several women doing so.

As far as the victims of communal assaults were concerned, in the majority of cases, they were acquainted with their assailants. This seems to have been a common feature of this type of violent crime.[48] However, one significant difference between lowland Scottish women and women elsewhere in relation to the victims involved in communal assaults was that, in Scotland, women did not solely attack other women. Rather there was an almost equal split between assaults carried out against males and assaults against females. This seems distinctly at odds with Peter Spierenburg's evidence for Amsterdam between 1650 and 1810 where he contends that women usually assault other women, and avoid attacking men. Female violence, he concludes, 'was same-sex violence'.[49]

The communal assaults that were indicted at the Scottish courts during the eighteenth and nineteenth centuries once again emphasise the readiness of lowland Scottish women to employ overt violence in their disputes with others. More often than not (in 65 per cent of cases), weapons were used in women's communal assaults. Unlike instances of domestic violence, the carrying of weapons was much more premeditated in this type of offence. Rather than spontaneously grabbing an implement that was close to hand, most of the women charged with communal assault had carried their chosen weapon some distance before the eventual affray actually took place. This not only suggests a considerable degree of planning on the part of the women concerned, but also a significant amount of determination on the part of the female assailants that if they needed to inflict injury in order to achieve their ends or to get their message across, they would clearly not flinch from doing so. A few examples of the types of communal assaults carried out between 1750 and 1815 will suffice to indicate the level of violence offered by lowland Scottish women when perpetrating assaults outside the home.

Janet Logan from Paisley and her sister Betty Deans had maintained a long-standing argument with a local man called John Chalmers over a sum of money which he had borrowed from them, but had not yet returned. On the 14 April 1764 the sisters set off to claim their money back, but upon reaching John Chalmer's house, he refused to make any payment to them. Consequently, Betty Deans pushed John down on the floor and held him there while Janet repeatedly thrashed him 'with a large iron poker about the legs, face and hands to the great effusion of his blood and danger of his life'. Not satisfied with having done this however, Janet and Betty then dragged

[48] See the conclusions of Ruff, *Violence in early modern Europe*, 117, and G. S. Rowe and J. D. Marietta, 'Personal violence in a "peaceable kingdom"', in Daniels and Kennedy, *Over the threshold*, 30–1.
[49] Spierenburg, 'How violent were women', 21, 27.

their victim over to the fire-place where they set his hair alight swearing to him that 'they would let him burn altogither' unless he returned to them the amount owed.[50]

At Wigtown Sheriff Court in 1810 Helen Hairstanes was indicted for the brutal assault of her neighbour Elizabeth McCluskey. A few days before the assault took place, the court heard how Elizabeth McCluskey had thrown 'stones and broken bottles' at the children of Helen Hairstanes and that Mrs McCluskey had been heard calling the defendant a 'vile whore' and saying that Helen's husband was 'only a cloak to her knavery.' In retaliation for this slight to her and her husband's character Helen marched round to Elizabeth McCluskey's house on 19 September 1810, where, using a set of sharpening stones, Helen beat Mrs McCluskey 'about the face and breast to the great effusion of her blood, causing her nose to be utterly flattened'.[51]

Mary Mitchell was indicted alongside her husband James Livingstone at the South Circuit of Justiciary in 1812. According to the victim, one David Clark, the couple had been trespassing upon his lands at Tormollan in the parish of Balmaghie within the Stewartry of Kirkcudbright. When David Clark challenged them about their improper conduct, Mary Mitchell struck him repeatedly with a rake and 'cut, wounded and bruised him in the head and in several parts of his body; and then the said Mary Mitchell cut him with a razor upon the right side of his face all to the great effusion of [his] blood and danger of his life'. As a result of this attack, David Clark was knocked to the ground, but none the less Mary Mitchell, who was now joined in the assault by her husband, continued 'to strike and beat him with a stick and kicked and beat him repeatedly with their feet, and it was with the utmost difficulty that the said David Clark made his escape'.[52]

Disputes involving women and their neighbours and acquaintances that resulted in violent assault were motivated by a variety of factors. These included money or disputes over landownership, property damage, trespassing, ridicule, slander and a prolonged history of bitterness between the parties involved. Unlike Scottish men, lowland women rarely seem to have got involved in drunken brawls, or at least they were not commonly indicted for that sort of behaviour. It was far more usual for Scottish women to have a specific grievance in mind when they perpetrated communal assault. Regularly, these women appear to have been acting in the defence of personal interests which they perceived to be under threat.

There are of course numerous examples throughout history and also in the present day of women going to vast and at times inordinate lengths to protect their families and livelihoods. It would be surprising to think that the 'protective' actions of women in lowland Scotland in the late eighteenth and early nineteenth centuries would be any different. Whether or not such 'threats'

[50] JC 26/174.
[51] SC 19/54/3.
[52] JC 26/355.

existed or whether these women suffered from paranoia or 'hypersensitivity of temperament' is more difficult to determine, as what one family sees as a menace another might disregard completely.

Overall, the evidence relating to the lowland Scottish women indicted for communal assault between 1750 and 1815 elaborates upon and extends the findings of Nancy Tomes in her study of violence amongst the working classes in nineteenth-century London. She argues that by behaving aggressively in a wide range of situations, women became empowered in their dealings with others. Certainly many women could not be regarded as fragile creatures in need of protection. Evidence to further substantiate Tomes's claims comes in the final category of non-fatal violence to be considered in this chapter – the assault of authority. Thus, as violent behaviour was not restricted to a modernising metropolis, historians should be persuaded to look further afield for the seeds of growing female power in the conduct of interpersonal relationships.

Assault against authority

The only exception to the general rule that men were less likely to report assaults committed against them if their attackers were women lies in the category of assaults against authority. In 82 per cent of the cases charged against lowland women, the assault of authority was coupled with the crime of deforcement. Deforcement is defined by Hume as 'the hindrance or resistance to officers of the law, in the execution of their duty'.[53] Together these two crimes were considered extremely serious offences by the Scottish law courts. As Hume explains, a crime of this nature

> cannot be considered by law as a venial transgression. The reprehension due to it, is not only on account of the high damage which may attend the hindrance, etc. in the particular instance; but also, and more especially, because it is a contempt of the authority of the King, as represented by his Court of Justice, and in the course of legal process; and is thus a matter of evil and very dangerous example, which tends to the unhinging of government, and to intercept the benefits of the state of civil union.[54]

It is clear that due to the seditious nature of this type of offence and the consequential gravity with which the authorities at law viewed the perpetrators of this crime, it is hard to entertain the possibility of an under-reporting of aggravated assault against authority, regardless of the sex of the assailant.[55] It should be remembered, however, that as this kind of crime against the person

[53] Hume, *Commentaries*, i, ch. xiii, p. 386.
[54] Ibid.
[55] For concurrence with this view see King, 'Punishing assault', 50, and J. M. Beattie, 'The pattern of crime in England, 1660–1800', *P&P* lxii (1974), 62.

was frequently committed by groups of offenders, it is conceivable that the victim would not be able to remember, recognise and therefore bring charges against all of his attackers. In its own way therefore, this type of assault adds to the overall doubt that the number of assaults indicted was an accurate reflection of the real incidence of that type of criminal activity.

Despite these caveats, the evidence for women's involvement in this type of offence in lowland Scotland between 1750 and 1815 is none the less significant. With the exception of infanticide, which has been long accepted as a gender-specific crime, there is no example in the existing historiography of a study where the number of indicted women surpasses the number of indicted men for a particular offence. Yet, at the Scottish Justiciary Court, 181 women were charged with assaulting officers of the law compared to 180 men. The significant proportion of lowland women indicted for this offence contrasts starkly with the evidence uncovered for the assault of authority elsewhere in Europe in the seventeenth, eighteenth and nineteenth centuries, where women only constituted a small proportion of the defendants concerned.[56] However, once again the evidence of the Justiciary Court in relation to 'less serious' crimes must be questioned in terms of how accurately it represents violent female criminality in Scotland during the pre-modern period. In the sample survey of other lowland Scottish courts, for instance, the trend for women to dominate in this type of offence was completely reversed, although there were far fewer cases uncovered. In the Justice of the Peace Courts, for example, only two cases of assault of authority were found and both of these involved men. In the Sheriff Court, on the other hand, there were forty-seven indictments for this offence. Only seven of these were charged against lowland women. In part the dominance of the Justiciary Court in indicting this offence can be explained by the seriousness with which it was regarded. Women in particular, it seems, were more likely than men to be brought to the highest court for transgressions against authority. The skew towards female offenders in the evidence from the Justiciary Court notwithstanding, it is clear that a substantial number of lowland women were indicted for this type of offence.

As was the case in instances of communal assault, the vast majority of assaults against authority were committed by married women, and in the main these offences were committed in rural areas. This latter conclusion is at odds with John Beattie's findings for eighteenth-century Surrey, where he contends that women in urban areas were far more likely to commit this type of offence than women in the countryside.[57] In lowland Scotland however, although the evidence shows a slight bias towards rural-based attacks (in 56 per cent of cases), this is not substantial. The evidence suggests that the location for assaults against authority in lowland Scotland was more commonly

---

[56] See, for example, Spierenburg, 'How violent were women?', 9; Walker, Crime, gender and social control, 76–7; and Beattie, 'The criminality of women', 85.

[57] Beattie, 'The criminality of women', 97.

dictated by circumstance and opportunity rather than any external factors. Certainly Beattie's claim that women were more socially restricted in rural Surrey at this time does not appear to have been mirrored north of the border in relation to assaults against authority.[58]

Another similarity with the characteristics of the defendants in communal assaults was that the overwhelming majority of lowland women indicted for the assault of authority had not acted alone. The groups involved varied in size from partnerships to large-scale mobs, but most commonly the group was made up of two to three women; sometimes the women were related and sometimes they were merely acquainted with one another. The perceived advantage of safety and strength in numbers as well as a common interest or motive, probably help to explain why 90 per cent of the indicted women (or 163 cases out of 181) had found it prudent to assault authority in company.

Unlike the other forms of assault analysed in this chapter, the victims of assaults against authority were normally strangers to their attackers and they were universally male. The apparent willingness of lowland women to attack male authority figures is interesting as it contradicts the long-held assumption that women only ever attacked other women in violent offences against the person. However, by its very nature, this particular form of assault necessitated attacking men. The most common victims of this crime in lowland Scotland were law officers trying to deliver warrants of arrest or customs and excise officers trying to confiscate illegal produce or to exact payment of duty on contraband produce, usually liquor. Neither of these roles were likely to be carried out by women in the eighteenth or early nineteenth century.

Perhaps the fact that women realised that they would be facing men in these sorts of attacks explains why they were so violent in carrying them out, as well as why they preferred to work in groups whilst doing so. Unlike in communal assaults, the weapons used by women in the defiance of authority were less premeditated in nature, and were more commonly items that were ready to hand in the outside environment. Sticks and stones were by far the weapons of choice in these instances, with nearly 94 per cent of attacks being carried out using these implements.

In addition, there does seem to have been a fair amount of 'symbolic ritual' in the assaults against authority figures. Not only were the men beaten, but they were also shamed by their assailants. Significantly, these methods of humiliation were fairly similar across the lowland region throughout the eighteenth and nineteenth centuries. They included rubbing dung in the face and hair of the victim, forcing the officer to eat and regurgitate any documentation he had brought, and also commonly, stripping the victim of all his clothes in the process of the attack. Interestingly, John Beattie uncovered similar forms of humiliation carried out against authority figures by women

[58] For further discussion see ibid. 97–100.

in eighteenth-century Surrey, suggesting that these methods were not solely restricted to Scottish women.[59]

The following examples help to illustrate the type of behaviour exhibited by lowland women in assaults on authority. The first is a case that was brought to the High Court of Justiciary in 1758 against seven women. John McChlery, an excise officer had come to Stranraer after prosecuting individuals from the local area who had been selling liquor without a licence. The sentences meted out to the offenders concerned involved the payment of fines, and McChlery had come to the area to collect the money owed. When he was in the process of doing this, on the 11 February 1758,

> Margaret McCulloch, Elizabeth McConnel, Elizabeth McNish, Agnes Semple, Janet Agnew, Margaret Agnew and Isobell Chalmer, did assemble together, many of them armed with rungs [clubs], sticks or other offensive weapons, and then and there did lay violent hands upon John McChlery, one or other of you sitting on his face and causing his nose to break and further attacking him in a lawless manner, rubbing manure in his hair, forcing warrants brought against you into his mouth and beating and bruising him ... to the great effusion of his blood and danger of his life; and also tearing the clothes from him, did drag him towards the sea, there to complete the wicked and malicious purpose formed against him, and which probably would have been accomplished to the utmost, had not some well-disposed persons interposed and rescued him out of your hands.[60]

The second example is a case brought before the South Circuit Court in 1781 charged against Robert Lindsay, Thomas Maxwell, Susan Agnew, Janet McGaa and Helen Alexander. Customs officers in Port William (Wigtown-shire) had seized a box of tea on the sea-shore which they believed had been smuggled without proper payment of duty. The pannels, on the other hand, claimed that the tea belonged to them, and accordingly, at the instigation of Helen Alexander, Robert Lindsay and Thomas Maxwell, attempted to rescue it whilst Susan Agnew and Janet McGaa

> did violently assault Hugh Hannah [customs officer] and forcibly held him down on the floor and beat him most cruelly with stones about the face and otherways upon his body to the great effusion of his blood and danger of his life. They then stripped him of his cloaths [clothes] and continued to beat and bruise him as before. As a result of this treatment Hugh Hannah lost an eye and was left in a most miserable condition.[61]

Some similarities can be drawn between the motives of the lowland women indicted for communal assault and those charged with the assault of authority, in that the women involved in these offences tended to be reacting to an antici-

---

[59] See ibid. 88.
[60] JC 26/161. My note in parenthesis.
[61] JC 26/223. My notes in parenthesis.

pated threat to either themselves or the livelihood of their families.[62] Predominantly, in lowland Scotland, the victims of assaults against authority were law officers, messengers, constables, sheriff-officers and the like attempting to serve warrants of arrest on the spouse, close-relative or acquaintance of their aggressor. The threat of the removal of the 'bread-winner' from the household or a loved one from the community was a startling enough prospect for these women to be stimulated into overt action.

Women were also involved in crimes in which the eventual intention was the seizure of goods (whether smuggled or otherwise) without payment of duty, an offence common in Scotland throughout the eighteenth- and nineteenth-century period.[63] Although the resulting assault and deforcement of revenue and excise officers was proportionately more often associated with male offenders, just over a quarter of the lowland Scottish women charged with assault of authority were accused of these types of offences.[64]

Apart from the zeal of the authorities in prosecuting offenders involved in assaults of this nature, and the protective actions of women, what other theories can be offered to explain the considerable level of female participation in these acts of manifest violence? Certainly female militancy of this type was not unknown in Scotland. Highland women, for example, were renowned for taking the lead in resistance against oppression in the context of the Highland Clearances. Malcolm MacLean and Christopher Carrell in *As an fhearann (From the land)*, for instance, show that women

> In the early decades of the nineteenth century led the men at Culrain and Gruids into the fray. They 'assaulted and humiliated' the sheriff-officers at Durness; in Loch-Shiel they single-handedly drove off an eviction party. In Glencairn the women set fire to the eviction notices. Twelve years later, in 1852, the women of Greenyards (on the same estate) lined up against the militia in front of their men and sustained severe injuries.[65]

In lowland Scotland female belligerence was not unknown either, as the evidence on assault has shown and as we will see in the next chapter on popular disturbances. Violence by women, especially that which involved the defiance of authority, may not have been regarded as unusual in Scotland, unlike elsewhere in Europe since the early modern period. It seems that Scottish women were expected to take the lead in acts of confrontation with

---

62 For further discussion see Walker, *Crime, gender and social order*, 80.

63 See, for instance, Donnachie, '"The darker side"', 15; L. M. Cullen, 'Smuggling in the north channel in the eighteenth century', *SESH* vii (1987), 9–26; and R. Goring, 'Eighteenth-century Scottish smugglers: the evidence from Montrose and Dumfries', *Review of Scottish Culture* iii (1987), 53–65.

64 For further discussion of this particular offence in eighteenth-century Scotland see Whatley, 'How tame were the Scottish lowlanders?', 6–14.

65 M. MacLean and C. Carrell (eds), *As an fhearann (From the land)*, Edinburgh 1986, 23. For further discussion and other examples see E. Richards, *A history of the Highland Clearances*, II: *Emigration, protest, reasons*, London 1985, esp. pp. 324–9, 341–2.

authority, as traditionally they had always done so. This conclusion suggests much about the Scots' regard for authority and the measure of their respect for the law within the social, economic and political conditions of a given period. Was Scotland less socially stable as a society as a result of this defi-ance of authority or more controllable, because the populace could vent their discontent on a regular basis? These issues will be explored in more detail in the conclusion to this volume.

In the case of aggravated assaults against law officers in which women participated in substantial numbers, it could be argued that in many instances the men whom these officers were trying to arrest (as it was generally a male accused) were hardly likely to make their job an easy one and must often have been in hiding, leaving the women to face the authorities. A more mundane explanation is that the relatively low levels of male participation in this particular offence could be attributed to their being out at work, away on business or overseas on military service when the authorities tried to arrest them. Whatever the reason, the officers' insistence on thoroughly and often recklessly searching the premises regardless of the woman's explanations for the absence of her spouse, may well have incited many women to enlist the help of others to deforce and assault the sheriffs and constables who were invading, disrupting and vandalising their households and property.

In cases of offences against revenue and excise officers, where men and women often joined forces in their attacks, but where females regularly made up the vanguard, it could be supposed that the offenders believed that the authorities would behave more leniently towards women on account of their sex. Alternatively, in simple economic terms, it may well have been the case that the household could not risk the male wage-earner being arrested. Women could be more easily replaced by a relative if taken into custody. Men, in their role as providers of the family income, could not. If women were perceived to be more economically expendable than men, this would go some way towards explaining why a large number of female defendants was involved in instances of assault of authority in lowland Scotland between 1750 and 1815.

Evidence from this chapter suggests that although more men than women were indicted for assault, this did not mean that women were unwilling to perpetrate the offence, or that they were less violent or aggressive when they did so.

While not deemed as serious as many of the other crimes against the person, 'common' assault was still regularly indicted at the Scottish courts; in fact it was the most frequently indicted violent offence brought to the courts' attention between 1750 and 1815 for both male and female defend-ants. Having said this, however, it is clear that a substantial proportion of instances of non-fatal violence never made it to trial, especially domestic assaults perpetrated by women. The community may well have frequently intervened to offer their own form of retributive humiliation as an alternative to legal recourse. In addition, husbands may have been reluctant to admit to being bullied by their wives and overall it seems likely that domestic assaults by women were largely unreported during the eighteenth- and nineteenth-century period. At any rate, when women did commit assault in the home, it was usually a hot-blooded reaction to given circumstances, and on occasion it could be brutal, violent and life-threatening.

Communal assaults against neighbours and acquaintances were certainly better reported than domestic incidents, although victims had recourse to bonds of caution for good behaviour if they did not want to expend time and money on a trial. The women involved in these offences usually worked in groups and knew their victims. Their attacks were fairly premeditated in nature. Lowland women tended to bring weapons along with them to carry out their assaults and chief among the motives for their violent behaviour was the defence of their reputations and/or the defence of family interests.

This latter rationale was also strongly evident in episodes involving the assault of authority. As with communal assaults, the women accused of this offence worked in groups and carried weapons, although on the whole their attacks were not usually planned in advance to any large extent. Certainly once again the defence of family interests was an important stimulus for these women, although some of the female defendants used their violence to help them 'rescue' contraband produce from customs and excise officers. It may not have been unusual for Scottish women to behave defiantly towards authority, as there is evidence of their substantive involvement in popular disturbances and in other militant episodes throughout the history of pre-modern Scotland.

Overall, women tended to be involved in a fair degree of 'everyday' violence in lowland Scotland between 1750 and 1815. They committed the same sorts of offences as their male counterparts, although their actions seem to have been more premeditated on the whole. Excepting perhaps domestic attacks, lowland women tended to assault for a specific reason, with a specific purpose in mind. Women rarely got involved in drunken brawling of the sort that typi-fied much of the male experience of assault. Lowland women, especially when assaulting 'authority', were motivated to protect their families and were regu-larly prepared to use violence to do so. Scottish men were probably motivated in the same way on occasion, but they were much more likely to be indicted for casual affrays than intentional disorder. The latter was clearly the domain of their female counterparts, or at least that was how the Scottish authorities liked to portray assaults which involved lowland women. Moreover, Scot-tish women were far more likely than their male counterparts to be indicted for non-fatal acts of aggression at the nation's supreme criminal court. This reflects the seriousness with which the Scottish authorities regarded violent female criminality of any kind during the pre-modern period.

6

Popular Disturbances

'Certainly a scots Rabble is the worst of its kind ... they are a hardened, refractory and Terrible people.'[1]

Popular protest of one kind or another has been a common phenomenon throughout history and it has received a fair amount of attention from historians as a result.[2] In Scotland, on the other hand, 'traditional' historiography has highlighted what has been termed an 'orthodoxy of passivity'.[3] Writers like Christopher Smout and Thomas Devine maintain that one of the most notable elements of lowland Scottish society, especially in relation to the eighteenth century, is the almost total absence of overt social discontent amongst the Scottish populace.[4] This notion of the 'uninflammability' of the Scots has recently been challenged, however, chiefly by the work of Christopher Whatley and to a lesser extent, Ian Whyte.[5] Although at first glance, the Scots might appear more quiescent in comparison to their counterparts south of the Tweed,[6] there is compelling evidence emerging which suggests that they were far less 'tame' than had previously been supposed.

From the bloodfeud and clan wranglings of the sixteenth century, the Covenanting rebellions of the mid-seventeenth century, the Levellers' revolt in Galloway in 1724 and the various Jacobite risings most prominent in the eighteenth century, through to the anti-clearance protests in the Highlands which began in the mid-nineteenth century and escalated thereafter, there

---

1 G. H. Healey (ed.), *The letters of Daniel Defoe*, Oxford 1955, 133, 140. The first part of the quotation is an extract from Daniel Defoe to Robert Harley, 24 Oct. 1706. The second part is an extract from Defoe to Harley, 2 Nov. 1706. During this period Defoe was visiting Edinburgh to comment on the circumstances leading up to the Union of 1707.
2 See, for instance, J. Stevenson, *Popular disturbances in England, 1700–1870*, London 1979; J. E. Archer, *Social unrest and popular protest in England, 1780–1840*, Cambridge 2000; R. Quinault and J. Stevenson (eds), *Popular protest and public order: six studies in British history, 1790–1920*, London 1974; and R. B. Shoemaker, *The London mob: violence and disorder in eighteenth-century London*, London 2004.
3 This orthodoxy is outlined in Whatley, 'How tame were the Scottish lowlanders', 3.
4 See, for instance, Smout, *A history of the Scottish people*, 303–10, 417, and T. M. Devine, 'Social stability and agrarian change in the eastern lowlands of Scotland, 1810–1840', *SH* iii (1978), 331–46.
5 See Whatley, 'How tame were the Scottish lowlanders?', 1–30, and *Scottish society*, chs iv, v; and I. D. Whyte, 'Scottish population and social structure in the seventeenth and eighteenth centuries: new sources and perspectives', *Archives* xx (1993), 30–41.
6 See A. Charlesworth (ed.), *An atlas of rural protest in Britain, 1548–1900*, London 1983, 48–121.

appears to have been something of a tradition of 'collective action' in Scotland.[7] This seems to have been largely ignored by proponents of the 'passivity' thesis. Further evidence relating to the first half of the eighteenth century, cites incidents such as the anti-Union and malt tax riots of the early 1700s, the Porteous riot of 1736, as well as a variety of anti-customs scuffles, food riots, religiously-motivated revolts and numerous forms of 'everyday' protest. This suggests that traditional thinking related to popular disturbances in Scotland is in need of revision, particularly with reference to the eighteenth-century experience.[8] This chapter extends and develops the emerging revisionist historiography of Scottish protest by looking at the types of collective action that lowland women were engaged in between 1750 and 1815.

In the late eighteenth and early nineteenth century, riots and tumults were common amongst the Scottish populace. Primarily this was because the general public had scant opportunity directly to influence those who had power over them.[9] It is clear from the Justiciary Court evidence of lowland Scotland between 1750 and 1815 that women were often involved in such activities. Yet women have been largely ignored by the historiography on popular disturbances, both in a Scottish context and indeed elsewhere.[10] Nevertheless, tantalising evidence of female involvement in popular protest can be glimpsed in some of the seminal works on crowd violence during the eighteenth and nineteenth centuries. Edward Thompson, for instance, quotes Robert Southey writing in 1807 that women were 'more disposed to be mutinous' than their male counterparts. He asserted that women 'stand less in fear of the law, partly from ignorance, partly because they presume upon the privilege of their sex, and therefore in all public tumults they are foremost in violence and ferocity'.[11]

Clearly, female participation in this type of behaviour is important in any attempt to understand the overall nature and incidence of women's involvement in violent criminal activity. However there are, in addition, three key characteristics identifiable from the indictments for popular disturbances

---

[7] For further details regarding these episodes see Brown, *Bloodfeud*; D. Stevenson, *Revolution and counter-revolution in Scotland, 1644–1651*, Edinburgh 2003; T. Brotherstone (ed.), *Covenant, charter and party: traditions of revolt and protest in modern Scottish history*, Aberdeen 1989; J. Leopold, 'The Levellers' revolt in Galloway in 1724', *Journal of the Scottish Labour History Society* xiv (1980), 4–29; B. Lenman, *The Jacobite risings in Britain, 1689–1746*, Aberdeen 1995; and E. Richards, *The Highland Clearances: people, landlords and rural turmoil*, Edinburgh 2000.

[8] See, for instance, Whatley, 'How tame were the Scottish lowlanders?', 1–30, and *Scottish society*, chs iv, v; and Logue, *Popular disturbances*.

[9] See Logue, *Popular disturbances*, 1.

[10] The exceptions to this general rule include brief references to riotous Scottish women: ibid. 36, 87, 106, 199–203; Houston, 'Women in the economy', 137–8; and Whatley, *Scottish society*, especially ch. v. For other work on women's involvement in collective action pertinent to this study see Dekker, 'Women in revolt', 337–62; Bohstedt, 'Gender, household and community politics', 88–122; and Thomas and Grimmett, *Women in protest*.

[11] E. P. Thompson, 'The moral economy of the English crowd in the eighteenth century', *P&P* 1 (1971), 116.

relating to lowland Scotland between 1750 and 1815, which warrant this subject being treated separately from the other offences against the person brought before the Justiciary Court at that time.

The first of these has less to do with the content of the records themselves than with the period under consideration. Charles Tilly has attempted to chart the nature and evolution of what he terms 'collective violence' in western Europe from the seventeenth century to the present day.[12] The period being considered here, 1750 to 1815, is important for his research. He categorised three main forms of 'collective violence'. The initial stage involved 'primitive' collective violence which was communal in nature and usually localised and small-scale (for example the family feud). This form of disturbance had almost completely died out by the modern period. The second stage, of what he termed 'reactionary' collective violence, was also communally based, but, in contrast, grew out of opposition to national socio-economic and political change (for example the food riot). This phase covers the entire period being studied here and extends to the 1830s when it is superseded by the final category, that of 'modern' collective violence, which is based not on communal association but on specific interest groups which promote change rather than resist it (for example the political demonstration).[13] Although Tilly's approach can be criticised for its rigidity, it does underline the importance of the mid eighteenth and early nineteenth centuries in the study of popular disturbances.

The second reason for examining popular disturbances separately from other crimes against the person is simply the number of women involved. After the crimes of assault of authority and infanticide, mobbing was the most frequently indicted violent offence charged at the Justiciary Court against lowland Scottish women between 1750 and 1815. Although only approximately one third of the male total of indicted individuals (125 females compared to 457 males), the numbers are still significant.[14]

Thirdly, and finally, the propensity for violence exhibited by the women brought before the Justiciary Court indicates the need for closer analysis of this type of offence. Although Southey and Thompson stated that women rioters in this period were ferociously violent, the violence that they were

---

12 See C. Tilly, 'Collective violence in European perspective', in H. D. Graham and T. D. Gurr (eds), *Violence in America: historical and comparative perspectives*, New York 1969, 83. For an exploration of Tilly's argument see S. J. Connolly, 'Violence and order in the eighteenth century', in P. O'Flanagan, P. Ferguson and K. Whelan (eds), *Rural Ireland, 1600–1900: modernisation and change*, Cork 1987, 57–8.

13 See Tilly, 'Collective violence', 89–97.

14 Although rioting could, on occasion, be indicted at the courts of lower jurisdiction in Scotland, in the main, if the episode involved the use of violence, the offence was brought before the Justiciary Court, as it was regarded as a crime against public order. This was as true for male defendants as female ones, and therefore the skew towards indicting violent female offenders at the Justiciary Court, evident in chapter 5 above, does not apply to popular disturbances and riot in the same way or to the same extent.

referring to was predominantly targeted against property. What seems to have been distinctive about the women of lowland Scotland on the other hand, was their universal willingness to resort to violence aimed at people.

The types of collective protest analysed are restricted to those for which lowland women were indicted before the Justiciary Court at this time. These were the food riot, the patronage riot and, to a far lesser extent, the industrial dispute. Nevertheless, it is hoped that by first addressing the legal context for this type of criminal activity and then going on to determine the general characteristics, methods employed and motives of the offenders related to each type of popular disturbance, comprehensive insight can be gained into the nature of this offence and the type of women who committed it. For example, can Edmund Burke's description of French rioters as 'all the unutterable abominations of the furies of hell, in the abased shape of the vilest women'[15] be ascribed to the eighteenth-century women of lowland Scotland?

The legal context and attitudes towards popular disturbances

The criminal act involved in popular disturbances, which separated it from the general category of assault, was that of mobbing, or, as it was sometimes quaintly referred to, the 'tumultuous convocation of the lieges'. In Scots law, as Baron Hume stated, 'Under this general appellation "of mobbing" … our practice seems to reduce the several degrees and stages of disorder, which are known in the law of England, by the names of *Riot, Rout and Unlawful Assembly*.'[16] He goes on:

> For whether the convocation proceed to execute their violent purpose, which the law of England calls a *riot*; or only take some step toward the execution, which is a *rout*; or have simply met with the intention of doing some mischief, which is an *unlawful assembly*; this is a consideration which, in our practice, serves to affect only the measure of the punishment, and in no-wise the proper style to be applied to the offence, in drawing the indictment: Provided always the meeting be attended with those circumstances of disorder and alarm, which makes it a punishable meeting.[17]

It is clear from Hume's comments that any description of what constitutes an act of mobbing was relatively complex in a Scottish legal context and clearly distinct from English understanding. Indeed, Hume provides no statutory definition of the crime of mobbing. Instead, he suggests four 'particulars' which must be apparent in the committal of the offence, in order for an indictment to be laid. The first is that a crowd of people must be assembled. Hume goes

15 G. Rudé, *The crowd in history, 1730–1848*, London 1981, 8.
16 Hume, *Commentaries*, ii, ch. xvi, p. 416.
17 Ibid. .

on to explain that 'it is, – in the appearance of power, as well as disposition to execute their unlawful purposes, of their own will and authority, – that the alarm and danger of such assemblies lie'.[18] In English common law the lowest number necessary to constitute a mob was three people.[19] However, in Scots law it appears to have been left to the discretion of individual prosecutors considering individual cases as to what numbers had to be involved in a specific offence in order for an indictment of mobbing to result.[20]

The second 'particular' advanced by Hume was that in order for a charge of mobbing to arise the crowd had to disturb the public peace, and behave in a violent or threatening manner so as to cause fear amongst the general populace.[21] Third, the assembly must not only tend towards violence and disorder, but it must also consist of individuals who have combined together for that purpose. As Hume explains, 'It is the *union* and resolution of a multitude, who are in league to defy authority, and execute their pleasure by means of force, – by these means which it belongs to the supreme power alone to employ, – that is the aggravated quality of the crime of mobbing.'[22] In this description mobbing was distinguished in Scots law from its English equivalent, which included participants in 'casual affrays' or 'quarrels' and even mere spectators of popular disturbances in charges of this nature.

The fourth and final 'particular' was that the disorder had to arise from a matter of 'private' concern. The word 'private' in this context referred to matters of specific or local interest, such as an attempt to reduce the price of grain in a certain market, rather than a more national concern or interest of the state, such as an attempt to challenge or depose the government, which would be considered sedition or treason.[23]

Although open to ambiguous interpretation and the manipulation of prosecutors, depending on the circumstances of a given case, these four 'particulars' cited by Hume were the basis in Scots law for an indictment of mobbing to be held valid by the Justiciary Court.

However, the court could also indict participants in popular disturbances via an entirely separate legal provision to that concerned with mobbing. The Riot Act of 1. Geo. I. c. 5 had evolved from four older Scots and English laws relating to collective protest, namely James II 1457 c. 77, Queen Mary 1563 c. 83, 1. Mary, stat. 2. c. 12 and 1. Eliz. c. 16. Once a magistrate had read the Riot Act, it was a capital offence if more than twelve individuals remained in an 'assembly' and did not disperse. The act also made it a non-clergyable felony if the crowd attempted to prevent the magistrate's proclamation or if any property damage was committed during the reading of the act.[24]

---

18 Ibid.
19 Stevenson, *Popular disturbances*, 5.
20 Hume, *Commentaries*, ii, ch. xvi, p. 416.
21 See ibid.
22 Ibid. 418.
23 See ibid.
24 See McLynn, *Crime and punishment*, 219.

Despite various peculiarities linked to the 1715 Riot Act, such as the fact that it did not apply if the rioters dispersed after fifty-nine minutes or if there were only eleven individuals assembled, it was frequently referred to in Justiciary Court indictments. It appears to have been particularly common for the prosecutor to apply the Riot Act charge if he had serious misgivings about his ability to achieve a conviction for mobbing in the face of an assize that he perceived to sympathise with those accused.

Thus the wide-ranging legal provision for popular disturbances suggests that the authorities were determined to control the incidence of this type of crime in pre-modern Scotland. Yet when cases actually came to trial, the attitudes of the courts did not necessarily reflect this resolve in terms of the punishments meted out to those convicted. It was extremely rare, for instance, for a convicted rioter to receive the ultimate sanction from Justiciary Court judges. Executions for this offence were rare for participants of either gender. It was far more common, in the initial decades of the eighteenth century, for riotous individuals to be imprisoned (sometimes at hard labour) or fined. From the 1760s onwards, however, banishment or transportation became the favoured sanction for these convicts, especially for women, although this could be coupled with flogging in episodes where the Scottish judges thought a show of judicial force was necessary.[25]

The increased use of transportation at this time was more a reflection of changing punishment preferences for crime in general than a shift in judicial attitudes towards rioting *per se*. The authorities considered the punishment of a few unruly offenders, through imprisonment or banishment, to be enough of a deterrent to other would-be rioters, and as a result the execution of rioters could be avoided. This was especially important if the rioters' cause was one that elicited widespread communal sympathy. Fierce disturbances could result from an unpopular hanging, as was exemplified by the Porteous riots in Edinburgh in 1736, and such instances had to be avoided in an age when there was a basic lack of resources for 'formal' social control throughout Scotland.[26]

The final reason why the authorities shrank from passing capital sentences upon rioters during the eighteenth century was because it was frequently very difficult to arrest and convict the individuals involved. The reasons for this will be investigated in the next section. Measuring the precise degree of culpability in an episode of collective action, for instance, was particularly hard to establish, and this meant that 'lesser' sanctions were commonly employed by the Scottish courts to demonstrate the maintenance of order, rather than anything more severe.

---

[25] For further discussion see Kilday, 'Women and crime', ch. vi.
[26] For further discussion on the Porteous riots see H. T. Dickinson and K. Logue, 'The Porteous riot: a study of the breakdown of law and order in Edinburgh, 1736–1737', *Journal of the Scottish Labour History Society* x (1976), 21–40. For further discussion on the lack of methods of formal social control see Whatley, 'How tame were the Scottish lowlanders?', 18–19, and Smout, *A history of the Scottish people*, 205–12.

The 'dark figure' of popular disturbances

Before scrutinising the first type of popular disturbance, the food riot, it is important to bear in mind the contribution of unknown or unreported crime (known as the 'dark figure' of criminal statistics) to our understanding of this type of offence. Popular disturbances are distinct in this respect from the other crimes against the person studied in this volume. Instead of instances of collective protest being hidden from the criminal records due to a combination of stealth and under-reporting, the instances of rioting and mobbing went undetected due to the behaviour and attitude of the authorities towards crime of a 'popular' nature. It should be stressed that up to this point no significant work has been carried out on the issue of the 'dark figure' of criminal statistics in relation to popular disturbances in Scotland. However, English and French evidence suggests that there are various reasons which can account for the apparent lethargy exhibited by the authorities in their pursuit and apprehension of offenders. Although these reasons cannot as yet be wholly validated for the lowland Scottish experience, it seems reasonable to suggest that they probably applied in that area to roughly the same extent as elsewhere.

First, and most simply, because of the numbers involved it was frequently difficult for the authorities to apprehend all the participants involved in a disturbance which may have comprised twenty, thirty or more rioters. There was an inadequate number of sheriffs, justices of the peace and town guards to maintain order in the first place, and it was often difficult to achieve just one arrest for any given offence.[27] It must have been far more onerous to bring a mob to justice. Consequently it was often left to the discretion and perception of individual officers to determine what constituted a popular disturbance in the first place, and thereafter which, if any, of the rioters could or should be apprehended.

Although the authorities regularly sympathised with the grievances of the protesters, their status and office generally obliged them to curb any illegal activities that took place. However, the legal provision for doing so, in the form of the Riot Act, did not make this task easy, since it placed the premium upon policing rather than punishment. Primarily this was because the main function of the act was to encourage rioters to disperse. This hindered the arrest of suspects, however, as the authorities had to seek out the rioters afterwards when they were obviously much harder to locate.[28]

The final reason for the prominence of the 'dark figure' in statistics relating to popular disturbances involves a degree of manipulation on the part of individual authority figures. As Roger Wells suggests, it is probably fair to say that

[27] See, for example, W. H. Fraser, 'Patterns of protest', in T. M. Devine and R. Mitchison (eds), *People and society in Scotland*, I: *1760–1830*, Edinburgh 1988, 274.
[28] See A. Booth, 'Food riots in the north-west of England 1790–1801', *P&P* lxxvii (1977), 105, and R. B. Shoemaker, 'The London "mob" in the early eighteenth century', *Journal of British Studies* xxvi (1987), 296.

the local JPs did not report every riot that took place. As JPs had to be seen to maintain order in local communities, their reputations would suffer if they had to involve the court authorities on a regular basis.[29]

There is another side to this argument. Local officials could actually have used the threat or reality of a popular disturbance as a means of leverage with governmental authorities in order to affect or induce a change of policy which would ultimately be to their long-term advantage. In this way, they may have worked in a kind of 'unconscious coalition' with the very criminals they were supposed to prevent from disturbing the peace in the first instance, and therefore would be less inclined to arrest them.[30] However, as yet no real evidence exists to substantiate this theory in a Scottish context, and it must remain speculation.

All these factors taken together suggest that the frequency of indictments for collective protest at the Justiciary Court may well bear little resemblance to the true incidence of crimes of that nature. Nevertheless, as long as this caveat is borne in mind, the evidence that is available remains crucial for an understanding of Scottish female criminality during the pre-modern period.

Food riots

According to John Stevenson, food riots were 'The most persistent and wide-spread disturbances in eighteenth century England.'[31] Women seem to have been commonly involved in these disturbances and on occasion they were the instigators of the disorder. According to John Beattie, this was because women's domestic duties necessitated an interest in the price and provision of foodstuffs.[32] Kenneth Logue contends that both of these statements are applicable to Scotland between 1780 and 1815 when food rioting was the most frequently recorded popular disturbance, and where 68 per cent of the women indicted for collective protest were participants in such activity.[33] In lowland Scotland between 1750 and 1815, 61 per cent (seventy-six cases out of 125) of the women charged with mobbing and/or riot were accused of being involved in food riots.[34] But what common characteristics can be

---

[29] See R. A. E. Wells, 'Counting riots in eighteenth-century England', *Bulletin of the Society for the Study of Labour History* xxxvii (1978), 68.

[30] For further discussion see J. Walter, 'Grain riots and popular attitudes to the law: Maldon and the crisis of 1629', in J. Brewer and J. Styles (eds), *An ungovernable people: the English and their law in the seventeenth and eighteenth centuries*, London 1983, 60.

[31] Stevenson, *Popular disturbances*, 91.

[32] See Beattie, 'The criminality of women', 88.

[33] My calculation on the evidence presented in Logue, *Popular disturbance*, 192. For further discussion of this type of popular disturbance in a Scottish context see Whatley, 'How tame were the Scottish lowlanders?', 14–20.

[34] Sixteen of these women were declared fugitate and failed to appear in court to face the charges against them. Nevertheless, sufficient information was provided in the Justi-

gleaned from the females appearing before the Justiciary Court for this type of offence?

First, and pre-eminently, in 95 per cent (seventy-two cases out of seventy-six) of the indictments, the defendants' occupation was not given. This does not mean however, that they were social misfits or criminal riffraff, as Gustav Le Bon believed was the case for the usual composition of the eighteenth-century crowd.[35] None of the women had previous convictions before the Justiciary Court and none of them was described as itinerant or vagrant.

The second common characteristic of the indicted lowland women was that, somewhat surprisingly, nearly two-thirds of them were unmarried. The reverse might well have been expected due to the frequent descriptions of food rioting as a crime which related to matters of family interest. Certainly, the stereotypical image of the European food rioter is that of a married woman rioting so that she could afford to feed her dependants.[36] The evidence here suggests, however, that many lowland Scottish women participated in food riots in order to promote their own personal convictions or those of the wider community in which they lived. This contention is borne out by the fact that a mere 3 per cent of female food rioters in lowland Scotland were accused of joining in this offence with family members. The remaining 97 per cent allegedly acted with acquaintances, neighbours or complete strangers belonging to the shared community where the lybelled disturbance took place.

It seems that the prevailing cause of the food riot was arguably more important than individual circumstances. In this respect, lowland women who perpetrated food riots were probably not unlike their European counterparts. Rather than reacting to a direct threat to personal or family interests, these women were more concerned with a common cause that they believed was worth fighting for. Perhaps married women were less willing to participate in violent activity when they were not specifically or personally threatened. Their family responsibilities may have been too great for them to risk involvement in this type of communal criminality. Instead, married women seem to have been happy to let other women campaign on their behalf, unless, of course, they felt sufficiently compelled to join in.

The final characteristic of the women indicted for popular disturbance in lowland Scotland was that while 58 per cent of them committed this activity in rural areas, 42 per cent did so in urban locations. Clearly, there is not a significant difference between the two categories. Women were just as willing to participate in food riots in towns as they were in the countryside. These

ciary Court record to include their crimes in the overall analysis. Proportionately, lowland women were involved in 31% of the food riots indicted by the Justiciary Court between 1750 and 1815. The only study to provide comparable data is John Bohstedt's work on women in English food riots between 1790 and 1810, where he found that 26% of the food rioters were female: 'Gender, household and community politics', 92.

[35] See G. Le Bon, The crowd: a study of the popular mind, London 1947 edn, 36.

[36] Beattie, 'The criminality of women', 88. See also Thomas and Grimmett, Women in protest, 28.

statistics compare favourably with the contemporary French and English experience of the so-called 'rebellions of the belly'. For, as George Rudé suggests, throughout the period 'the food riot remained as the typical and constant expression of popular discontent; and this was true of the village as it was of the city and market town'.[37]

Although comparisons with other studies must be treated with a great deal of care, the evidence indicates that the lowland Scottish women indicted for food rioting displayed some characteristics which seemed to differ from contemporary assumptions and expectations of that type of criminal activity elsewhere in Europe. However, it is in the very nature of their protesting that an even greater distinction lies.

One of the most common assertions made by historians of popular disturbances is that food riots were largely disciplined, restrained and peaceful. It was unusual for the crowd to display overt aggression, but if acts of violence were perpetrated by food rioters they were typically directed at property and not people.[38] According to John Bohstedt, women in particular were especially reluctant to be overtly violent when participating in food riots.[39] However, these characteristic features of food rioting in England and France were not mirrored in the actions of the women of lowland Scotland between 1750 and 1815. In every single case that was brought before the Justiciary Court at this time, a violent act had allegedly been perpetrated by the accused. Indeed, in 86 per cent of cases (sixty-five out of seventy-six), the women were not only charged with mobbing and/or rioting, but were also charged with aggravated assault. The remaining 14 per cent (eleven cases out of seventy-six) were accused of violent property damage.

The fact that females appear to have been treated slightly more leniently than men by the authorities for this type of non-fatal violence, might explain women's high involvement in violent acts of food rioting.[40] It could also be argued that the reason for the proportionately high rates of violent activity amongst these cases was because they were Justiciary Court indictments, and therefore more likely to detail 'serious' offences. Nevertheless, if a comparison is made from the indictment evidence along gender lines, lowland Scottish women do appear proportionately more violent than their male counterparts. Only 45 per cent (seventy-six cases out of 168) of the male food rioters were charged with assault, whilst the majority of those accused, 55 per cent (ninety-two cases out of 168), were indicted for violent property damage.

There were generally two key food rioting methods employed by the women of lowland Scotland. The most popular was the attempt to prevent the move-

---

[37] Rudé, *The crowd in history*, 21–2. For the English experience in this respect see Bohstedt, 'Gender, household and community politics', 106–13.

[38] For further discussion see Stevenson, *Popular disturbances*, 105, and Beattie, *Crime and the courts*, 133.

[39] See Bohstedt, 'Gender, household and community politics', 104.

[40] See Kilday, 'Women and crime', especially ch. vi.

ment of foodstuffs. Exporting foodstuffs when local provisions were scarce and expensive must have caused widespread resentment in certain areas. This led some rioters to prevent the transportation of produce destined for markets in neighbouring areas or locations further afield. As John Stevenson explains, 'the sight of grain being moved out of an area or shipped from small ports could easily excite popular indignation'.[41] This was no less the case in lowland Scotland where more than 60 per cent of the indictments for food rioting charged against women were alleged to have been committed in areas with transhipment points.

The prevention of the movement of foodstuffs, especially for export, was indeed a general feature of food rioting at this time. A few examples to illustrate this, some involving women, occurred at Lyme in the west of England in 1766, Tayside in December of 1772, Conray and Bangor Ferry in Caernarvonshire in February of 1795 and also in Montrose in December of 1812.[42] None of these instances, however, exhibited violence to the extreme level that was employed by the women of lowland Scotland during the mid-eighteenth and early nineteenth century in attempting to prevent the movement of foodstuffs.

The general behaviour of the women indicted for this type of food rioting was not dissimilar to that displayed in the following three examples.[43] Jean Cochrane, Elizabeth McWhinnie, Jean Hannah, Agnes Duncan, Janet Iron, Mary Clark, Isabell Hutchison and Elizabeth Keay appeared at the High Court of Justiciary in 1763. They were charged with mobbing and destroying the rigging of a ship at the port of Stranraer laden with grain for export. After this it was alleged that they did proceed 'in a most violent and lawless manner' to assault four members of the ship's crew 'to the great effusion of the men's blood and the danger of their lives'. One of the crew members lost an eye in the incident, and another found 'several of his tuith [teeth] to be missing'. The women had used parts of the ships' broken rigging to attack the men in this instance.[44]

In 1796 Agnes Byers, Katherine Miller and Janet Nicol were brought before the South Circuit Court of Ayrshire. They were charged with mobbing and trying to prevent grain being loaded onto a ship in Port William in Mochrum, Wigtownshire. The women were accused of stoning members of the ship's crew and attacking them with 'rungs [stout sticks] and beating them with their bare fists to the gret [great] effusion of the men's blood and the danger of their lives in a most ferocious and violent manner'. One crewman, Robert

41 Stevenson, *Popular disturbances*, 94. See also Logue, *Popular disturbances in Scotland*, 32.
42 For further discussion of these episodes see Stevenson, *Popular disturbances*, 95; S. G. E. Lythe, 'The Tayside meal mobs, 1772–3', *Scottish Historical Review* xlvi (1967), 32; D. J. V. Jones, 'The corn riots in Wales, 1793–1801', *Welsh Historical Review (Cylchgrawn Hanes Cymru)* ii (1965), 328; and Logue, *Popular disturbances*, 18.
43 Of all lowland female food rioters 61% participated in this type of food riot.
44 JC 26/170. My note in parenthesis.

Cross had one of his ears ripped off in this incident by Janet Nicol, who claimed in her testimony to the court that she had merely been 'getting a chuggle [tug] of his hair'.[45]

Also, in April of 1801, Marion Milligan, Agnes Glover and Marion Ireland appeared before the South Circuit Court of Dumfries. The women were charged with mobbing and tumult, and that having arrived at a ship 'lying with a Cargo of potatoes and other articles bound for Liverpool ... in the harbour of Kirkcudbright', they boarded and 'forcibly entered' the vessel. Then, after having 'broke open the hatches, they did from thence violently seize and carry away a quantity of Potatoes amounting to Twelve Bolls or thereby'. The women took the said potatoes, and at an unspecified location 'did distribute them without any authority at a price they deemed "just"'. However, not satisfied with these measures, the three women decided to search the town of Kirkcudbright for Thomas Sproat, the farmer whose foodstuffs were being exported. Upon finding the said Mr Sproat, the women 'without the smallest provocation and in the most wanton, violent and outrageous manner did assault the person of the said Thomas Sproat. ... After forcibly dragging him by the hair from his house to the Harbour of Kirkcudbright, the women did then and there throw the said Mr Sproat headlong into the River, to the great danger of his life and injury of his person.' The women thereafter 'continued to throw stones at the man in his most perilous situation'.[46]

This evidence is consistent with John Walter's assessment that ports became focal points for the tensions building up in a given community.[47] In addition, the material from lowland Scotland between 1750 and 1815 demonstrates that in the case of women at least, these tensions could easily erupt into violent acts being perpetrated upon those involved in the movement of foodstuffs.

The French term for the second method frequently employed by food rioters is 'taxation populaire'. This kind of price-fixing by collective action also falls into two separate categories: the reduction of prices through bargaining with the grain-seller in the market-place (using violence or the threat of violence); and, more commonly, the confiscation of the foodstuff by the rioters to be sold by them at what they believed to be a 'just' price.[48] This type of approach was not just employed in mid eighteenth- and early nineteenth-century Britain but was an international phenomenon. Examples of 'taxation populaire' occurred at Kilkenny in 1766, in Castillon in May

---

[45] JC 26/285. My additions in parenthesis.
[46] JC 26/310.
[47] Walter, 'Grain riots and popular attitudes to the law', 75.
[48] For a fuller discussion of this type of food riot see Rudé, *The crowd in history*, 23; R. B. Rose, 'Eighteenth-century price riots and public policy in England', *International Review of Social History* vi (1961), 277–92; and J. Stevenson, 'Food riots in England, 1792–1818', in Quinault and Stevenson, *Popular protest and public order*, 57.

1773, in Boston, Massachusetts, in July 1777, in Delph in the north-west of England in July 1795 and also in Merthyr Tydfil in September 1800.[49]

Once again, however, in each of these instances it is argued that the women involved exhibited restraint rather than violence. In lowland Scotland, as was often the case elsewhere, any money pocketed by the rioters in the sale of the grain was generally returned to the relevant farmer or meal-seller concerned. None the less particularly violent methods were employed by women in order to be given the right to set the aforesaid 'just' price in the first instance.

Again, the following examples are typical of the actions displayed by women indicted for this type of food riot.[50] At the High Court of Justiciary in 1771 Agnes McKetterick, Mary Murdoch, Jean McClauchrie, Ann Brown, Jean Milligan, Margaret Newal and Doline Bendall were charged, along with six males, with 'riot, tumult and convocating the lieges'. The rioters allegedly broke into a warehouse in Bridgend of Dumfries and 'in a masterful and most predacious manner did take away a considerable part of the meal stored within'. With the aid of carts, horses and sacks, which they had brought with them, they carried the meal to the Trades Hall in Dumfries 'in order to sell it at such a price as they should judge to be reasonable'. When a group of the local authorities tried to prevent this from occurring, the accused did allegedly 'attack and assault magistrates, Justices of the Peace and a party of soldiers, with Sticks, Stones and other Offensive Weapons and did Wound and bruise many of them to the effusion of their Blood and danger of their Lives'. After the Riot Act had been read to no avail, the magistrates who 'were in fear for the preservation of their Lives' ordered 'a party of the Military to fire' on the rioters by which an unspecified person was killed and many others wounded.[51]

At the South Circuit Court held at Dumfries in 1800 Susan McNaught, Jean Haining, Elizabeth Lindsay and a John Blacklock were indicted. They were charged with mobbing and the aggravated assault of a Dalbeattie (Kirkcudbrightshire) meal-monger, in an attempt to convince him to reduce his prices to 'a fair level for the common good'. When he refused, they threw him down to the ground, stamped on his head and beat him with sticks 'to the great effusion of his blood and danger of his life', whilst thereafter rubbing 'all manner of mainner [manure] over his person' until he relented to their demands.[52]

Similarly, Ann Lyon, Agnes Kirkwood, Agnes Brown, Grizel Baird, Elizabeth Cowan and Mary Gibson were brought before the South Circuit Court

---

[49] For further discussion of these episodes see Connolly, 'Violence and order in the eighteenth century', 54; Ruff, Crime, justice and public order, 152; D. Hoerder, Crowd action in revolutionary Massachusetts, 1765–1780, London–New York 1977, 360; Booth, 'Food riots', 93; and Jones, 'The corn riots in Wales', 332.

[50] Of all lowland female food rioters 39% participated in this type of food riot.

[51] JC 3/37.

[52] JC 26/305. My note in parenthesis.

held at Ayr in 1801. They were charged with mobbing and of having confiscated meal from a farmer in Newmills in Ayrshire. They did this by hitting him on the back of the head with a rake and 'thereafter beating him about the body with sharp stones and with their bare-fists to the great effusion of his blood'. They thereafter sold the meal 'in a tumultuous manner' outside the house of the said Ann Lyon, at what they considered to be 'a just price'.[53]

The Justiciary Court evidence relating to food riots employing 'taxation populaire' in lowland Scotland indicates that, rather than discipline being the norm, women on occasion targeted individual members of the community for violent assault in order to achieve their aims. Having said this, however, there is a distinct lack of material in the Justiciary records relating to female involvement in the damage of mill and warehouse property or the simple looting and spoiling of foodstuffs. The evidence suggests that lowland men were far more likely to be involved in this kind of wilful property damage.[54] In addition to this is the aforementioned readiness of food rioters to return any money obtained from the sale of confiscated goods.

What all this evidence suggests is that although readily violent in their behaviour female food rioters in the lowlands of Scotland between 1750 and 1815 were not simply being boisterous. Indeed, as John Beattie points out, 'the crowd's willingness to act violently was not acquired for the occasion, or was simply made palatable by the safety of numbers, but that it arose from a general view of the acceptability of certain kinds of violence'.[55] The analysis must now seek to explain why food riots were deemed necessary in the first place and to discover the reasons why the violence employed in such activities was considered 'acceptable' by the participants involved.

Initially at least it would appear to be relatively easy to assume that the key motivation for participation in food riots was a critical food shortage caused by poor harvests during a period of rapid population increase. It may appear unsurprising that women commonly participated in food riots as they, more than anyone, recognised the implication of high prices: they bought the food. Consequently it would seem that individuals, but particularly females, needed no other motive than scarcity and high prices to encourage their participation in food riots.[56] However, this statement can itself be questioned.

---

[53] JC 26/311.

[54] In indictments for food rioting in lowland Scotland between 1750 and 1815, men were more likely to face the additional charge of vandalism (55% of the total indicted) whereas women were more likely to be charged in addition with assault (86% of the total indicted).

[55] Beattie, *Crime and the courts*, 133. For more in-depth analysis of the sociological theories related to collective action see Le Bon, *The crowd*, and especially S. Milgram and H. Toch, 'Collective behaviour: crowds and social movements', in G. Lindzey and E. Aronson (eds), *The handbook of social psychology*, IV: *Group psychology and phenomena of interaction*, Reading, MA–London 1969, 507–610.

[56] See, for instance, Stevenson, *Popular disturbances*, 101; Archer, *Social unrest and popular protest*, 36; and Bohstedt, 'Gender, household and community politics', 101.

If basic 'economic pressure' was the key factor behind participation in food riots, as is often suggested,[57] why did some disturbances occur not only when there was a sufficient grain supply to meet demand, but also when the price of that grain was at a relatively normal level? Evidence from the lowland Scottish experience of this category of popular disturbance includes the food riots at Stranraer, Wigtownshire, in 1763, Newark, Renfrewshire, in 1781, Carstairs, Lanarkshire, in 1797, and Beith, Ayrshire, in 1801.[58] Indeed, in his attempt to answer the question 'Were "hunger" rioters really hungry?' Dale Edward Williams could find no evidence of a direct causal relationship between poverty and protest. It is his contention that hunger caused by high prices was not a 'sufficient' explanation for the motives of food rioters.[59] The available evidence from the Justiciary Court records appears to concur with Williams's thesis. There is not one indictment where women simply pillaged a warehouse and made off with the meal inside, nor is there an example of women craving 'lower prices', only 'just' or 'fair' ones.

Edward Thompson has criticised the interpretation of popular disturbances espoused by commentators such as Max Beloff, Robert Wearmouth and Charles Wilson, who contend that food riots were caused by a knee-jerk reaction to economic factors.[60] He states that

> It is of course true that riots were triggered off by soaring prices ... or by hunger. But these grievances operated within a popular consensus as to what were legitimate and what were illegitimate practices in marketing, milling, baking, etc. This in turn was grounded upon a consistent traditional view of social norms and obligations, of the proper economic functions of several parties within the community, which taken together, can be said to constitute the moral economy of the poor. An outrage to these moral assumptions, quite as much as actual deprivation, was the usual occasion for direct action.[61]

---

[57] For proponents of this view see Jones, 'The corn riots in Wales', 323–45; Smout, A history of the Scottish people, 209; and Whatley, Scottish society, 193–4.

[58] See, in order of appearance, JC 26/170; JC 26/225; JC 26/293; JC 26/309. For evidence of regional grain prices and supply capabilities see respectively Flinn, Scottish population history, appendix B, at pp. 495–7; R. Mitchison, 'The movements of Scottish corn prices in the seventeenth and eighteenth centuries', Economic History Review 2nd ser. xviii (1965), 278–91; and A. J. S. Gibson and T. C. Smout, Prices, food and wages in Scotland, 1550–1780, Cambridge 1995, chs iii–v.

[59] For further discussion see D. E. Williams, 'Were "hunger" rioters really hungry? Some demographic evidence', P&P lxxi (1976), 70–5. For an extension of this argument see J. Walter and K. Wrightson, 'Dearth and the social order in early modern England', P&P lxxi (1976), 22–42.

[60] Thompson, 'The moral economy', 76. See also the references in n. 58 above.

[61] Thompson, 'The moral economy', 78–9. For criticism of this argument see A.W. Coats, 'Contrary moralities: plebs, paternalists and political economists', P&P liv (1972), 130–3; E. F. Genovese, 'The many faces of the moral economy: a contribution to a debate', P&P lviii (1973), 161–8; and J. Bohstedt, 'The pragmatic economy, the politics of provision and the "invention" of the food riot tradition in 1740', in A. Randall and A. Charlesworth

It was this perceived erosion of traditional 'paternalism' and customary rights that existed between supplier and consumer which frequently gave the food rioters what Thompson defined as a 'legitimizing notion' for their participation in such popular disturbances and which made violence wholly acceptable.[62]

Increasingly, farmers, millers, meal merchants and the like were seen by the general populace as being engaged in certain 'malpractices' involved with the supply of foodstuffs. Although of obvious benefit and profit to the distributor such practices were considered unfair by, and detrimental to, the consumer at large. Weight tampering, degrading the quality of the meal, selling and buying in bulk to the highest bidder and thus by-passing the market place and the demands of the poor, and also fore-stalling where grain, potatoes and other foodstuffs were hoarded to enable the farmer to rapidly increase prices in times of scarcity, were all techniques practised throughout the mid-eighteenth and early nineteenth century by those who sold provisions. As the impact of the market and free-trade economy grew, so did the frequency of these 'practices', enabling suppliers to maximise profits at the consumers' expense.[63]

It appears to have been the case that when scarcity and high prices (or the threat of them) existed, and were combined with these 'malpractices' by foodstuff dealers, the possibility of collective protest increased and the use of violence within food riots was considered a 'justified' means to an end.

The theory that on the whole female food rioters were not merely boisterous in their behaviour is confirmed by the fact that many of the lowland Scottish women who had sold confiscated food stuffs at a 'fair' price returned the money. Not only were they avoiding charges of theft by doing so, but more significantly they were reaffirming their position in the relationship between provider and consumer which the former had neglected. Rather than riotous behaviour for its own sake, therefore, the lowland women indicted for participating in food riots at the Justiciary Court between 1750 and 1815 appeared to be acting in defence of rights which they considered to have been abused or to be under serious threat.

Patronage riots

In England during the eighteenth-century period, there were numerous popular disturbances connected with religious issues. Infamous examples include the Sacheverell riots of 1710, the Gordon riots of 1780 and the

---

(eds), *Moral economy and popular protest: crowds, conflict and authority*, Basingstoke 2000, 55–92.

[62] See Thompson, 'The moral economy', 78.

[63] For further discussion see ibid. 76–136; Logue, *Popular disturbances*, ch. i; Lythe, 'The Tayside meal mobs', 26–36; and Booth, 'Food riots', 84–107.

Priestley riots of 1791.[64] In contemporary Scotland disturbances of a religious nature focused to a large extent on the repercussions of the Patronage Act of 1712. Indeed, according to Kenneth Logue, 'The question of lay patronage bedevilled the Church of Scotland from the Tory Patronage Act of 1712 until the Disruption of 1843.'[65]

By the previous Act concerning Patronages of 1690, heritors paid a 600 merks composition to the patron.[66] In return, and although under the supervision of the presbytery, heritors were given the authority to propose ministers for positions in vacant parishes. However, concerns were soon raised that the terms and conditions of the 1690 act were not being met, and as a result that 'measure' was replaced. The problem with the original patronage legislation was that patrons were not receiving the payment due to them. Consequently, the 1712 act restored the powers of nomination to patrons whilst reserving to congregations the right to dissent from the choices made. If disagreement persisted, the matter was to be resolved by the presbytery. However, in the course of the eighteenth century the rights of congregations were increasingly ignored and nominations made by patrons were commonly accepted by the ecclesiastical courts without reference to the views of the laity.[67] This was the key factor which often resulted in collective action being adopted by parishioners. Furthermore, in order to assert their perceived 'rights', it appears that congregations were not averse to violence.[68]

Logue has traced female participation in anti-patronage riots in Scotland in areas as far apart as Newburgh in Fife (1785) and Assynt in Sutherland (1813).[69] His evidence reflects the fact that 19 per cent of the women who participated in popular disturbances between 1780 and 1815 were involved in patronage disputes.[70] What can be said of the women of lowland Scotland indicted for this offence before the Justiciary Court between 1750 and 1815?

Some 30 per cent (thirty-eight cases out of 125) of the women indicted for popular disturbances relating to lowland Scotland were accused of being anti-patronage rioters. Certain characteristics of these women can be identified. First, in every single case the anti-patronage riot was committed by women in rural areas. This has obviously much more to do with the location of certain parishes, and less to do with a proven propensity of country

---

[64] See Stevenson, *Popular disturbances*, esp. chs iv, vii. For the Priestley riots in particular see R. B. Rose, 'The Priestley riots of 1791', *P&P* xviii (1960), 68–88.

[65] Logue, *Popular disturbances*, 168. For further discussion of patronage riots see C. G. Brown, *The social history of religion in Scotland since 1730*, London 1987, 29–31, 103–4, and Whatley, *Scottish society*, 168–170.

[66] See ch. 5, n. 46.

[67] For further discussion see Ferguson, *Scotland*, 13, 111, and Logue, *Popular disturbances*, 168.

[68] See, for example, Fraser, 'Patterns of protest', 283; Logue, *Popular disturbances*, 168; and Whatley, *Scottish society*, 168–70.

[69] Logue, *Popular disturbances*, 169, 199–200.

[70] My calculation on the evidence ibid. 192.

women to be more aggressive than their urban counterparts. The conclusion that rural areas predominated as locations for patronage disputes seems to be confirmed for Scotland as a whole, regardless of gender, by the work of Kenneth Logue.[71]

The second characteristic of note is that, as was the case with female food rioters, in a high proportion of the indictments charged against women involved in lowland Scotland's patronage disputes, the occupation of the accused was not given. In only 5 per cent of the indictments was the defendant's occupation recorded. Certainly, in this respect, the indicted women do not appear to have been tied down by family commitments. The majority were unmarried. In addition to this, the fact that some 87 per cent of them allegedly committed the disturbances, not with relatives, but with friends, neighbours or total strangers, reflects the communal or personal orientation of the patronage riot. Once again, perhaps, married women were more reticent about getting involved in popular protest when the issue at stake did not have a directly detrimental affect on their interests or the welfare of their families.

The final characteristic of the female patronage rioters of lowland Scotland between 1750 and 1815 was their willingness to resort to violence. Although not as significant as in the case of food rioters, 63 per cent of the women involved in patronage disputes were charged with aggravated assault as well as other breaches of the peace. The remaining 37 per cent were accused of violent property damage and violent threats, as well as lesser charges of tumultuous behaviour. Once again, it appears to have been accepted by the indicted women of lowland Scotland that, in defence of lost rights, the use of violence was legitimate. Just how that violence was put into practice will now be examined.

The methods employed by patronage rioters to express their views on the issue were relatively straightforward both in conception and practice. The fundamental aim of the lowland Scottish women and other rioters elsewhere was to prevent the man selected by the patrons from becoming minister to the congregation. The methods used in this type of popular disturbance merely reflected this aim. A few examples help to illustrate this.

In 1751 Rebecca Gillies, Martha Gray, Jean Weir, Elizabeth Martine, Grizell Vessie, Agnes Wilson, Grizell Wilson, Agnes Meek, Isobel Paton, Jean Frizell (alias Fraser), Jean Aitken and Isobel Forrest, along with a number of men, appeared before the High Court of Justiciary in Edinburgh. They were charged with the 'riotous and tumultuous opposition to Mr Robert Dick', selected by John Lockhart of Lee Esquire, patron of the parish church of Lanark to be minister there. They first tried to prevent Mr Dick from entering the village:

---

[71] Ibid. ch. vii.

Armed with Clubs, Sticks and other offensive Weapons ... they mett [met] with the said Mr Robert Dick on the country road to the parish of Old Monkland ... where with force and violence and many horrid Oaths and Imprecations and threatening Expressions they compelled him to away, and would not suffer him to enter the village and perform Divine service there.

When latterly the said Mr Dick attempted once more to enter the parish, he was met with even more resistance. The rioters 'sett [set] the fire Bell a ringing' and 'beat a drum' to assemble the people. They then 'in a most riotous and disorderly manner' attacked the minister and his two companions by 'throwing stones through the streets and from the steeple near the Church, and also by beating them with Clubs and Sticks to the great effusion of their blood and danger of their lives'. Furthermore, and as an additional precautionary measure, the women 'barricaded and made fast the Church Doors to prevent the Minister getting Access thereto and swore to bring the building down about his ears if he ever set foot therein'.[72]

Similarly, in 1790, the following women appeared before the South Circuit Court of Ayr: Janet Montgomery, Marion Baillie, Helen Taylor and Janet Miller. They were charged with 'riotously and tumultuously assembling for the purpose of obstructing' Mr John Duncan's admittance as minister for the parish of Ardrossan. They were accused of attacking the patrons of the parish who had come to introduce the new minister to the congregation:

By throwing dirt and stones at the gathered patrons, they were by that means forcibly driven out of the area... In the course of the attack, ... Doctor James Woodrow got a severe stroke on the head with a stone, which cut and bled him, ... Patrick Kelso got his hand cut by a stone, which bled much, Robert Clark got a blow on the side with a stone, and Robert Barclay along with the said Mr John Duncan were thrown into the gutter, and wounded to the great effusion of their blood.[73]

Similar instances could be cited. At New Monkland, Lanarkshire, in 1768 two women and two men were subsequently indicted and at Greenlaw, Renfrewshire, in 1770 five women were eventually brought before the Justiciary Court.[74] The methods employed by the women of lowland Scotland reflect their willingness to resort to violence in attempting an outward show of public sentiment on the issue of patronage. The motivations behind their behaviour must now be investigated.

According to William Mathieson, congregations 'looked with repugnance on patronage as an intrusion of secular, if not of political, influence into the spiritual domain, and they shrank from the harshness and oppression which

[72] JC 3/27. My additions in parenthesis.
[73] JC 26/257.
[74] See JC 13/16; JC 26/192/1.

its exercise involved'.[75] In light of the Justiciary Court evidence, 'shrank' is scarcely an accurate reflection of the actions of women of lowland Scotland. Nevertheless, the 1750 to 1815 period was one where the perceived 'rights' of parishioners were increasingly being ignored in favour of those of the patrons. It was this flagrant disregard exhibited by the patrons which agitated congregations and which, in their own opinion, legitimised their subsequent actions.[76] Clearly, the basic motivation for patronage rioting was the simple fact that parishioners did not readily accept changes being forced on them against their will. This was especially true when there appeared to be no formal course of redress open to them. Ministers could be opposed for a whole range of reasons. Perhaps their own personal views were unpopular, the religious or political persuasion of their patrons caused offence, or the precise nature of their presentation provoked discontent. Indeed, due to the general 'controversy' and bitter resentment surrounding the way in which a minister could be appointed, he may well have been forced to share the general outlook and opinions of the landowner and to see himself as the laird's mouthpiece.[77]

In this context Christopher Whatley and Callum Brown argue that there seems to be a correlation between patronage disturbances and the main phases of agricultural development.[78] In addition, as patronage riots were ultimately directed towards landowners, Whatley and Brown believe that they can be accurately described as 'the most significant Scottish equivalent to rural protest in the rest of the British Isles'.[79] The nominated minister, adopting the role of the 'laird's mouthpiece', was seen by the local population as being party to the views of the landowner and therefore a suitable target for protest against agrarian change.

The evidence of the Justiciary Court neither directly supports nor refutes these arguments. However, in the relatively few instances where the direct testimony of the accused individual is provided, the women unanimously refer to the loss of their 'privilege of selection' as being the key rationale behind their actions.[80]

Although few in number and less frequently indicted than food rioters, the women of lowland Scotland charged with patronage rioting displayed just as much aggression as the women who participated in the other popular disturbances brought to the Justiciary Court's attention during the 1750 to 1815

[75] W. L. Mathieson, *The awakening of Scotland: a history from 1747 to 1797*, Glasgow 1910, 196.

[76] For further discussion see Fergusson, *Scotland*, 121.

[77] See the conclusions in Logue, *Popular disturbances*, 168, and Smout, *A history of the Scottish people*, 216.

[78] See, for example, Whatley, 'How tame were the Scottish lowlanders?', 21.

[79] Brown, *The social history of religion*, 104. See also Whatley, 'How tame were the Scottish lowlanders?', 21. This view has been challenged by Devine in *The transformation of rural Scotland*, 159–60, but Whatley has countered Devine's comments in *Scottish society*, 169–70.

[80] See, for example, JC 26/164.

period. It seems that the principal motivation for their behaviour concerned the election of ministers to parishes by patrons, without the congregations' consent or against its wishes. As a result, the women considered their 'rights' to have been abused and they therefore felt fully justified in the action they decided to take, be it violent or otherwise. It is this 'legitimising notion' which links all indicted female participation in popular disturbances in lowland Scotland between 1750 and 1815.

Other disturbances

After food and patronage riots have been accounted for, 9 per cent (eleven cases out of 125) of the total number of lowland women indicted for popular disturbances remain to be discussed. All of these women except one were involved in simple assaults against authority which had been deemed riotous by the law officers concerned. As this subject area has already been dealt with in depth in the previous chapter, and as there is virtually no difference in the characteristics, patterns of behaviour or motives of these women compared to those analysed previously, it would be unproductive to address the activities of these women once more.

The remaining case is none the less significant. Agnes Urie was indicted for her part in an industrial disturbance that occurred in Paisley in 1773. Charged with eleven male weavers, she was not a weaver herself, although she was married to one. It was alleged that

> at the time lybelled, there was an unlawful Combination amongst the Weavers in Paisley in order to prevent Weavers from working until the price of the work was regulated and fixed, whereby many persons who were willing to work were intimidated from taking out kains [canes] or webs, and a great Interruption to the trade of Paisley was occasioned for eight weeks.

For her part, Agnes Urie was specifically charged with 'being concerned in a Mob who insulted and assaulted James Robertson [a blackleg weaver from Maxweltoun]'.[81]

The details concerning the case are somewhat sketchy. In addition, the strike as a form of popular disturbance was rare in lowland Scotland between 1750 and 1815. Kenneth Logue could find not one example of a woman being involved in industrial disturbances in the whole of Scotland between 1780 and 1815, and recorded the participation of only twenty-two males.[82] Clearly, this kind of popular disturbance was not only male-dominated but must surely have increased in incidence after 1812 when demonstrations and

---

81 JC 13/19. My notes in parenthesis.
82 Logue, *Popular disturbances*, 192. For female participation in English industrial disputes in the eighteenth century see Bohstedt, 'Gender, household and community politics', 115–19.

strikes gradually replaced communal-based disorder. In this instance, Agnes Urie had much in common with her fellow countrywomen in her attempts to publicly 'demonstrate' or present what she considered to be a legitimate grievance, in that she in turn employed what she believed to be 'legitimate means' in her attempt to have that grievance addressed.

The absence of lowland women in protests other than food riots or anti-patronage disputes deserves further attention. Why were these Scottish women not involved in other forms of popular disturbance between 1750 and 1815? Perhaps women were less often indicted for riotous behaviour as the authorities believed that women were acting on behalf of men, either their husbands or other male relatives, rather than for their own ends. In this way it could be argued that women rioters were not directly responsible for their actions and therefore they should and could not be prosecuted for their behaviour.[83] However, this theory of the 'hidden' nature of female riotous activity does not explain why some women were indicted for certain types of protests and not others.

Perhaps the forms of protest women chose to be involved in were a reflection of the aspects of community life with which were closely associated in the period under review, namely the market and the church. When women's lives and the environments they experienced became more expansive and more fluid, especially from the nineteenth century onwards, this perhaps meant that women began to be involved in other types of protest which, by that time, were coming to have more meaning or significance to them.[84] Certainly women were more commonly involved in industrial, social and political disturbances during the mid-to-late nineteenth century than they had been in the period before.[85]

There could perhaps be a simpler explanation. This study only looks at the records of lowland popular disturbances indicted at the Justiciary Court between 1750 and 1815. Yet many riots which involved women may have been deemed less grievous by the authorities and thus dealt with in the lower courts as episodes of breach of the peace or disorderly conduct. As a result, women's involvement in popular protests during the 1750 to 1815 period (especially when there was an absence of overt violence) may be significantly underestimated by this study. Sources other than court indictments may also have much to tell us about women's involvement in formal protest, especially in episodes concerning matters other than food or patronage.[86]

---

[83] For this theory see A. Wood, *Riot, rebellion and popular politics in early modern England*, Basingstoke 2002, 106.

[84] For this theory see Bohstedt, 'Gender, household and community politics', 113–19. For a study of the changing nature of women's lives in nineteenth-century Scotland see E. Gordon, 'Women's spheres', in W. H. Fraser and R. J. Morris (eds), *People and society in Scotland*, II: *1830–1914*, Edinburgh 1997, 206–35.

[85] See Thomas and Grimmett, *Women in protest*, chs ii–vi and the postscript.

[86] For instance, lowland women seem to have been actively involved in a militia riot in

Finally, of course, there were the numerous forms of 'everyday' protest that were simply ignored by authorities and never formally recorded. Usually covert in nature, we will never know the true extent to which women were involved in these more subtle rebellions, although evidence suggests that women could be just as mutinous in their everyday lives as their male counterparts, especially, it seems, when they had a 'legitimate' grievance to voice.[87] Women did not necessarily have to voice these complaints in a collective form of overt and violent protest like a riot or mob. Instead, they could on occasion make private protests to their masters, their husbands or the local authorities that were more tactful, more peaceful and arguably perhaps more effective in getting their message across.

Perhaps due to the persistent historical tradition of collective protest in Scotland, from the mid-eighteenth to the early nineteenth century Scots law provided two charges to enable the prosecution of those involved: mobbing and rioting. Indictments involving these charges were the third most frequently prosecuted offence against the person for which lowland women were brought before the Justiciary Court at that time.

These women participated in two significant types of popular disturbance – the food riot and the patronage riot. The characteristics of the women involved were that in the main their occupation was not given in the indictment, they were unmarried and they committed this type of offence, not with other family members, but with members of the community in which they lived whom they may or may not have been acquainted with. This suggests the existence of common aims which were not restricted to the defence of family or personal interests as was the case in the other crimes against the person previously analysed. A further characteristic of this type of offence, one that was distinctive to participants in food riots, was that there was a roughly equal split between those committed by women in rural areas and those committed in urban areas. In the case of patronage riots, all the women who were indicted came from rural areas. This distinction is probably not a reflection of a greater propensity for rural lowland women to be 'disruptive' in this respect but it is more likely to be simply indicative of the location of 'vacant' parishes.

In general terms the methods and motives of the women involved in popular disturbances varied according to the activity they were engaged in and the specific ends they had in view. The common factor in all such activities, however, seems to have been the fundamental belief in the legitimacy of their actions in response to what they perceived as the erosion of 'traditional

---

Tranent (East Lothian) in 1797 which is not apparent from the indictment records of the Justiciary Court: K. J. Logue, 'The Tranent militia riot of 1797', *Transactions of the East Lothian Antiquarian and Field Naturalists' Society* xiv (1974), 37–61.

[87] See, for instance, Thomas and Grimmett, *Women in protest*, 24; Houlbrooke, 'Women's social life', 176–7; and Whatley, 'How tame were the Scottish lowlanders?', 21.

rights and customs' which they had previously and justifiably enjoyed. This 'legitimising notion' was reflected in the willingness of these women to resort to violence in their attempts to address this anomaly. The significant difference between lowland Scottish women and those studied elsewhere is that in the overwhelming majority of cases this violence was directed specifically at person rather than property. This violence was legitimised by customary action, rather than disarmed by it.

Returning to the views of Edmund Burke and Robert Southey cited at the beginning of this chapter, it is conceivable that the victims of these riotous attacks by the women of lowland Scotland could have readily described their assailants as 'all the unutterable abominations of the furies of hell, in the abased shape of the vilest women'.[88] However, whether these women were more inclined to resistance than their male counterparts is not apparent from the Justiciary evidence. Certainly the indicted lowland women could not be described as 'uninflammable' in their methods of collective action. Rather, their actions shatter the 'orthodoxy of passivity' promoted by some Scottish historians for the eighteenth-century period. Yet women's involvement in popular disturbances should not be exaggerated.[89] For, although women appear to have been more violent than men when carrying out collective protest, they only make up one third of the total number indicted for this type of offence. Although this caveat must be borne in mind, what is clear none the less is that a study of the nature and incidence of women's involvement in popular disturbances gives a fascinating insight into their popular mentality in the pre-modern period, an insight which no other type of crime can afford.

---

[88] Rudé, *The crowd in history*, 8.
[89] For further discussion of the assertion that women's involvement in popular disturbances has been exaggerated see Bohstedt, 'Gender, household and community politics', 89; Thomas and Grimmett, *Women in protest*, 32–4; W. Thwaites, 'Women in the market place: Oxfordshire, c.1690–1800', *Midland History* ix (1984), 36; and J. Rendall, *The origins of modern feminism: women in Britain, France and the United States, 1780–1860*, Basingstoke 1985, 201.

7

Robbery

'Unlike the sneak-thief, the robber encounters his victims face to face, and is prepared to risk his life fighting. A <u>man</u> who commits robbery must be brave as well as desperate, and bravery of that kind is a distinguishing characteristic of <u>the English</u>.'[1]

It is widely held amongst historians of female criminality that the incidence of women's participation in crimes against property was far greater than their participation in crimes against the person.[2] However, the evidence from the Justiciary Court records demonstrates that the situation in lowland Scotland between 1750 and 1815 was very different. Less than a third of the women indicted were charged with an offence against property. Nearly two-thirds, on the other hand, were charged with crimes against the person, with the remaining women indicted for offences against public justice, such as failing to appear in court as a trial witness. It should be remembered, however, that the prominence of crimes against the person in relation to this study is to a large extent a reflection of the province of the Justiciary Court. As it dealt with indictments for the most 'serious' offences, it was therefore more inclined to prosecute a murder than an act of petty theft.[3]

Despite their apparent lack of participation in property crime in relation to offences against the person, women in lowland Scotland were still indicted for the former felony in large numbers. Clearly, in order to achieve a fuller understanding of violent female criminality in this part of Scotland during the period being studied, women's involvement in violent property offences must be addressed.

---

[1]   C. Plummer (ed.), *The governance of England by Sir John Fortesque*, Oxford 1885, 141–2. Author's emphasis added.

[2]   See, for example, works such as Hanawalt, 'The female felon', 251–73; Sharpe, *Crime in seventeenth century England*; Ruff, *Crime, justice and public order*; Henry, *Dublin hanged*; Beattie, *Crime and the courts in England*; and King, *Crime, justice, and discretion*.

[3]   This is not to say that indictments for non-violent property crime were rarely brought to the Justiciary Court or were solely dealt with by the inferior Scottish courts, but rather it is an attempt to explain why indictments for crimes against the person so greatly outnumber those against property. In any case, violent crimes against property, which will be dealt with in this chapter, were far more likely to be indicted at the Justiciary Court than within any other jurisdiction, due to their supposedly 'serious' nature. Consequently, there is no gendered skew in the number of defendants charged at the Justiciary Court as was arguably the case in the indicted episodes of common and aggravated assault seen in chapter 5 above.

Property crimes committed with the use of violence accounted for nearly a third of all property offences indicted in relation to lowland Scotland between 1750 and 1815. Women accounted for some 38 per cent of the total number of indictments for this type of crime. Although obviously less than the incidence of male indictments, and bearing in mind the limitations of comparisons with other research using different sources from those employed here, this figure (in proportional terms) is considerably higher than any of the findings from other studies of female involvement in this type of criminality.[4] Certainly, female participation in violent property crime in mid eighteenth- and early nineteenth-century lowland Scotland merits closer attention.

The crimes that fall into the category of violent property offences are robbery, arson and plagium (child-stealing). As robbery is the only one of the three which regularly involved direct physical violence, it will form the sole focus for this chapter. In any event, only a miniscule number of women were indicted for the other two offences, certainly not enough to warrant their detailed investigation in this analysis.

More than any other type of offence committed in the pre-modern period, robbery caused the greatest consternation amongst authorities and contemporary commentators alike.[5] Chiefly this was because this offence not only threatened an individual's personal safety but also their personal 'status' or wealth as well. Regularly, then, the nature and incidence of robbery was used as a gauge of how 'criminal' society was in general at a given period of time. Robbery was not an offence solely restricted to the English, however, as Sir John Fortesque implies in the opening quotation to this chapter. It was a crime regularly indicted in Scotland during the pre-modern period, and was reserved – almost exclusively – to the jurisdiction of the Justiciary Court.

Fortesque was also mistaken in his assertion that robbery was solely a male activity. Once again the women of lowland Scotland buck the trend about what is known and 'expected' of female criminals in the pre-modern period. A substantial number of women were indicted for robbery in this region during the eighteenth century. In addition, the evidence suggests that the levels of violence employed by Scottish women who robbed were unparalleled in brutality and ferociousness even in comparison with those of their male counterparts in Scotland and elsewhere. It is clear that the degree of aggression used by women in robbery offences at this time was greater than that employed in any other crime for which they were indicted, including murder. These women were clearly not behaving according to 'gendered' prescriptions of femininity.

This chapter explores the phenomenon of female robbers in Scotland between 1750 and 1815. First, attitudes towards robbery are explored, together with the incidence of the offence. The analysis will then turn to the typical

---

4   See the references in n. 2 above.
5   See Beattie, *Crime and the courts*, 148, and Emsley, *Crime and society*, 54.

characteristics of the women involved, the techniques they employed and the reasons for their behaviour. The evidence presented reinforces suggestions that we should quickly abandon gendered 'notions' of behaviour. By providing a unique insight into women's criminal behaviour away from the domestic sphere, this chapter testifies further to the aggressive nature of Scottish criminal women. Arguably, rather than behaving 'appropriately' for their sex, lowland women robbers behaved on a par with the most aggressive of men.

The legal context and attitudes towards robbery

It is possible to define robbery as 'the taking and carrying away of personal property of another from the person and against his will, by force or violence, or by assault and putting in fear, with intent to steal'.[6] As this offence regularly involved direct physical confrontation between the victim and offender, robbery was regarded as one of the most serious crimes committed for trial.

In English law, the key factors involved in determining whether an act of robbery fell under the statutory provision of the 1691 Robbery Act were the monetary value of the plunder and the location from which the goods were stolen.[7] In *ancien régime* France matters were yet more complicated. There, an offence was deemed a robbery or aggravated theft depending on a variety of circumstances. These included the nature of the object stolen, the way in which the crime was committed, the place and time the robbery occurred and even the status or rank of the individuals involved.[8]

In Scotland, robbery (or stouthrief) was a 'capital crime at common law' and there were two simple and logical qualifications for an indictment of this nature to arise.[9] First, something had to be stolen and, second, the thief must have used violence. The violence alluded to here did not necessarily have to be applied to the victim for a robbery indictment to result. If the victim had surrendered his/her possessions merely because of the threat of being assaulted, this was enough to constitute a robbery according to the principles of Scots law.[10]

The period 1750 to 1815 is an important one in the study of this type of violent property crime. During this time, there was an unprecedented wave

6   J. E. Conklin, *Robbery and the criminal justice system*, Philadelphia 1972, 4.
7   See P. Linebaugh, *The London hanged: crime and civil society in the eighteenth century*, London 1993, 54.
8   For further discussion see Ruff, *Crime, justice and public order*, 113.
9   Stouthrief was the old name (unique to Scots law) for theft carried out with open force. It was no different from robbery in terms of the actual crime carried out, and was commonly used to refer to robbery offences in early eighteenth-century indictments. This was simply a reflection of the preferred vocabulary of court scribes rather than a distinction of semantics. For further discussion see Hume, *Commentaries*, ii, ch. ii, p. 104.
10 See ibid. ii, ch. ii, pp. 104–5, and Anderson, *Criminal law of Scotland*, pt II, 183.

of popular concern in Britain at a nationally perceived epidemic of robberies. It was widely recognised that the security of the highways was essential to communications and to the growing commerce of the kingdom. Consequently, if people were unable to travel along public roads without fear of being robbed, this would have serious implications for trade in an increasingly market-based economy.[11] In addition to this, the extensively published comments of contemporary English writers made individuals fear for their own public safety. Henry Fielding, writing in 1751, stated that 'I make no doubt, but that the streets ... and the roads ... will shortly be impassable without the utmost hazard.'[12] He complained that 'I am to be assaulted, and pillaged, and plundered ... I can neither sleep in my own house nor walk the streets, nor travel in safety.'[13]

Were these comments mere hyperbole? Victor Gatrell would appear to think so. He states that 'the power of the law has always been measured in some degree by the safety of the highway, and then as now, as a result, public alarm at the incidence of violent robbery in public spaces was often disproportionate to the actual frequency of the offence'.[14] Both John Beattie and James Sharpe agree with Gatrell. In terms of actual indictments at least, they argue that violent robbery was relatively rare in early modern England.[15]

The findings of studies elsewhere in Europe, however, do not concur with this view but rather substantiate the fears and opinions of Fielding and his contemporaries. According to Julius Ruff for instance, robbery seems to have thrived in the *ancien régime* court of Libourne in south-west France during the eighteenth century,[16] while Brian Henry infers that Dublin between 1780 and 1795 was notoriously rife with violent thieves; indeed he contends that most of the property crimes brought to court were street robberies.[17]

How does Scotland, and the lowland region in particular, fit into this picture? In total 188 indictments relating to robbery were brought before the Justiciary Court in lowland Scotland (at a fairly regular rate) between 1750

---

[11] For further discussion see A. Macfarlane, *The justice and the mare's ale: law and disorder in seventeenth century England*, Oxford 1981, 136.

[12] H. Fielding, *An enquiry into the causes of the late increase of robbers & etc.*, London 1751, 2.

[13] Ibid. 3. For more on the so-called 'moral panics' which emanated from this perceived increase in robbery offences in Britain during the eighteenth and nineteenth centuries see, for instance, P. King, 'Newspaper reporting, prosecution practice and perceptions of urban crime: the Colchester crime wave of 1765', *C&C* ii (1987), 423–54; R. Sindall, *Street violence in the nineteenth century: media panic or real danger?*, Leicester 1990; and J. Davis, 'The London garotting panic of 1862: a moral panic and the creation of a criminal class in mid-Victorian England', in Gatrell, Lenman and Parker, *Crime and the law*, 190–213.

[14] V. A. C. Gatrell, 'The decline of theft and violence in Victorian and Edwardian England', in Gatrell, Lenman and Parker, *Crime and the law*, 317.

[15] See Beattie, *Crime and the courts*, 147, and Sharpe, *Crime in seventeenth-century England*, 104.

[16] See Ruff, *Crime, justice and public order*, 115.

[17] For further discussion see Henry, *Dublin hanged*, 100–10.

and 1815. Although this number is far below what might be considered an epidemic, it does not suggest that this type of violent property crime was altogether rare in incidence either. In terms of Justiciary Court evidence at least, the lowland experience of robbery in the mid-eighteenth and early nineteenth centuries appears to relate to neither of the extremes exhibited by contemporary England, France or Ireland, and it consequently warrants closer analysis.

Initially, however, it is important to point out that there are several reasons why the number of indictments for robbery and stouthrief was not an accurate reflection of the incidence of this type of violent property crime.[18] The first of these is directly linked with the perceived nature of female criminality in these offences.

According to John Beattie, women were essentially involved in robbery as decoys or look-outs. As a result he claims that many women implicated in robberies in this way were never arrested or prosecuted by the authorities. Consequently it is probable that indictment figures for robbery significantly under-represent the involvement of women.[19] In addition, women who acted as decoys by seducing their male victims also contributed to the under-reporting of robbery and/or stouthrief in another way. This was because this type of deception was based on the victim's desire to engage in illicit sexual relations; as a result he would be less inclined to report his misfortune to the authorities. Many of the women involved therefore went undetected.[20]

Another reason for the incidence of robbery being under-reported was the frequent and apparently successful attempt, by blatant threat to the victims or bribery of the prosecutors, to ensure that an indictment was never laid against a suspect individual in the first place.[21] Offenders could easily use part of the profit from their appropriated plunder as inducement to those in authority willing to turn a blind eye to the crimes committed. However, given the intense public concern about this type of violent property crime during the 1750 to 1815 period, the use of bribery was probably not as widespread as alarmists like Henry Fielding tried to suggest.

Probably more commonly, threats made against the victims of robbery and stouthrief caused these types of crimes to be under-reported. It is clear from the Justiciary Court evidence that robbers often worked in gangs. They did this, not only to commit the violent act of theft itself, but also to have contacts who could fence the stolen goods or who would harbour them in so-

---

[18] For further discussion of the contribution of property crimes to the 'dark figure' or unquantifiable level of criminal statistics see C. Herrup, 'New shoes and mutton pies: investigative responses to theft in seventeenth-century east Sussex', HJ xxvii (1984), 811–30.

[19] See Beattie, 'The criminality of women', 90.

[20] Pollak, The criminality of women, 29–30.

[21] For further discussion see Fielding, An enquiry into the causes, 4.

called 'flash-houses' after the crime had taken place.[22] In this way a network was created, implicating all concerned in some form of criminal activity. It was not just the robbers themselves who had to avoid apprehension, but also their accomplices in the wider criminal sphere. Consequently, the threats made against the victims could be carried out by a wide variety of individuals, thus giving these apparent menaces more credence and resulting in a reluctance to report this type of offence to the authorities.

A further reason for the hidden incidence of robbery is suggested by Victor Gatrell. He states that: 'Robbery of the poor was doubtless less often reported than robbery of the not-so-poor, and the relationship between known cases and those actually committed is unlikely to have been a close one.'[23] It is logical to assume that this must often have been the case in lowland Scotland between 1750 and 1815, as elsewhere in the country at that time.

That said, the brutal intensity of violence which frequently attended robbery offences was enough motivation for a substantial number of individuals to be indicted before the Justiciary Court. Furthermore, the fact that informers were known to betray their fellow robbers if victims or prosecutors offered them enough incentives to make it worth their while goes some way towards redressing the balance between committed and indicted violent property crimes of this type.

The association between robbery and acts of abject violence had another implication in terms of the legal context for this type of offence. Individuals convicted of robbery were more likely to be executed and less likely to be pardoned than any other type of offender.[24] Linked to the contemporary fears referred to earlier, and because of the regular brutality in evidence during the perpetration of this type of crime, judges were unlikely to show mercy to a robber. This was especially true of the Scottish women indicted for the offence. In eighteenth-century England women convicted of serious felonies were shown greater leniency than those convicted of minor ones, to avoid executing many women. In Scotland, on the other hand, penal policy was somewhat different.[25] Once a lowland woman stepped outside the boundaries of expected 'feminine' behaviour, she would be given overtly brutalised punishments as a visual 'lesson' to the populace. For female robbers (as well as their male contemporaries) this meant the regular adoption of aggravated punishments, such as dismemberment of the limbs prior to execution, gibbeting of the offender's remains and post-mortem public dissection and anatomisation. It is a significant detail that limb dismemberment and gibbeting were not

---

[22] For further discussion on the use of gangs in robberies see Beattie, *Crime and the courts*, 252–63.

[23] Gatrell, 'The decline of theft and violence', 317.

[24] See, for instance, J. Rule, *Albion's people: English society, 1714–1815*, London 1992, 238.

[25] See, for instance, Morgan and Rushton, *Rogues, thieves and the rule of law*, 122–3; and King, 'Gender, crime and justice', and *Crime, justice, and discretion*, 232–7, 261–2, 274–85.

meted out to female offenders for any other crime except robbery. This is another reflection of how seriously the crime was deemed by the authorities of the day, and how repugnant they regarded the members of the 'fairer-sex' who perpetrated it. It is now pertinent to turn specifically to the Scottish lowland women indicted for robbery before the Justiciary Court between 1750 and 1815, and to ask how commonly these women were involved in this type of offence, and what means they employed to carry it out.

Incidence of female robbery and methodology

As far as female participation in robbery is concerned, there is, according to Otto Pollak, a distinct lack of evidence. He explains that robbery is 'considered a specifically male offence since it represents the pursuit of monetary gain by overt action and thus combines in the criminal sphere two roles which in our culture have been generally assigned to men'.[26] However, as has already been shown in relation to the crimes against the person studied in previous chapters, between 1750 and 1815 Scottish women were frequently involved in various types of so-called 'overt action' for a multitude of reasons. Whether their motivation for violent activity extended to that of 'monetary gain' must now be examined, and not merely dismissed as emphasising the bounds of appropriate female behaviour.

Of the total number of people accused of robbery and stouthrief in lowland Scotland 35 per cent were women.[27] This proportion seems remarkably high in comparison with other studies of this form of violent property theft during the pre-modern period. John Beattie's sample survey of the Surrey assizes between 1663 and 1802, for instance, discovered that women accounted for a mere 8 per cent of the total number of robbery indictments.[28] Peter King, on the other hand, found that less than 2 per cent of robbery offenders in Essex between 1740 and 1804 were female,[29] while Garthine Walker's study of early modern Cheshire failed to find any robbery indictments charged against women.[30] It would appear, then, that Scottish lowland women were much more willing to indulge in this type of violent property crime than many of their English counterparts, at least according to the evidence of the Scottish Justiciary Court.[31]

---

[26] Pollak, *The criminality of women*, 29.

[27] Fifty-four lowland Scottish women were indicted at the Justiciary Court for robbery and 11 were indicted for stouthrief. All of these women appeared in court to answer the charges against them. Of the men similarly charged, 115 were indicted for robbery and 8 were indicted for stouthrief.

[28] Beattie, 'The criminality of women', 91.

[29] King, *Crime, justice, and discretion*, 196.

[30] G. Walker, 'Women, theft and the world of stolen goods', in Kermode and Walker, *Women, crime and the courts*, 81–105, and *Crime, gender and social order*, ch. v.

[31] For further evidence of the low incidence of female involvement in robbery outside

It is important to note that none of the Scottish lowland women indicted before the Justiciary Court were classified as highway robbers. Although the types of robberies committed were not necessarily differentiated in the court's records (as the legal qualifications for a robbery indictment did not require it), there is still no instance, either in the charges levelled or in the witness testimony, of any woman described as being on horse-back. Highwaywomen seem to have been rare. According to John Beattie, 'The essential requirements for successful highway robbery were good horsemanship and skill with weapons, especially pistols, and neither were accomplishments that women acquired easily in their youth.'[32]

Beattie's explanation appears convincing in this respect. However, his argument breaks down in regard to the women of lowland Scotland when he concludes that when women did participate in robbery offences, they rarely took a violent or direct part in the crimes. Female robbers, he argues, avoided direct confrontation with victims and preferred to adopt subsidiary roles in the committal of the offence.[33] This view of women's ancillary participation in robbery is commonly held. Carol Wiener, writing of late Elizabethan Hertfordshire, for instance, states that 'The types of larcenies in which women were best represented were probably the ones in which the least bravado and initiative were involved.'[34] James Sharpe also adheres to this view, arguing that women tended to behave cautiously when perpetrating robberies in early modern England. Sharpe believes that rather than being the instigators or aggressors, women favoured remaining in the background, acting as decoys or lookouts for male accomplices.[35] Surely, however, the idea that women only ever played minor roles in the perpetration of violent property thefts is too conveniently aligned with traditional gendered notions of women as passive, subordinate participants in the spheres of criminality and wider society? Yet, as previous chapters have shown, this stereotype can be readily refuted, at least in a Scottish context.

Whilst it may be true that many Scottish women might have acted as decoys in robberies and were simply never apprehended, for the reasons previously suggested, this can only ever be mere conjecture. What is certain, however, is that the women who were actually indicted for robbery before the Justiciary Court between 1750 and 1815 not only demonstrated initiative

Scotland see Ruff, *Violence in early modern Europe*, 234; E. Hobsbawm, *Bandits*, London 2000, 7; and G. Spraggs, *Outlaws and highwaymen: the cult of the robber in England from the Middle Ages to the nineteenth century*, London 2001, 265.

[32] Beattie, 'The criminality of women', 90. For further discussion see Spraggs, *Outlaws and highwaymen*, 265.

[33] See Beattie, 'The criminality of women', 90, and *Crime and the courts*, 238.

[34] Wiener, 'Sex roles', 42.

[35] See Sharpe, *Crime in early modern England*, 109. For further discussion of the view that women played only minor roles in robbery offences see Walker, 'Women, theft and the world of stolen goods', 82–3; Hobsbawm, *Bandits*, 147; and Ruff, *Violence in early modern Europe*, 235.

and courage in their unlawful practices in this respect but also showed an overwhelming readiness to resort to shocking levels of brutality in this type of violent property crime.

In total 72 per cent (forty-seven cases out of sixty-five) of the women indicted in relation to crimes committed in lowland Scotland were not only charged with robbery (a violent crime in itself), but were also charged with aggravated assault. In this respect the actions of these women appear to compare with those of the male 'footpad' robbers prevalent in eighteenth-century London. Footpads were the criminals most feared by London society. They were armed robbers who travelled on foot and operated in gangs. As foot-pads could not leave the crime scene very quickly, they regularly attempted to reduce their chances of apprehension by rendering their victim incapacitated through extreme acts of violence. As a result they were regarded with horror and repugnance.[36]

The general methods employed by the women of lowland Scotland in robberies did not vary to any great extent from crime to crime. As was the case in 'footpad' robberies, the women simply subdued their target with what-ever violence or force was deemed necessary in order to steal his or her posses-sions. Although this was the method universally employed by the indicted women, the degree of violence offered by the robbers varied from case to case depending on the individuals involved, as the following examples demon-strate.

In September 1814 Mary McCall, Ann Robertson, Francis Smith and Mary Lawrie were indicted at the South Circuit Court of Ayrshire. They were accused of having 'wickedly and feloniously robbed and assaulted Alex-ander Simpson Innkeeper in West Kilbride by violently knocking him over the head with a large stick and beating him about the body with their bare fists and then presently ... abstracting a gold watch and pocket book from his person'.[37]

Similarly, Elizabeth Barron, James McAlpine and James Cumming appeared at the West Circuit Court in October 1780. The three were charged with having robbed and assaulted a farmer named Robert McNish in the centre of Glasgow in June of the said 1780. The victim testified that

> the two men seized me by both arms and one of them put his hand upon my mouth. In that situation, they dragged me into a closs [close] where a woman came up, said 'God damn you I will knock out your brains', and with the two men keeping me pushed to the ground, she did presently hold a knife to my throat, did strike me several blows with her bare fist and did bite and tear at my face to the great effusion of my blood and danger of my life rendering me almost senseless. She then wickedly and most feloni-

36 For further information regarding 'footpads' see McLynn, *Crime and punishment*, 5–6; Spraggs, *Outlaws and highwaymen*, 154–5; and D. Brandon, *Stand and deliver: a history of highway robbery*, Stroud 2001, 165, 171.
37 JC 26/366.

ously did open two buttons of my upper coat and did take from a pocket my pocket book in which there were nine guinea notes from the bank of Scotland and some papers. She also took out of my left breeches pocket a small bag containing fifteen or sixteen shillings in silver and took out of my upper coat pocket a silk and thread handkerchief.[38]

Again, at the High Court of Justiciary in 1766 appeared Mary Ross, Catherine Campbell and Jean Stewart. They were charged with 'feloniously and wickedly robbing and assaulting Hugh Craig on the road to Stewarton in Ayrshire'. The indictment read that 'Mary Ross and Catherine Campbell did violently beat the said Hugh Craig over the head with a pistol and did repeatedly stab him in the legs with a pitchfork to the great effusion of his blood and imminent danger of his life, while the said Jean Stewart did carry off the saddle-bags which the said victim had been carrying, which contained items of silk finery.'[39]

Finally, and again at the High Court of Justiciary, but this time in 1788, Agnes Walker and Mary Robieson were indicted for robbery and aggravated assault. They were charged that they did 'feloniously and wickedly attack Isobell Templeton, Postmistress in Wigtown, by laying hold of her, setting her hair alight and after attempting to cut off her nose to the great effusion of her blood, did threaten to slice off both her ears with a razor, unless she surrendered the envelopes and parcels in her possession to you, some of which contained bank notes, which she duly did'.[40]

Numerous other examples could be cited here but they would not reflect any variations in the actual methods employed by the women of lowland Scotland. Rather than using violence as a means to an end, these women seemed to relish inflicting hurt and injury on their victims. In this respect lowland women robbers behaved in a manner usually only expected of the most brutal of male criminals. Moreover, the evidence from the Justiciary Court suggests that the violence employed by Scottish women in these robbery indictments was more exaggerated than their behaviour in the other offences for which they were charged in the pre-modern period. Much of the intensity of violence on display can be explained by the need to incapacitate the victim proficiently, in order to facilitate a clean getaway. In addition, however, as Gillian Spraggs points out, as society was 'conditioned' to regard women as unthreatening, obedient and passive individuals, it follows that women robbers had to be *more* violent and aggressive than would be expected, in order to scare the victim to part with their possessions and thereby to commit their crime efficiently and effectively.[41] Gender was a hindrance rather than a help in these

---

[38] JC 13/22.
[39] JC 26/177.
[40] JC 26/250.
[41] See Spraggs, *Outlaws and highwaymen*, 267.

instances, and the excessive violence women perpetrated must often have been an attempt to substantiate their credibility as 'serious' robbers.

The evidence gleaned from the indictments of female robbers does not suggest that these women could be termed 'professional criminals' in terms of the skills they used in carrying out this type of violent property offence. The contemporary fear of a rise in 'professional' criminals was not mirrored in the actions of the female robbers brought to court in terms of the ways in which they perpetrated their crimes. The tactics in evidence were more often based on the opportunistic nature of the offence, and were reactions to the prevailing circumstances, rather than examples of established techniques and well-rehearsed approaches.[42] Where a degree of professionalism in their actions does appear, however, is in the premeditation necessary to carry out these crimes. Robberies involved a fair degree of forethought relating to the selection of targets, methods of appropriation, means of escape and techniques of disposal.[43]

In addition to this, the actions of the women robbers of lowland Scotland could be considered premeditated as 89 per cent (fifty-eight cases out of sixty-five) of those indicted were charged with the possession of a violent weapon. This weapon could be anything from a large stick to a firearm. As John Conklin indicates, 'Robbery offenders often carry weapons, primarily to make the crime easier to commit. The weapon creates a buffer zone between the offender and the victim, (in the form of a "psychological prop" [44]), permits the offender to make good on his [or her] threat to the victim, and helps to insure the offender's escape from the scene of the crime.'[45]

Whether professional or otherwise, however, the methods employed by the female robbers of lowland Scotland between 1750 and 1815 indicate that they could hardly be considered to lack aggression. Furthermore, rather than acting as decoys or look-outs, the women indicted before the Justiciary Court were more often than not the actual and direct perpetrators of the violent acts associated with the crimes of robbery and stouthrief, even in situations where their accomplices and co-accused were men. Before going on to suggest why Scottish women behaved in this fierce manner, we should find out more about the women themselves. Were there any characteristics of the women indicted for robbery which enable an offender profile to be drawn?

[42] For further discussion of the non-professional elements of robbery offences see Morgan and Rushton, Rogues, thieves and the rule of law, 84–6; B. J. Davey, Rural crime in the eighteenth century: north Lincolnshire, 1740–1780, Hull 1994, 22; and Gatrell, 'The decline of theft and violence', 316–33.

[43] See Conklin, Robbery, 101; Ruff, Violence in early modern Europe, 220–1; and Linebaugh, The London hanged, 210.

[44] Conklin, Robbery, 108.

[45] Ibid. 122. My note in parenthesis.

Defendant characteristics

There are five essential characteristics which emerge from the Justiciary Court material concerning female robbery defendants. Firstly, the majority of the women, some 74 per cent (forty-eight cases out of sixty-five) were unmarried. Secondly, in some 88 per cent (fifty-seven cases out of sixty-five) of the indictments the occupation of the female defendants is unclear. Certainly the women of lowland Scotland indicted for robbery and stouthrief do not conform to the stereotypical robbers elsewhere in Europe, as regards their 'occupational' description during the 1750 to 1815 period. In *ancien régime* France at this time, for instance, many of those charged with theft (aggravated or otherwise) were vagrants and vagabonds.[46] Although in the majority of cases their occupation was not given, none of the women indicted before the Justiciary Court were described in similar terms. Nor were any of them accused of being or reputed to be smugglers. Yet, Cal Winslow claimed that in contemporary England, a number of those involved in robbery were primarily smugglers, raising money to finance future smuggling endeavours.[47]

The third characteristic apparent from the Justiciary evidence was that there was no substantial difference between the number of robberies committed by Scottish lowland women in urban and in rural areas. The figures were 55 per cent (thirty-six cases out of sixty-five) and 45 per cent (twenty-nine cases) respectively. This evidence is perhaps surprising as robbery is usually seen as being more commonly perpetrated in urban areas.[48] However, if we consider it to be an essentially 'opportunistic' crime, then it is clear that for the robber the key to the committal of the offence was the availability of a worthwhile target and not the actual *locus operandi* itself.

The penultimate characteristic of the Scottish lowland women accused of robbery concerns the victims targeted. Unlike other crimes of violence where the victim and the perpetrator are commonly known to one another, robbery is distinct as it is normally committed by a predatory stranger.[49] This was overwhelmingly the case in the indictments studied here. It is clear from the testimony of the accused individuals that the women did not select their targets from any prior acquaintance or knowledge of the victim. Rather, they used the victim's general appearance as a gauge of the potential profitability of a given violent theft.

The final notable feature of lowland Scottish females indicted for robbery and stouthrief was that there was not a single instance of a woman being indicted alone. Fifty-seven per cent (thirty-seven cases out of sixty-five) of

---

[46] See Ruff, *Crime, justice and public order*, 120–3.
[47] See C. Winslow, 'Sussex smugglers', in Hay, Linebaugh, Rule, Thompson and Winslow, *Albion's fatal tree*, 155.
[48] See, for instance, Spraggs, *Outlaws and highwaymen*, 88–90, and Brandon, *Stand and deliver*, 171.
[49] For further discussion see Conklin, *Robbery*, p. viii.

these women were indicted with acquaintances and 43 per cent (the remaining twenty-eight cases) were indicted with close family relatives (although not husbands, as has already been shown). As described previously, most robbers worked in gangs. The main reason for this was that it was widely held that if certain tasks involved in the robbery could be delegated, the chance of success, both in terms of the theft itself and the subsequent escape, were greatly enhanced. On average, in gangs involving Scottish lowland women there were between three and four members, sometimes all women, sometimes including men.[50]

According to John Beattie and Frank McLynn these gangs were flexible and impermanent in terms of membership. Individuals could return to legitimate occupations if they wished and groups could be dispersed quickly if one of their number was arrested by the authorities.[51] The Justiciary Court material does not provide adequate substantive or critical evidence of the seemingly casual nature of robber gangs. What is apparent from the indictments, however, is that when the women of lowland Scotland set out to rob they did so in company.

The use of gangs in the committal of robberies implies the existence of criminal networks, or groups of individuals who did not participate in the act of robbery itself, but were facilitators. These networks were the chief concern of pre-modern commentators, who alluded to the presence of a 'criminal class' at work in eighteenth- and more especially nineteenth-century society: groups of men and women who made a living out of committing crime. For these individuals, robberies were deliberate acts rather than desperate ones, and for that reason they were loathed and feared in equal measure.[52]

The underground and covert nature of criminal networks means that it is commonly very difficult to determine from indictment evidence either the extent of their incidence or the nature of their component parts. However, close analysis of the Justiciary Court material reveals much about female participation. By looking at indictments for the crime of resett, for instance, it is possible to discern the significant role women played in criminal networks as the receivers of stolen goods gleaned after a robbery.

Eighteenth-century English commentators voiced their awareness, and indeed their concerns, about the link between robbery or theft and resett. In the 1720s Bernard Mandeville observed that 'the mischief that one man can do as a thief, is a very trifle to what he may be the occasion of, as an agent ...

---

50 For further discussion of criminal gangs see Beattie, *Crime and the courts*, 252–63.

51 See ibid. 257, and McLynn, *Crime and punishment*, 10.

52 For further discussion on the existence of criminal networks and/or a criminal class in relation to violent property crimes see Spraggs, *Outlaws and highwaymen*, 94–5; Brandon, *Stand and deliver*, 60–1, 158–60; Morgan and Rushton, *Rogues, thieves and the rule of law*, 77–8, 85–95; J. J. Tobias, *Crime and industrial society in the nineteenth century*, London 1967, ch. iv and pp. 97–106; and Gatrell, 'The decline of theft and violence', 316–33.

of felons'.[53] Then, in 1751, Henry Fielding argued that 'one great encourage-ment to theft of all kinds is the ease and safety with which stolen goods may be disposed of'.[54] The receiving of stolen goods was clearly regarded by both society in general and the authorities in particular, as both a widespread and a serious offence. It is curious, therefore, that so little attention has been paid to the crime of resett by historians and criminologists of the period from the mid-eighteenth century to the early nineteenth. What is even more surprising about this *lacuna* is that resett was one of the relatively few offences predomi-nantly committed by females.

None of the male robbers indicted at the Justiciary Court were described as resetters, although 45 per cent (or 29 cases out of 65) of the women were. In addition, of the individuals indicted solely for the non-violent property offence of resett committed as a result of a robbery, women outnumbered men by more than four to one. These figures appear comparable to those provided by Brian Henry for late eighteenth-century Dublin. He maintained that more than 60 per cent of the resett cases brought to court and recorded in the *Hibernian Journal*, were alleged to have been committed by women.[55] Henry also contends that these women were habitual offenders.[56] This appears to be true of the women resetters of lowland Scotland, as all but one had previous convictions for the same crime. Similarly, all but one were described as being 'habite and repute resetters' in the documentation presented to the court and all but two were indicted on multiple charges of the offence. These details suggest that the women indicted at the Justiciary Court for this type of activity were clearly 'professional' in their criminality. It seems that female resetters were capable of making a living from their crimes,[57] and this is substantiated by the fact that only two of the women from lowland Scotland were described as having alternative occupations.

Resett via robbery was relatively easy to commit. The women simply received the stolen goods into their possession, temporarily harboured them and then sold them on to others via established networks. According to Garthine Walker, 'Women's role as receivers has been linked to their posi-tion within the household, yet the association has largely been with notions of female dependence and familial obligation rather than with their own economic activities or their interactive social position within the commu-

---

[53] B. Mandeville, *An enquiry into the causes of the frequent executions at Tyburn and etc.*, London 1725, 8.

[54] Fielding, *An enquiry into the causes*, 105.

[55] My calculation on the evidence presented in Henry, *Dublin hanged*, 57. For other studies which confirm the dominance of women in this type of illegality (although scant statistics are presented to enable comparative analyses) see Linebaugh, *The London hanged*, 145; Walker, 'Women, theft and the world of stolen goods', 91; and Taylor, *Crime, policing and punishment*, 47.

[56] Henry, *Dublin hanged*, 57.

[57] For further discussion see ibid. 59, and Tobias, *Crime and industrial society*, 106–12.

nity.'[58] However, not only did the women of lowland Scotland commit this offence in collusion with others, they also predominantly did so with members of their immediate family. This evidence is somewhat at odds with the view of Garthine Walker, and suggests that the sophisticated systems of fencing in existence were more commonly made up of a network of family members than independent criminal entrepreneurs.[59]

There were several reasons why resett via robbery was considered a viable crime by Scottish women. By the eighteenth century it was far easier to dispose of luxury items, as trade and commercial links existed between local, regional and national markets. In addition, itinerant salesmen and tinkers, who visited villages and towns in increasing numbers during the early modern period, could be encouraged to move stolen property from place to place in a relatively 'foolproof fashion' with no questions asked.[60]

The attraction of resett as a relatively easy way to provide an individual with a lucrative source of income must have been tempting to both male and female alike in Scotland during this period. In addition, the fact that females appear to have been more actively concerned with household budgets and expenditures than their male counterparts suggests that women often participated in resett as they knew the value of goods and were therefore perceived as being able to obtain a better price for stolen items from prospective buyers.[61] This theory cannot be substantiated from the Justiciary Court evidence alone, however. The gender disparity in resett indictments may simply reflect the fact that women had more time to set up and be involved in the type of criminal enterprises necessary to facilitate this crime, and by implication, that they were more motivated to perpetrate it. What is more certain is that the evidence suggests that women were willing to be involved in criminal networks and robber gangs, especially in relation to crime of resett. The extent of women's involvement in this particular type of criminality was more substantial than that of their male counterparts, even given the contribution of resett to the unknown figure of criminal statistics.

---

58 Walker, 'Women, theft and the world of stolen goods', 92. See Pollak, *The criminality of women*, 87, for the type of argument Walker criticises. For further discussion of networks related to the crime of resett see Tobias, *Crime and industrial society*, 106.
59 A point also advanced by Otto Pollak in *The criminality of women*, 87. Both Brian Henry and Carol Wiener contend that resett was rarely committed by women acting alone in the early modern period, although they make no reference to family alliances: Henry, *Dublin hanged*, 57; Wiener, 'Sex roles', 42–3, 49.
60 For further discussion see M. Weisser, *Crime and punishment in early modern Europe*, Hassocks 1979, 118, and Rule, *Albion's people*, 228.
61 For further discussion see Walker, 'Women, theft and the world of stolen goods', 89–94.

Motivation

Historians contend that offenders chose to commit robbery rather than other types of property crime because the plunder involved was usually lucre. According to John Conklin, this meant that robbers avoided the time-consuming, inconvenient and risky process of converting property into cash.[62] Whilst this may have been true for men, and although the women of lowland Scotland frequently robbed their victims of money, they also often stole light and readily portable items such as pocket watches, hats, gloves and silk goods. As was the case in late eighteenth-century Dublin, 'Robbers stole a dizzying array of saleable items. They were motivated by greed as well as need, wanting things just to keep up with the changing fashions. A flourishing black market followed in the footsteps of a rapidly expanding consumer society ... reflecting the materialism of the age.'[63] Therefore although offenders participated in robberies in order to be provided quickly and directly with cash, it appears that women particularly favoured this type of property theft to supply them with immediate and fashionable additions to their wardrobes, and to provide them with the alternative opportunity of lucrative resett at a later stage.

The motivations of the individuals indicted for robbery and stouthrief at the Justiciary Court are difficult to discern from the evidence. Most historians contend that the motivations for robbery are linked to economic conditions.[64] Julius Ruff, for instance, asserts that in eighteenth-century France offenders committed robbery as a form of supplementary employment which could add to their meagre wages.[65] John Beattie, on the other hand, cites two particular contemporary economic factors which resulted in people participating in property crimes in England. These were respectively the high price of staple goods and the relative opportunities for employment.[66] As has been shown in the previous chapter regarding popular disturbances, prices were certainly high during this period and from time to time provisions became relatively scarce for the lower sections of society in the country as a whole, most markedly after episodes of warfare.[67] These facts give some support to Beattie's assertions of the motives behind robbery and other property offences.[68]

However, despite the fact that people moved from place to place carrying

---

[62] Conklin, *Robbery*, 87.

[63] Henry, *Dublin hanged*, 108. For a detailed study of the types of goods stolen by women see Walker, 'Women, theft and the world of stolen goods', 81–105.

[64] See, for example, Beattie, 'The criminality of women', 103; Davey, *Rural crime*, 21; and Laurence, *Women in England*, 260.

[65] See Ruff, *Crime, justice and public order*, 120.

[66] See Beattie, 'The criminality of women', 103.

[67] For further discussion of the link between warfare and the incidence of property crimes see Hay, 'War, dearth and theft, 117–60.

[68] It should be noted that as most of the Scottish women indicted for robbery were single, the types of economic pressure they faced would be less family-orientated and more personal in nature.

143

significant amounts of money and valuable goods in their possession, and therefore the targets for the would-be robber were numerous, most robberies were relatively 'small-scale' in terms of the value of the plunder taken.[69] As a result, in order to make a reasonable profit from this type of criminal venture, the offender had to commit robbery on a regular basis. For many involved in this type of criminal activity, robbery must have become a regular part of life. Robbers had to commit their crimes habitually in order to survive. As a result, increasingly over time they became both immune to economic fluctuations and largely liberated from the pressures of poverty.[70]

In this way, therefore, the initial stimulus for a robber to commit a violent property theft may have been linked to his or her inability to find work or to the prevalent high prices. As time passed, however, these primary motivations were sometimes replaced by a fundamental dependence upon robbery as a way of life and as a means of providing for an individual's survival. In this way, robbery can be seen as a form of full-time self-employment or career. The need to commit an act of robbery repeatedly in order to make the illegality financially viable would imply that (as contemporaries feared) there were many 'professional' offenders committing robbery on a regular basis throughout the country. However, only a quarter (sixteen cases out of sixty-five) of the lowland women indicted for robbery were described as recidivists. This data seems to suggest that although there were individuals who relied on robbery as a 'way of life', there were many more men and women who participated in robbery only when the desperation of their circumstances forced them to do so.[71] The brutal level of violence displayed by Scottish lowland women committing robberies may often have been a reflection of the sheer panic and despair that drove them to commit the offence in the first instance.

In his essay on the causes of robbery in eighteenth-century London, the contemporary commentator Henry Fielding offered various other suggestions as to why men and women were involved in this type of criminal activity.[72] First, he argued that the flaunting of luxuries by the upper class encouraged the lower orders to crave possession of items which they simply could not afford. Secondly, he suggested that the widespread drunkenness of society caused people to be more violent and therefore made them more willing to carry out robberies. Next, he pointed to the great increase in the numbers of gambling houses that occurred during the eighteenth century as a cause of robbery, in that debtors often turned to this type of crime in their desperate

---

69   See Henry, *Dublin hanged*, 107; Ruff, *Violence in early modern Europe*, 218; and Gatrell, 'The decline of theft and violence', 325–7.

70   See Hay, 'War, dearth and theft', 134.

71   For further discussion see King, *Crime, justice and discretion*, 216.

72   Similar sentiments were also voiced by Daniel Defoe and Bernard Mandeville at this time. See Defoe, *Augusta triumphans*, and *Street robberies consider'd: the reason of their being so frequent, with probable means to prevent 'em*, London 1728, and Mandeville, *Enquiry into the causes*.

attempts to recoup their losses. Fielding also claimed that inadequate poor law provision, reflected in the vast number of wandering vagabonds, motivated destitute individuals to commit this type of violent property theft. Finally, the inability of the authorities to break down criminal networks effectively or to apprehend, prosecute or convict individuals was also said to encourage robbery. These inefficiencies, along with the frequent pardoning of the few culprits who were actually declared guilty, motivated robbers to re-offend as they perceived they could readily get away with their crimes. In addition, according to Fielding, the weakness of the judicial system also encouraged previously innocent individuals to engage in violent property crime as it seemed unlikely that they would ever be caught.[73]

Whether any of these stimuli affected the women of lowland Scotland charged before the Justiciary Court between 1750 and 1815 is difficult to ascertain. Certainly, unlike their male counterparts, none of the women were described in their indictments as being drunk at the time of their offence or as owing substantial amounts of money, and none were referred to as vagabonds or vagrants. Nevertheless, as has been shown above, in terms of the types of goods stolen perhaps Scottish women did crave items of luxury to an extent. Also, given the fact that 25 per cent of the women indicted were charged with having committed more than one robbery offence, Fielding was perhaps right to suggest that the weakness of those in authority encouraged some robbers to re-offend. However, it could also be said that they did this out of entrepreneurial spirit, in order to make their criminal activities financially worthwhile, but in any case, these individuals were in the minority of those indicted. It is more probably the case that it was economic factors (whether stemming from hardship, greed or criminal dependency) which encouraged women to rob from their contemporaries in the pre-modern period.

An investigation of robbery is crucial to the study of violent female criminality. It is a crime which historians and criminologists have largely associated with male behaviour, with women playing only auxiliary roles in the process, rarely getting involved in the act of violent property theft itself. Yet Scottish women were more than willing to perpetrate direct acts of robbery, often in as shocking and as brutal a manner as their male counterparts. In comparison to all the other crimes of violence for which women were indicted, robbery provides a unique insight and perspective into female felony. Robbery offences enable us to analyse women's criminality in a non-domestic environment, where personal gain rather than the defence of family interests was the explanation for their illegality. Clearly, this is unlike any of the other offences analysed in this study.

During the eighteenth and nineteenth centuries, robbery more than any other offence caused intense concern and unease amongst the legal authorities and contemporary commentators of the day. Although perhaps not viable

[73] For further discussion see Fielding, An enquiry, 6–188.

in terms of incidence, the vicious way Scottish lowland women carried out robberies at this time does suggest that commentators may have been more accurate than historians had first thought. Certainly, complaints about the existence of a 'professional' class of robbers dominating the criminal experience of British society cannot be proven on the basis of Scottish Justiciary evidence alone, although there is substantive evidence to suggest women's involvement in criminal networks, particularly in relation to the fencing of stolen goods.

Overall, the Justiciary Court evidence suggests that, irrespective of motive, the women of lowland Scotland between 1750 and 1815 were determined to commit successful robberies. In so doing they were not only prepared to display direct confrontational aggression towards their victims but were more than willing to employ physical violence, regardless of the degree of severity, to bring about the desired result. In this respect the female robbers of Scotland appear to be distinct from their relatively sedate English, Irish and French contemporary counterparts. In lowland Scotland the 'ultra-violence' displayed by female robbers suggests that the brutality they meted out was not just fashioned to commit the crime effectively. Rather, these women seemed to revel in wreaking pain and misery on their victims and in this way they behaved like the fiercest of their male contemporaries, and not like members of the so-called 'gentler' sex at all. Even within the seemingly more aggressive context of Scottish women's criminality, Scottish women who robbed were regularly more uncompromising and bloodthirsty than their belligerent criminal sisters elsewhere.

Conclusion

What, then, can be concluded from this investigation of the previously murky and uncharted world of eighteenth-century Scottish female criminality? Whilst remembering the limitations of studying crime outlined in the intro-duction, the bare facts are that some 4,223 individuals from lowland Scotland were indicted at the Justiciary Court between 1750 and 1815. In total 967 (23 per cent) of them were women and 3,256 (or 77 per cent) were men. Clearly, as elsewhere in Europe in the pre-modern period, men far outnum-bered their female counterparts for indicted criminal activity – in this case by more than three to one. However, further analysis of the evidence about the type of crime for which each gender was indicted, reveals startling and unique results. Of the 1,990 Scottish individuals indicted for violent offences at the Justiciary Court between 1750 and 1815, 1,294 were men and 696 were women.[1] Although numerically men once again outnumbered women, this meant that proportionately 72 per cent (696 cases out of 967) of the total number of women indicted were charged with a violent offence compared to 40 per cent (1,294 cases out of 3,256) of men. Lowland Scottish females were proportionately more than twice as likely as their male counterparts to be indicted for a violent crime. This conclusion profoundly challenges the commonly held opinion that in comparison to males, female criminals were very rarely brought to court charged with violent criminal behaviour.

Of course, the proportional significance of violent women in this anal-ysis can in part be explained by the use of Justiciary Court indictments. As the Justiciary Court was the highest court dealing with criminal matters in pre-modern Scotland, it was more likely to deal with individuals who had committed the most serious offences. Thus, evidence produced from the proceedings of the Justiciary Court will reflect the grave nature of the crimes which fell within that jurisdiction, and will be skewed towards indictments for violent offences rather than petty ones. In addition, as the actions of violent women were considered both illegal and unfeminine, they were more likely to be indicted at the Justiciary Court than any lesser jurisdiction, thus enabling their behaviour to be publicly condemned and officially disciplined. It seems that evidence from the Justiciary Court may well suffer from a gendered bias, which tells us more about the perceived need to indict violent women at the

---

[1] These figures include nineteen individuals, four of whom were indicted for arson and fifteen who were charged with plagium or child-stealing. Under eighteenth-century Scots law, these offences were categorised as violent property crimes. However, as none of the indicted instances involved the use of violence, they did not warrant specific attention in this book.

most superior court, rather than a greater predilection on the part of Scottish women for violence and violent behaviour. This rationale must go a long way towards explaining why proportionately Scottish women were more likely than men to be indicted for a violent offence between 1750 and 1815.

In order to investigate further the gender disparity in violent offences, this book analysed the crimes against the person for which lowland individuals were indicted. These were homicides, infanticides, assaults, popular disturbances and robberies. From this analysis, several general characteristics of the lowland female defendants in particular become apparent. First, the majority of the women indicted for violent offences were unmarried. Second, nearly two-thirds of the women committed their criminal activities with the aid of others (including family members) rather than acting alone. Third, and finally, there was a favoured *locus operandi* for female offending. In general terms there was no significant difference between the number of indicted crimes committed in urban areas compared to rural ones. Interestingly, however, the majority of criminals did slightly favour the countryside over the town. Certainly this conclusion appears to be at odds with the commonly held belief that crime in pre-modern Europe was almost exclusively an urban phenomenon.

In addition to providing details about the defendants themselves, the Justiciary Court material gives information on the methods and motives behind the criminal activities of the indicted lowland women. These factors clearly varied from case to case depending upon the circumstances. On the whole, however, and with particular reference to violent crimes, it can be said that although the accused women behaved just as aggressively as their male counterparts in carrying out that type of offence, when they did so, it was usually with a particular intention in mind. Rather than being involved in random, drunken disputes with strangers, as was so often the case with the indicted Scottish men and men throughout Europe, the actions of lowland women were habitually premeditated. Their crimes were usually committed against people they knew, and were often in the defence of personal or family interests.

In sum then, three factors distinguish the actions of indicted lowland criminal women from those of their European counterparts during the eighteenth and early nineteenth centuries. First, women were proportionately more likely than men to be indicted for a violent offence at the Scottish Justiciary Court. Second, lowland women were overtly aggressive when committing violent offences. Third, when Scottish women perpetrated violent crime, it was not exclusively in the defence of family interests. Taken together, these characteristics suggest that indicted lowland women were more inclined to be violent than the evidence for other European countries has generally demonstrated. How can this be explained?

Certainly there does not seem to be a single, simple causal explanation for the nature of violent female criminality in lowland Scotland. None of the indicted women, for instance, was described as being drunk at the time of her offence, and only a tiny proportion were deemed insane by the clerks of the Justiciary Court. Traditional explanations for the absence of women involved in violent criminality during the pre-modern period are linked to their apparently limited social activity. John Beattie and Peter Spierenburg argue, for instance, that as women in the eighteenth century were largely confined to the domestic sphere, they rarely became embroiled in disputes involving the use of violence. That type of social 'experience', they argue, was essentially restricted to men.[2] Yet, in the Scottish context at that time, aside from homicide, women were commonly involved in violent criminality outside the domestic arena. Clearly, lowland women transcended the limited social experience ascribed to them by Beattie and Spierenburg.

In the light of the extensive involvement of women in Scotland's economic development, perhaps it is more appropriate to argue that fewer 'social' restrictions seem to have been placed on Scottish women in the pre-modern period than elsewhere. For instance, Scottish women seemingly encountered few barriers to entering the world of work, and, indeed, they were seen as an essential part of the workforce during the period of Scotland's industrial revolution. In addition, Scottish women were also increasingly and regularly involved in legal, political and civic matters, suggesting that their experiences were not solely restricted to the demands of the domestic sphere.[3]

This context could provide us with one line of explanation as to why Scottish women were seemingly more violent in their criminal endeavours than women elsewhere. Scottish women were entering a wider economic and social sphere in the pre-modern period, and they were engaging in social interaction with and alongside men at that time. Their enhanced public presence meant that lowland women had similar 'experiences' to lowland men. In this world, violent possibilities more readily came their way and they found themselves called upon to display or refute aggression when it appeared. Within this public world women faced more challenges to their economic, social and family security and consequently, on occasion, they were prepared to be overtly aggressive in order to safeguard their status. Scotland during the pre-modern period was a society in economic flux and women's participation in the public world could be precariously balanced between prosperity and ruin. Such vulnerability could seemingly induce violent behaviour amongst lowland women, with only minimal provocation. Women's economic independence took lowland women outside the domestic sphere so that they increasingly saw themselves as potentially the equals of men. Enhanced social interaction meant that in the course of their everyday lives these women were repeatedly exposed to instances of criminality and by implication to violence.

[2] For further discussion see Beattie, 'The criminality of women', 84, and Spierenburg, 'How violent were women?', 24–5, 27. See also McLynn, *Crime and punishment*, 122–3; Finch, 'Women and violence', 28–30; and Shoemaker, *Gender in English society*, 299–300.
[3] For further discussion see chapter 1 above and especially Whatley, 'Women and economic transformation', 19–40.

In consequence, aggressive behaviour may have become more acceptable and even, perhaps, normal for some lowland women.

The seemingly more violent disposition of these Scottish women does indeed imply that they had ignored, or were unaware of, the gendered notions of femininity so widely espoused by contemporary popular literature. Was this ignorance deliberate, or were these women genuinely naïve about how they were expected to behave? This latter suggestion seems unlikely given the strength and breadth of religiously inspired and moral disciplinary mechanisms in the lowland region at the time.[4] Yet, in a sense, the distinctively intense nature of Scottish religiosity during the pre-modern period may well have contributed to the aggressive nature of female criminality in the lowland region at that time. Since the Reformation Scotland had enthusiastically embraced the rigid doctrine and strict discipline of Calvinist teaching. The staunch nature of religious fervour in Scotland meant that congregations were readily familiar with the concept of predestination where the godly few had been 'elected' to enjoy the benefits of the 'heavenly' afterlife, whereas the rest of the population were regarded as 'reprobates' doomed to the everlasting torments of the fires of hell. Sermons which espoused the notion of predestination emphasised that election had occurred before time began and that an individual could do nothing to change his or her fate.[5]

The Scottish Church went to great lengths to promote the orthodox message of Calvinism, most commonly through harsh discipline and rigorous doctrinal 'lessons'.[6] In this stark context of intense religious indoctrination, women may have regarded violent behaviour as immaterial, especially if they considered their actions to be legitimate or justified, and particularly if they believed that they had already been consigned to the position of the damned. It could perhaps be argued that lowland women sometimes found themselves flouting moral and religious doctrine because, in any event, they feared or even believed themselves to be doomed. Perhaps this is why Rosalind Mitchison and Leah Leneman recorded so much resistance and dissent towards lowland church authorities during the pre-modern period in relation to sexuality and bastard bearing.[7] Did the impact of religious fervour in Scotland paradoxically give women more freedom to express themselves, particularly those who felt themselves driven way outside the religious pale? Were individuals behaving in an aggressive way because they believed that their actions would

[4] See, for instance, Mitchison and Leneman, *Sexuality and social control*, and Todd, *The culture of Protestantism*.
[5] For further discussion see D. MacCulloch, *Reformation: Europe's house divided, 1490–1700*, London 2003; Todd, *The culture of Protestantism*; and C. Parker, 'The moral agency and moral autonomy of church folk in the Dutch Reformed Church of Delft, 1580–1620', *Journal of Ecclesiastical History* xlviii (1997), 44–7.
[6] See, for instance, M. Graham, *The uses of reform: 'godly discipline' and popular behaviour in Scotland and beyond, 1560–1610*, Leiden 1996, and I. B. Cowan, *The Scottish Reformation: Church and society in sixteenth-century Scotland*, London 1982.
[7] Mitchison and Leneman, *Sexuality and social control*, 145–6, 243.

have little impact on them in the afterlife – irrespective of whether they were elect or reprobate?

Certainly, it is difficult to measure the nature of the relationship between religious sentiment and the actions of the violent women encountered in this book. Arguably, however, as the harsh nature of Calvinist doctrine was a distinctive and widespread feature of Scottish social life, it may well have had some part to play in explaining why lowland women appear to have been more violent than their counterparts elsewhere in Europe during the eighteenth and nineteenth centuries. It should of course be remembered here that the Kirk's function as an agency regulating morals was still important well into the nineteenth century.

Perhaps it was the perceived motives of these women that were all-important in making their actions appear distinctively aggressive. Scottish women, as outlined in chapter 6, do have an established history of involvement in resistance to oppression and in the use of popular protest for the protection of family interests. Perhaps violent behaviour was simply an accepted part of Scottish female culture in the pre-modern period in situations where the use of aggressive and violent tactics was merited. There was, after all, a clear absence of random violence committed by the indicted women of lowland Scotland. Most of their felonious activity was targeted against specific individuals for specific reasons.

The nature of seasonal employment in post-Enlightenment Scotland meant that men could be absent from their families for extended periods of time during the course of a given year.[8] Consequently women were far more likely than men to encounter sheriff officers, excise men and other officials on a regular basis. Women caught up in these confrontations with men were often both desperate and powerless. They wanted to protect their social and economic status and that of their families, and they had seen at first hand what men could get away with in the context of brawls, tumults and disputes. Yet, at the same time, as women, they were expected to behave in a prescribed manner, adhering to the principles of femininity which were regularly assigned to them.

It could be argued then, that during the pre-modern period female power and female choices in Scotland were in a state of flux. In this context there appears to have been a fundamental mismatch between expectation and reality. Women saw how they could behave whilst interacting within the 'masculine' environment and the authorities reminded them of how they *should* behave, encouraging female activity to be restricted and confined to the domestic sphere. Lowland women may have attempted to rebel against any attempt to relocate them within the home, by rejecting the instructions of moral and judicial commentators and by being overtly violent from time to time when committing criminal acts, most commonly when confronted with figures of authority.

---

8   Devine, *The transformation of rural Scotland.*

Arguably, by behaving in this way, lowland women were not merely imitating the generally more arbitrary actions of the men they encountered in the wider social spheres in which they increasingly came to operate. Rather, their behaviour tended to be premeditated and, in their minds at least, legitimised and justified. In the context of defending family interests, it is clear from defendant testimony that many of the indicted lowland women did not believe that they were doing anything wrong in attacking officers of the law. Certainly, they did not regard the use of violence as being in any way 'significant' or indeed 'sinful'. The evidence makes it clear that these women did not consider violence to be especially abhorrent or in any way abnormal.

Explanations that thus attempt to analyse why Scottish lowland women appear to have been more violent than women elsewhere, are none the less problematic. First, only a small proportion of the female population participated in violent criminality. If violence was an accepted or normalised part of female culture, why were not more women willingly involved in it? Conventional explanations of women's motivation do not help since not all the indicted lowland women had committed an act of violence in the defence of family interests. Some committed violence for personal gain or for self-interest.

Moreover, none of these explanations is unique to Scottish lowland women. Recent historiography has shown that women south of the border and elsewhere led much less restricted lives than historians had previously thought.[9] Women across Europe were quite willing to flout gender norms in a variety of specific situations, and they were traditionally involved in collective protest in the defence of interests which mattered to them, in the same way as their Scottish sisters.[10] In other areas of historical investigation the attitudes and behaviour of women has already been seen as distinctive during this period. Historians of witchcraft have regularly noted how contemporary writers across the confessional divide remarked upon the special gullibility and potential waywardness of women.[11] This persists beyond the era traditionally associated with the witch-hunts in Europe and further afield.

An additional issue for further research relates to the arguments around the potential paradoxes within Scottish Calvinism which could apply equally to lowland men just as much to lowland women. Seen alone, therefore, none of these arguments can wholly or properly account for the seemingly distinctly violent nature of lowland women. They none the less comprise a series of educated guesses based upon a close reading of the context in which this violence and these crimes occurred.

[9] For further discussion see chapter 1 above; O. Hufton, *The prospect before her: a history of women in western Europe*, London 1995; and D. Simonton, *A history of European women's work: 1700 to the present*, London 1998.

[10] For further discussion see Ruff, *Violence in early modern Europe*; ch. vi above; Houlbrooke, 'Women's social life', 171–89; Dekker, 'Women in revolt', 337–62; and A. Farge, 'Protesters plain to see', in Davis and Farge, *Women in the west*, iii. 489–505

[11] Larner, *Enemies of God*, 92–5.

CONCLUSION

Placing these findings in a European-wide context requires an engagement with the concept of the 'civilising process' which has been regularly employed by historians of crime such as James Sharpe and Peter Spierenburg. This strives to explain the changing nature of governance, authority, manners and criminality, as well as attitudes to all these during the pre-modern period.[12] According to Norbert Elias, the 'civilising process' was the key mechanism whereby politeness and etiquette grew in importance to become the corner-stones of socio-cultural development across Europe. Elias argued that through the 'civilising process' discipline became self-acquired and was necessary for an individual's viability in a changing world. The urban middling sort estab-lished regimes of manners that enhanced their own burgeoning social status and opportunities for power thereby marginalising those beneath them. As a result of this, the absence of conformity to species of 'manners', politeness and norms of behaviour was frowned upon and became the reason for forms of exclusion. Elias suggests that societies were only able to function effectively because individuals eventually disciplined themselves to interact with their social betters.[13]

Elias suggests that the 'civilising process' had been established as early as the fifteenth century in some especially advanced parts of western Europe. However, the actions of lowland Scottish women suggest that aspects of this process were still alien to Scottish society even as late as the eighteenth and early nineteenth centuries. For many individuals violent behaviour remained both inherently useful and necessary at this time. This supposition is espe-cially intriguing, given the extent of Scotland's reputation for intellectual innovation and humanism during the Enlightenment period. Indeed, one of the most prominent Scottish Enlightenment thinkers, Adam Smith, seemed in his writings to be fully aware of the economic benefits of the concept of civilised restraint.[14] Smith demonstrably believed that material prosperity would, by definition, civilise and tame what he saw as the wildness and back-wardness of his own nation.

Yet it seems incontrovertible that certain elements of the 'civilising process' are not recognisable in Scotland during the late pre-modern period. This contention is supported by recent work carried out by John Carter Wood on violent crime in England during the nineteenth century.[15] Carter Wood suggests that even by the end of the Victorian period, aspects of the 'civilising process' were not present amongst the lower orders in England.[16]

12 See J. A. Sharpe, 'Crime in England: long-term trends and the problem of moderni-zation', and P. Spierenburg, 'Long-term trends in homicide: theoretical reflections and Dutch evidence, fifteenth to twentieth centuries', in Johnson and Monkkonen, Civilization of crime, 17–34, 63–105.
13 For further discussion see Elias, The civilizing process.
14 See Adam Smith, Wealth of nations (1776), ed. E. Cannan, Chicago 1976 edn, i. 437.
15 J. Carter Wood, Violence and crime in nineteenth-century England: the shadow of our refine-ment, London–New York 2004.
16 Ibid. 145–6.

Rather, he argues that the civilising narrative, which idealised rationality and self-restraint, interacted or clashed with a customary and more plebeian narrative, which legitimised physical violence and confrontation as a way of dealing with disputes.[17] For many, violence was still seen as a legitimate response to circumstance well into the modern industrial era and according to Carter Wood, this was just as true for women as for men at that time.[18]

The material presented in this volume suggests that the 'clash' between civilised and customary interpretations of violence and aggressive behaviour may have begun much earlier north of the Tweed than the evidence for England would have predicted. An absence of restraint and self-discipline, combined with a customary belief in the legitimacy of violent behaviour (evident amongst lowlanders at least), may well have encouraged the Scottish authorities to impose closer order and discipline on the populace during the eighteenth century. This was essentially promoted through the procedures of established institutions such as the Kirk and the Scottish legal system. Evidence to support this contention can be found in the especially high conviction rate for violent offences in Scotland. Unlike the more flexible 'Bloody Code' south of the Tweed, there was little chance of mitigation for violent offenders in Scotland. This seems to have been especially true for women who had been charged with violent offences in this period.[19]

John Carter Wood rejects the idea that the eighteenth century was the key turning point in attitudes towards violence. He argues instead that the post-Enlightenment period was more concerned with promoting campaigns against sin and moral degeneracy and, as a result, 'violence' as a social concern was not invented until the late nineteenth century.[20] However, in Scotland the evidence from this study suggests that during the eighteenth-century period both violence and immorality were regarded as fundamental social evils by the authorities and had to be controlled by the Church and the law courts of the day.

Perhaps, then, instead of it being the case that lowland women were distinctively more violent than women elsewhere, the apparent greater propensity for violence amongst Scottish women was a reflection of other concerns. Perhaps it dawned upon Scotland's rulers that in order to promote and emphasise the 'enlightened' nature of the Scottish nation after 1750, the lingering 'dark side' of the pre-Enlightenment had to be publicly exposed and eradicated. As a result, justices and magistrates had to make more pointed examples of those who broke the rules. As violent women blatantly ignored the gender norms promoted by contemporary society, they had as a result to be disciplined, condemned and, if necessary, cast out. Consequently, lowland women appear to posterity to have been more violent because they were more

17 Ibid. chs 1–3 and pp. 3–4, 15.
18 Ibid. 61, 75.
19 For further discussion see Kilday, 'Women and crime', ch. vi.
20 Carter Wood, *Violence and crime*, 13–14, 27–9, and ch. 1 n. 19.

likely to be brought before the 'supreme' Justiciary Court. In part this was a consequence of their actual behaviour, but it was also because the Scottish authorities believed that the exemplary suppression of unruly women would send a clear message to the rest of society.

If women, as the 'moral guardians' of society, were unable to acquire the machinery of self-discipline, the authorities had to be seen to be still more severe. If women could be made to become 'civilised' by watching the fate of their convicted sisters, perhaps the rest of this society would follow. The eighteenth-century English concern that the physical punishment of women did not serve as a deterrent because it encouraged pity and hostility amongst the populace clearly does not seem to have been shared north of the border.[21] Scottish authorities were far more likely to sentence violent women than men to corporal or capital punishment. In addition, the types of mitigation open to English female criminals (such as the notion of *feme covert*) were not evident in Scotland to anywhere near the same extent.[22]

If modernisation was urgent for Scotland, as the writings of men like Adam Smith suggest, why did the 'civilising process' falter during a period when Scotland was at the forefront of intellectual and philosophical progress, and when the nation was experiencing an incomparable economic transformation? There is insufficient room here to explore this question in detail, but a few pointers may be given. Perhaps all the elements necessary to establish an effective 'civilising process' were not in place in Scotland by 1815. Scotland had long been considered a backward nation in socio-economic and political terms in the run-up to the Union of 1707. It was only really during the eighteenth century that extensive progress began to be made. Arguably, the benefits of this rapid economic development did not come to fruition until the politically stable period after the Napoleonic Wars.[23] It was also around this time that the Scottish courts began to adopt more summary forms of justice and more tempered forms of punishment for convicted felons – both male and female.[24]

It is possible, therefore, that Scottish society was too unevenly developed before 1815 to fully assimilate a 'civilising process'. Thus historians should consider this conclusion, along with the work of Carter Wood, as suggesting that the 'civilising process' was not a homogeneous event. In places and in specific legal contexts it took effect significantly later than has been previously suggested. Violence – both judicial and interpersonal – was still seen as legitimate throughout Scottish society. The 'clash' between civilised and customary interpretations of violence, which arguably began during the eighteenth century north of the border, remained largely unresolved well into

---

[21] See Beattie, *Crime and the courts*, 436.
[22] See chapter 3 above and Kilday, 'Women and crime', ch. vi.
[23] See, for instance, Whatley, *Scottish society*, ch. vi.
[24] See Donnachie, '"The darker side"', 5–24, and Crowther, 'Criminal precognitions', 75–84.

the next century and beyond. In this latter respect the Scottish experience may have had much in common with its southern counterpart which also failed to become fully 'civilised' during the pre-modern period, according to the evidence provided by John Carter Wood.[25] This suggests that the stereotypical image of pre-modern Scotland as an ungovernable 'other' nation was little more than chauvinistic propaganda on the part of the English, as their own adoption of a common culture of refinement and self-restraint at this time was piecemeal and episodic.

The theory of the 'civilising process' is yet to be explored fully in relation to pre-modern society, and pre-modern Scotland in particular. Certainly, as John Carter Wood argues, the concept was not an all-embracing one. For any 'process' of this nature to succeed, it cannot remain static, but rather it needs to react to and change with the circumstances that confront it.[26] Perhaps, then, it is an exaggeration to say that the 'civilising process' was wholly unsuccessful in Scotland between 1750 and 1815: it may have had fragmentary or episodic degrees of success in particular areas of the country at different times. As yet the long-term value of this theory in understanding criminality (and women's behaviour especially) still remains somewhat unclear.

Evidence from the Justiciary Court suggests that Scottish women were more violent than their counterparts elsewhere in terms of their proportional involvement in serious offences. To an extent, this is a reflection of their actual criminality, perhaps best explained by enhanced levels of social interaction and economic independence which historians of crime have yet fully to acknowledge. However, this anomaly may also be partly explained by a greater propensity on the part of the judicial authorities to indict violent women at Scotland's supreme criminal court. Whether this tendency was caused by the unsuccessful assimilation of what we would term a 'civilising process' must probably remain speculative. Certainly, it does appear that the Scottish authorities were more severe in their treatment of the women brought before them on charges of violent crime than authorities elsewhere in Europe during the eighteenth and early nineteenth centuries. This goes some way towards explaining why so many women were indicted, convicted and punished in exemplary ways for violent offences at that time in contrast to the decades after 1815. Whether the reason for this earlier, sterner attitude can be understood through the absence of a well-established 'civilising process' deserves further research, but the explanatory possibilities remain intriguing none the less.

Overall, this book has afforded a significant insight into violent criminal activity in Scotland during the period from the mid-eighteenth century to the early nineteenth. However, the work done here is merely a starting point. How representative the conclusions are for all indicted violent crime in lowland Scotland can only be fully determined when other scattered and

---

[25] Carter Wood, *Violence and crime*, esp. chs i–iv and p. 146.
[26] Ibid. 5, 17–18.

fragmentary sources are made to yield further evidence. Similarly, the lowland experience of crime, and in particular female crime, must eventually be set alongside that of other areas of eighteenth-century Scotland and further afield. Nevertheless the evidence of this book has shown that the history of crime in Scotland is a subject worthy of considerably more detailed study in its own right. Its many novel features, around such issues as the legal context and the involvement of women in criminal activity, cannot be ignored, nor can the Scottish experience of crime be assimilated simply or conveniently into 'British' criminological history. Scotland must now take its place in the wider histories of crime, as an area that offers a distinct perspective on the issues of criminality, gender and the law.

Bibliography

Unpublished primary sources

Edinburgh, National Archives of Scotland
Justice of the Peace Court records, 1750–1815

East Lothian	JP 2/2	Quarter Sessions minute books
Kirkcudbright	JP 1/2	Quarter Sessions minute books
	JP 2/4	Monthly court books
Midlothian	JP 4/2	Quarter Sessions minute books
	JP 4/4	Monthly court books (including small debt court)
	JP 4/6	Court books
Selkirk	JP 13/2	Quarter Sessions minute books
West Lothian	JP 15/2	Quarter Sessions minute books
	JP 15/5	Miscellaneous court documents
Wigtown	JP 17/2	Quarter Sessions minute books

Justiciary Court records, 1750–1815

JC 3	Books of adjournal, series D
JC 4	Books of adjournal, series E
JC 7	High Court minute books, series D
JC 8	High Court minute books, series E
JC 12	South Circuit minute books
JC 13	West Circuit minute books
JC 18	Register of lawburrows
JC 20	Signet minute books
JC 22	Circuit appeal registers
JC 24	Remissions
JC 25	Petitions
JC 26	Processes
JC 42	Appointments and commissions
JC 45	Productions

Sheriff Court records, 1750–1815

Haddington	SC 40/51	Criminal record
	SC 40/54	Criminal processes
Hamilton	SC 37/50	Record of criminal jury trials
Paisley	SC 58/1	Ordinary court minute and act books
	SC 58/22	Processes
	SC 58/50	Criminal records
	SC 58/54	Criminal processes
	SC 58/55	Miscellaneous criminal papers

Peebles	SC 42/23	Criminal sederunt books
Selkirk	SC 63/44	Criminal record and copy indictments
Stirling	SC 67/44	Criminal register
	SC 67/45	Criminal process
	SC 67/46	Bail bonds
	SC 67/47	Miscellaneous criminal papers
Wigtown	SC 19/54	Criminal libels and indictments

Official documents and publications (in date order)

Acts of the parliaments of Scotland, iii, xi, Edinburgh 1814, 1824
Parliamentary papers, x, xi, London 1812, 1814-15

Newspapers and periodicals

The Cornhill Magazine

Contemporary books and articles

Allestree, R., *The whole duty of man, laid down in a plain and familiar way for the use of all but especially the meanest reader*, London 1716

Anon., *A warning to the wicked or Margaret Dickson's welcome to the gibbet*, Edinburgh 1724

Arber, E. (ed.), *The English scholar's library of old and modern works*, no. ii, London 1895.

Bartholomew, J. (ed.), *The gazetteer of the British Isles: statistical and topographical*, Edinburgh 1887

Bruce Trotter, R. de, *Galloway gossip 80 years ago*, Dumfries 1901

Cobbe, F. P., 'Wife-torture in England', *Contemporary Review* (Apr. 1878), 55–87

Defoe, D., *Augusta triumphans: or, the way to make London the most flourishing city in the universe*, London 1728

———— *Street robberies consider'd: the reason of their being so frequent, with probable means to prevent 'em*, London 1728

Fielding, H., *An enquiry into the causes of the late increase of robbers & etc.*, London 1751

Fordyce, J., *The character and conduct of the female sex*, London 1776

Healey, G. H. (ed.), *The letters of Daniel Defoe*, Oxford 1955

Hume, D., *Commentaries on the laws of Scotland, respecting crimes*, i, ii (1797), Edinburgh 1844 edn, repr. 1986

Johnson, C., 'An essay on the signs of murder in new born children', *Edinburgh Medical and Surgical Journal* x (1814), 394

Knox, J., *The first blast of the trumpet against the monstrous regiment of women* (1558), London 1895

Lewis, S., *A topographical dictionary of Scotland comprising the several counties, islands, cities, burgh and market towns, parishes and principal villages with historical*

160

and statistical descriptions; embellished with engravings of the seals and arms of the different burghs and universities, i, ii, London 1846

Mackenzie, G., *Law and customs of Scotland in matters criminal*, Edinburgh 1678

Mandeville, B., *An enquiry into the causes of the frequent executions at Tyburn and etc.*, London 1725

Ormond, G. W. T., *The Lord Advocates of Scotland*, i, Edinburgh 1883

Owen, M. E., 'Criminal women', *Cornhill Magazine* xiv (1866), 153

Plummer, C. (ed.), *The governance of England by Sir John Fortescue*, Oxford 1885

Smith, A., *Wealth of nations* (1776), ed. E. Cannan, Chicago 1976 edn

Reference works

Charlesworth, A. (ed.), *An atlas of rural protest in Britain, 1548–1900*, London 1983

Craigie, W. A. and A. J. Aitken (eds), *A dictionary of the older Scottish tongue from the twelfth century to the end of the seventeenth*, Chicago 1964

Grant, W. and D. D. Murison, *The Scottish national dictionary*, Edinburgh 1965

Raynor, P., B. Lenman and G. Parker, *Handlist of records for the study of crime in early modern Scotland (to 1747)*, London 1982

Robinson, M. (ed.), *The concise Scots dictionary*, Aberdeen 1985

Secondary sources

Abrams, L., 'From demon to victim: the infanticidal mother in Shetland, 1699–1802', in Brown and Ferguson, *Twisted sisters*, 180–203

Allan, D., *Scotland in the eighteenth century: union and Enlightenment*, Harlow 2002

Amussen, S. D., 'Gender, family and the social order, 1560–1725', in A. Fletcher and J. Stevenson (eds.), *Order and disorder in early modern England*, Cambridge 1987, 196–217

⸻ '"Being stirred to much unquietness": violence and domestic violence in early modern England', *Journal of Women's History* vi (1994), 70–89

Anderson, A. M., *The criminal law of Scotland*, 2nd edn, Edinburgh 1904

Anderson, E. A., 'The "chivalrous" treatment of the female offender in the arms of the criminal justice system: a review of the literature', *Social Problems* xxiii (1976), 350–7

Andrew, D. T., 'The code of honour and its critics: the opposition to duelling in England, 1750–1850', *SH* v (1980), 401–13

Archer, J. E., *Social unrest and popular protest in England, 1780–1840*, Cambridge 2000

Arnot, M. L. and C. Usborne, 'Why gender and crime? Aspects of an international debate', in Arnot and Usborne, *Gender and crime*, 1–43

⸻ and C. Usborne (eds), *Gender and crime in modern Europe*, London 1999

Bailey, J., *Unquiet lives: marriage and marriage breakdown in England, 1660–1800*, Cambridge 2003

Barker, H. and E. Chalus, 'Introduction', to Barker and Chalus, *Gender in eighteenth-century England*, 1–28

_____ and K. Harvey, 'Women entrepreneurs and urban expansion: Manchester, 1760–1820', in Sweet and Lane, *Women and urban life*, 111–30

_____ and E. Chalus (eds), *Gender in eighteenth-century England: roles, representations and responsibilities*, London–New York 1997

Beattie, J. M., 'The pattern of crime in England, 1660–1800', *P&P* lxii (1974), 47–95

_____ 'The criminality of women in eighteenth-century England', *JSH* viii (1975), 80–116

_____ *Crime and the courts in England, 1660–1800*, Oxford 1986

_____ *Policing and punishment in London, 1660–1750: urban crime and the limits of terror*, Oxford 2001

Bohstedt, J., *Riots and community politics in England and Wales, 1790–1810*, Cambridge, MA–London 1983

_____ 'Gender, household and community politics: women in English riots, 1790–1810, *P&P* cxx (1988), 88–122

_____ 'The pragmatic economy, the politics of provision and the "invention" of the food riot tradition in 1740', in A. Randall and A. Charlesworth (eds), *Moral economy and popular protest: crowds, conflict and authority*, Basingstoke 2000, 55–92

Booth, A., 'Food riots in the north-west of England, 1790–1801', *P&P* lxxvii (1977), 84–107

Boyd, K. M., *Scottish church attitudes to sex, marriage and the family, 1850–1914*, Edinburgh 1980

Brandon, D., *Stand and deliver: a history of highway robbery*, Stroud 2001

Briggs, J. and others, *Crime and punishment in England: an introductory history*, London 1999

Brodie-Innes, J.W., 'Some outstanding differences between English and Scots law, III: The origins and the courts of law', *JR* xxvii (1915), 175–94, 312–27

Brotherstone, T. (ed.), *Covenant, charter and party: traditions of revolt and protest in modern Scottish history*, Aberdeen 1989

——— D. Simonton and O. Walsh (eds), *Gendering Scottish history: an international approach*, Glasgow 2000

Brown, C. G., *The social history of religion in Scotland since 1730*, London 1987

——— *Religion and society in Scotland since 1707*, Edinburgh 1997

Brown, K., *Bloodfeud in Scotland, 1573–1625: violence, justice and politics in early modern society*, Edinburgh 1986

Brown, Y. G. and R. Ferguson (eds), *Twisted sisters: women, crime and deviance in Scotland since 1400*, East Linton 2002

Cage, R. A., *The Scottish poor law, 1745–1845*, Edinburgh 1981

Cairns, J. W., 'Historical introduction', in K. Reid and R. Zimmermann (eds), *A history of private law in Scotland, II: Obligations*, Oxford 2000, 14–184

——— 'Legal theory', in A. Broadie (ed.), *The Cambridge companion to the Scottish Enlightenment*, Cambridge 2003, 222–42

Campbell, R., 'Sentence of death by burning for women', *Journal of Legal History* v (1984), 44–59

Campbell, R. H., *Scotland since 1707: the rise of an industrial society*, Edinburgh 1985

Carlen, P. and A. Worrall, *Gender, crime and justice*, Milton Keynes 1987

Carter Wood, J., *Violence and crime in nineteenth-century England: the shadow of our refinement*, London–New York 2004

Castan, N., 'Criminals', in Davis and Farge, *Women in the west*, 475–88

Chalus, E., 'The rag plot: the politics of influence in Oxford, 1754', in Sweet and Lane, *Women and urban life*, 43–64

Chitnis, A. C., *The Scottish Enlightenment: a social history*, London 1976

Churches, C., 'Women and property in early modern England: a case study', *SH* xxiii (1998), 165–80

Clark, A., *Working life of women in the seventeenth century*, 3rd edn, London 1992
———— *Women's silence, men's violence: sexual assault in England, 1770–1845*, London–New York 1987
_____ 'Humanity or justice? Wifebeating and the law in the eighteenth and nineteenth centuries', in C. Smart (ed.), *Regulating womanhood: historical essays on marriage, motherhood and sexuality*, London–New York 1992, 187–206

Clark, S., *Women and crime in the street literature of early modern England*, Basingstoke 2003

Coats, A.W., 'Contrary moralities: plebs, paternalists and political economists', *P&P* liv (1972), 130–3

Cockburn, J. S. (ed.), *Crime in England, 1550–1800*, London 1977
_____ 'Patterns of violence in English society: homicide in Kent, 1560–1985', *P&P* cxxx (1991), 70–106

Conklin, J. E., *Robbery and the criminal justice system*, Philadelphia 1972

Conley, C. A., 'No pedestals: women and violence in late nineteenth-century Ireland', *JSH* xxviii (1995), 801–18

Connolly, S. J., 'Violence and order in the eighteenth century', in P. O'Flanagan, P. Ferguson and K. Whelan (eds), *Rural Ireland, 1600–1900: modernisation and change*, Cork 1987, 42–61
_____ 'Albion's fatal twigs: justice and the law in the eighteenth century', in R. Mitchison and P. Roebuck (eds), *Economy and society in Scotland and Ireland, 1500–1939*, Edinburgh 1988, 117–25

Cooper, T. M., *Select Scottish cases of the thirteenth century*, Edinburgh–London 1944

Cornish, W. R. and G. de N. Clark, *Law and society in England, 1750–1950*, London 1989

Cowan, I. B., *The Scottish Reformation: Church and society in sixteenth-century Scotland*, London 1982

Coutts, W., 'Wife and widow: the evidence of testaments and marriage contracts, c.1600', in Ewan and Meikle, *Women in Scotland*, 176–86

Craig, M., *Damn' rebel bitches: the women of the '45*, Edinburgh 1997

Croft Dickinson, W., 'The High Court of Justiciary', in *Introduction to Scottish legal history*, 408–12

Crowther, M. A., 'Criminal precognitions and their value for the historian', *Scottish Archives: Journal of the Scottish Records Association* i (1995), 75–84

Cullen, L. M., 'Smuggling in the north channel in the eighteenth century', *SESH* vii (1987) 9–26

Daly, M. and M. Wilson, *Homicide*, New York 1988

Daniels, C. and M.V. Kennedy (eds), *Over the threshold: intimate violence in early America*, London–New York 1999

Datesman, S. K. and F. R. Scarpitti, *Women, crime and justice*, Oxford 1980

Davey, B. J., *Rural crime in the eighteenth century: north Lincolnshire, 1740–1780*, Hull 1994

Davies, S. J., 'The courts and the Scottish legal system,1600–1747: the case of Stirlingshire', in Gatrell, Lenman and Parker, *Crime and the law*, 120–54

Davis, J., 'The London garotting panic of 1862: a moral panic and the creation of a criminal class in mid-Victorian England', in Gatrell, Lenman and Parker, *Crime and the law*, 190–213

Davis, N. Z. and A. Farge (eds), *A history of women in the west*, III: *Renaissance and Enlightenment paradoxes*, Cambridge, MA.–London 1993

D'Cruze, S., *Crimes of outrage: sex, violence and Victorian working women*, London 1998

_____ (ed.), *Everyday violence in Britain, 1850–1950: gender and class*, Harlow 2000

Dekker, R. M., 'Women in revolt: popular protest and its social basis in Holland in the seventeenth and eighteenth centuries', *Theory and Society* xvi (1987), 337–62

Delumeau, J., *Sin and fear: the emergence of a western guilt culture, 13th–18th centuries*, trans. E. Nicholson, New York 1990

DesBrisay, G., '"Menacing their persons and exacting their purses": the Aberdeen justice court, 1657–1700', in D. Stevenson (ed.), *From lairds to louns: country and burgh life in Aberdeen, 1600–1800*, Aberdeen 1986, 70–90

Devine, T. M., 'Social stability and agrarian change in the eastern lowlands of Scotland, 1810–1840', *SH* iii (1978), 331–46

_____ 'Unrest and stability in rural Ireland and Scotland, 1760–1840', in R. Mitchison and P. Roebuck (eds), *Economy and society in Scotland and Ireland, 1500–1939*, Edinburgh 1988, 126-39

_____ 'Urbanisation', in Devine and Mitchison, *People and society*, 27–52

_____ *Clanship to crofters' war: the social transformation of the Scottish Highlands*, Manchester 1994

_____ *The transformation of rural Scotland: social change and the agrarian economy, 1660–1815*, Edinburgh 1994

_____ *The Scottish nation, 1700–2000*, London 1999

_____ and R. Mitchison (eds), *People and society in Scotland*, I: *1760–1830*, Edinburgh 1988

Dickinson, H.T. and K. Logue, 'The Porteous Riot: a study of the breakdown of law and order in Edinburgh, 1736–1737', *Journal of the Scottish Labour History Society* x (1976), 21–40

Dickinson, J. R. and J. A. Sharpe, 'Infanticide in early modern England: the court of great sessions at Chester, 1650–1800', in Jackson, *Infanticide*, 35–51

Dickinson, W. C. (ed.), *Sheriff Court book of Fife, 1515–1522*, Edinburgh 1928

Dingwall, H., 'The power behind the merchant? Women and the economy in late seventeenth-century Edinburgh', in Ewan and Meikle, *Women in Scotland*, 152-64

Dolan, F. E., *Dangerous familiars: representations of domestic crime in England, 1550–1700*, Ithaca, NY–London 1994

Donaldson, G., 'The legal profession in Scottish society in the sixteenth and seventeenth centuries', *JR* n.s. xxi (1976), 1–19

Donnachie, I., '"The darker side": a speculative survey of Scottish crime during the first half of the nineteenth century', *SESH* xv (1995), 5–24

────── 'Profiling criminal offences: the evidence of the Lord Advocate's papers during the first half of the nineteenth century in Scotland', *Scottish Archives: Journal of the Scottish Records Association* i (1995), 85–92

Dove Wilson, J., 'Historical development of Scots law', *JR* viii (1896), 217–41

Eales, J., *Women in early modern England, 1500–1700*, London 1998

Eisner, M., 'Modernisation, self-control and violence: the long-term dynamics of European homicide rates in theoretical perspective', *British Journal of Criminology* xli (2001), 618–38.

Elias, N., *The civilizing process: the history of manners and state formation and civilization*, trans. E. Jephcott, Oxford 1994

Elton, G. R., 'Introduction: crime and the historian', in Cockburn, *Crime in England*, 1–14

Emsley, C., *Crime and society in England, 1750–1900*, London 1996

Erickson, A. L., *Women and property in early modern England*, London 1993

Ewan, E., '"For whatever ales ye": women as consumers and producers in late medieval Scottish towns', in Ewan and Meikle, *Women in Scotland*, 125–36

────── 'A realm of one's own? The place of medieval and early modern women in Scottish history', in Brotherstone, Simonton and Walsh, *Gendering Scottish history*, 19–36

────── and M. M. Meikle, 'Introduction: a monstrous regiment of women', in Ewan and Meikle, *Women in Scotland*, pp. xix–xxx

────── and M. M. Meikle (eds), *Women in Scotland, c. 1100–c. 1750*, East Lothian 1999

Farge, A., 'Protesters plain to see', in Davis and Farge, *Women in the west*, 489–505

Farmer, L., *Criminal law, tradition and legal order: crime and the genius of Scots law, 1747 to the present*, Cambridge 1997

Feeley, M., 'The decline of women in the criminal process: a comparative history', *Criminal Justice History: An International Annual* xv (1994), 235–74

────── and D. L. Little, 'The vanishing female: the decline of women in the criminal process, 1687–1912', *Law and Society Review* xxv (1991), 719–57

Ferguson, W., *Scotland 1689 to the present*, Edinburgh 1990

Ferraro, J. M., 'The power to decide: battered wives in early modern Venice', *Renaissance Quarterly* xlviii (1995), 492–512

Finch, A., 'Women and violence in the later Middle Ages: the evidence of the officiality of Cerisy', *C&C* vii (1992), 23–45

Findlay, J., *All manner of people: the history of the justices of the peace in Scotland*, Edinburgh 2000

Finlay J., 'Women and legal representation in early sixteenth-century Scotland', in Ewan and Meikle, *Women in Scotland*, 165-75

Finn, M., 'Women, consumption and coverture in England', *HJ* xxxix (1996), 703–22

Flinn, M. W. (ed.), *Scottish population history: from the seventeenth century to the 1930s*, Cambridge 1977

Foyster, E. A., 'Silent witnesses? Children and the breakdown of domestic and social order in early modern England', in A. Fletcher and S. Hussey (eds), *Childhood in question: children, parents and the state*, Manchester 1999, 57–73

────── 'Creating a veil of silence? Politeness and marital violence in the English household', *Transactions of the Royal Historical Society* xii (2002), 395–415

Francus, M., 'Monstrous mothers, monstrous societies: infanticide and the rule of law in Restoration and eighteenth-century England', *Eighteenth Century Life* xxi (1997), 133-56

Fraser, W. H., 'Patterns of protest', in Devine and Mitchison, *People and society*, 268–91

Freeman, M. D. A., *Violence in the home*, Farnborough 1979

Gaskill, M., *Crime and mentalities in early modern England*, Cambridge 2000

Gatrell, V. A. C., 'The decline of theft and violence in Victorian and Edwardian England', in Gatrell, Lenman and Parker, *Crime and the law*, 238–370

—————— *The hanging tree: execution and the English people, 1770–1868*, Oxford 1994

—————— B. Lenman and G. Parker (eds), *Crime and the law: the social history of crime in western Europe since 1500*, London 1980

Genovese, E. F., 'The many faces of the moral economy: a contribution to a debate', *P&P* lviii (1973), 161–8

Gibson, A. J. S. and T. C. Smout, *Prices, food and wages in Scotland, 1550–1780*, Cambridge 1995

Gillespie, R., 'Women and crime in seventeenth-century Ireland', in M. MacCurtain and M. O'Dowd (eds), *Women in early modern Ireland*, Edinburgh 1991, 43–52

Gilmour, I., *Riots, risings and revolution: governance and violence in eighteenth-century England*, London 1992

Gordon, E., 'Women's spheres', in W. H. Fraser and R. J. Morris (eds), *People and society in Scotland, II: 1830–1914*, Edinburgh 1990, 206–35

Gordon, W. M. and T. D. Fergus (eds), *Legal history in the making: proceedings of the Scottish legal history conference, Glasgow, 1989*, London 1991

Goring, R., 'Eighteenth-century Scottish smugglers: the evidence from Montrose and Dumfries', *Review of Scottish Culture* iii (1987), 53–65

Gowing, L., 'Secret births and infanticide in seventeenth-century England', *P&P* clvi (1997), 87–115

—————— *Domestic dangers: women, words, and sex in early modern London*, Oxford 1998

Graham M. F., 'Women and the church courts in Reformation-era Scotland', in Ewan and Meikle, *Women in Scotland*, 187–200

—————— *The uses of reform: 'godly discipline' and popular behaviour in Scotland and beyond, 1560–1610*, Leiden 1996

Hamilton, H., *An economic history of Scotland in the eighteenth century*, Oxford 1963

Hammerton, A. J., 'The targets of "rough music": respectability and domestic violence in Victorian England', *G&H* iii (1991), 23–44

Hanawalt, B., 'The female felon in fourteenth-century England', *Viator: Medieval and Renaissance Studies* v (1974), 251–73

Harding, A. (ed.), *Law-making and law-makers in British history*, London 1980

Harrison, J. G., 'Women and the branks in Stirling, c. 1600–c. 1730', *SESH* xviii (1998), 114–31

Hay, D., 'War, dearth and theft in the eighteenth century', *P&P* xcv (1982), 117–60

—————— 'Master and servant in England: using the law in the eighteenth and nineteenth centuries', in W. Steinmetz (ed.), *Private law and social inequality in the industrial age: comparing legal cultures in Britain, France, Germany and the United States*, Oxford 2000, 227–64

_____ P. Linebaugh, J. R. Rule, E. P. Thompson and C. Winslow (eds), *Albion's fatal tree: crime and society in eighteenth-century England*, London 1975

Heidensohn, F., *Women and crime*, Basingstoke 1996

Helmholz, R. H., 'Infanticide in the province of Canterbury during the fifteenth century', in R. H. Helmholz (ed.), *Canon law and the law of England*, London 1987, 157–68

Henderson, T., *Disorderly women in eighteenth-century London: prostitution and control in the metropolis, 1730–1830*, London 1999

Hendry, J., 'Snug in the asylum of taciturnity: women's history in Scotland', in I. Donnachie and C. Whatley (eds), *The manufacture of Scottish history*, Edinburgh 1992, 125–42

Henry, B., *Dublin hanged: crime, law enforcement and punishment in late eighteenth-century Dublin*, Dublin 1994

Herrup, C., 'New shoes and mutton pies: investigative responses to theft in seventeenth-century east Sussex', *HJ* xxvii (1984), 811–30

―――― *The common peace: participation and the criminal law in seventeenth-century England*, Cambridge 1987

Hill, B., *Eighteenth-century women: an anthology*, London 1984

―――― *Women, work and sexual politics in eighteenth-century England*, Oxford 1989

Hobsbawm E., *Bandits*, London 2000

Hoerder, D., *Crowd action in revolutionary Massachusetts, 1765–1780*, London–New York 1977

Hoffer, P. C. and N. E. C. Hull, *Murdering mothers: infanticide in England and New England, 1558–1803*, New York 1984

Honeyman, K., *Women, gender and industrialisation in England, 1700–1870*, Basingstoke 2000

Houlbrooke, R. A., 'Women's social life and common action in England from the fifteenth century to the eve of civil war', *C&C* i (1986), 171–89

Houston, R. A., 'Women in the economy and society of Scotland, 1500–1800', in Houston and Whyte, *Scottish society*, 118–47

―――― *Social change in the age of Enlightenment: Edinburgh, 1660–1760*, Oxford 1994

_____ and I. D. Whyte, 'Introduction', to Houston and Whyte, *Scottish society*, 1–36

―――― and I. D. Whyte (eds), *Scottish society, 1500–1800*, Cambridge 1989

Hufton, O., 'Women and violence in early modern Europe', in F. Dieteren and E. Kloek (eds), *Writing women into history*, Amsterdam 1990, 75–95

_____ *The prospect before her: a history of women in western Europe*, London 1995

Hull, N. E., *Female felons: women and serious crime in colonial Massachusetts*, Urbana, ILL.–Chicago 1987

Humfrey, P., 'Female servants and women's criminality in early eighteenth-century London', in Smith and others, *Criminal justice in the old world and the new*, 58–84

Hunt, M., 'Wife beating, domesticity and women's independence in eighteenth-century London', *G&H* iv (1992), 10–33

_____ '"The great danger she had reason to believe she was in"', in V. Frith (ed.), *Women and history: voices of early modern England*, Ontario 1997, 81–8

Hunt, M. R., *The middling sort: commerce, gender and the family, 1680–1780*, Berkeley–London 1996

Hurl-Eamon, J., 'Domestic violence prosecuted: women binding over their husbands for assault at Westminster quarter sessions, 1685–1720', *Journal of Family History* xxvi (2001), 435–54

_____ *Gender and petty violence in London, 1680–1720*, Columbus Ohio 2005

Ingram, M., 'Ridings, rough music and the "reform of popular culture" in early modern England', *P&P* cv (1984), 79–113

_____ 'Ridings, rough music and mocking rhymes in early modern England', in B. Reay (ed.), *Popular culture in seventeenth-century England*, London–Sydney 1985, 129–65

_____ '"Scolding women cucked or washed": a crisis in gender relations in early modern England?', in Kermode and Walker, *Women, crime and the courts*, 48–80

Introduction to Scottish legal history (Stair Society xx, 1958)

Irvine Smith, J., 'Criminal procedure', in *Introduction to Scottish legal history*, 426–48

Jackson, M., *New-born child murder: women, illegitimacy and the courts in eighteenth-century England*, Manchester 1996

_____ (ed.), *Infanticide: historical perspectives on child murder and concealment, 1550–2000*, Aldershot 2002

Johnson, E. and E. Monkkonen (eds) *The civilization of crime: violence in town and country since the Middle Ages*, Urbana, ILL. 1996

Jones, D. J. V., 'The corn riots in Wales, 1793–1801', *Welsh Historical Review (Cylchgrawn Hanes Cymru)* ii (1965), 323–45

_____ *Crime in nineteenth century Wales*, Cardiff 1992

Kelly, J., 'Infanticide in eighteenth-century Ireland', *Irish Economic and Social History* xix (1992), 5–26

Kermode, J. and G. Walker (eds), *Women, crime and the courts in early modern England*, London 1994

Kilday, A.-M., 'Maternal monsters: murdering mothers in south-west Scotland, 1750–1815', in Brown and Ferguson, *Twisted sisters*, 156–79

King, P., 'Newspaper reporting, prosecution practice and perceptions of urban crime: the Colchester crime wave of 1765', *C&C* ii (1987), 423–54

_____ 'Female offenders, work and life-cycle change in late-eighteenth-century London', *C&C* xi (1996), 61–90

_____ 'Punishing assault: the transformation of attitudes in the English courts', *Journal of Interdisciplinary History* xxvii (1996), 43–74

_____ 'Gender, crime and justice in late eighteenth- and early nineteenth-century England', in Arnot and Usborne, *Gender and crime*, 44–74

_____ *Crime, justice and discretion in England, 1740–1820*, Oxford 2000

Knelman, J., *Twisting in the wind: the murderess and the English press*, Toronto–London 1998

Knox, A., '"Barbarous and pestiferous women": female criminality, violence and aggression in sixteenth- and seventeenth-century Scotland and Ireland', in Brown and Ferguson, *Twisted sisters*, 13–31

Lachance, A., 'Women and crime in Canada in the early eighteenth century,

1712–1759', in L. A. Knafla (ed.), *Crime and criminal justice in Europe and Canada*, Ontario 1981, 157–77

Langbein, J. H., 'Albion's fatal flaws', *P&P* xcviii (1983), 96–120

Larner, C., *Enemies of God: the witch-hunt in Scotland*, London 1981

Laurence, A., *Women in England, 1500–1760: a social history*, London 1994

Lawson, P., 'Property crime and hard times in England, 1559–1624', *Law and History Review* iv (1986), 95–127

⸻ 'Patriarchy, crime and the courts: the criminality of women in late Tudor and early Stuart England', in Smith, May and Deveraux, *Criminal justice*, 16–57

Le Bon, G., *The crowd: a study of the popular mind*, London 1947

Leneman, L., '"A tyrant and a tormentor": violence against wives in eighteenth- and nineteenth-century Scotland', *C&C* xii (1997), 31–54

⸻ and R. Mitchison, 'Scottish illegitimacy ratios in the early modern period', *Economic History Review* 2nd ser. xl (1987), 41–63

⸻ *Alienated affections: the Scottish experience of divorce and separation, 1684–1830*, Edinburgh 1998

Lenman, B., *The Jacobite risings in Britain, 1689–1746*, Aberdeen 1995

⸻and G. Parker, 'Crime and control in Scotland, 1500–1800', *History Today* xxx (1980), 13–17

Leopold, J., 'The Levellers' revolt in Galloway in 1724', *Journal of the Scottish Labour History Society* xiv (1980), 4–29

Levack, B. P., 'The proposed union of English law and Scots law in the seventeenth century', *JR* n.s. xx (1975), 97–115

⸻ 'English law, Scots law and the Union, 1603–1707', in Harding, *Lawmaking*, 105–19

⸻ *The formation of the British state: England, Scotland, and the Union, 1603–1707*, Oxford 1987

⸻ 'Law, sovereignty and the Union', in R. A. Mason (ed.), *Scots and Britons: Scottish political thought and the Union of 1603*, Cambridge 1994, 213–37

Linebaugh, P., 'The Tyburn riot against the surgeons', in Hay, Linebaugh, Rule, Thompson and Winslow, *Albion's fatal tree*, 65–118

⸻ *The London hanged: crime and civil society in the eighteenth century*, London 1993

Logue, K. J., 'The Tranent militia riot of 1797', *Transactions of the East Lothian Antiquarian and Field Naturalists' Society* xiv (1974), 37–61

⸻ *Popular disturbances in Scotland, 1780–1815*, Edinburgh 1979

⸻ 'Eighteenth-century popular protests: aspects of the people's past', in E. J. Cowan (ed.), *The people's past*, Edinburgh 1980, 108–30

Lynch, M., *Scotland: a new history*, London 1992

Lythe, S. G. E., 'The Tayside meal mobs, 1772–3', *Scottish Historical Review* xlvi (1967), 26–36

⸻ and J. Butt, *An economic history of modern Scotland, 1100–1939*, Glasgow 1975

MacCormick, N., 'Law and enlightenment', in R. H. Campbell and A. S. Skinner (eds), *The origins and nature of the Scottish Enlightenment*, Edinburgh 1982, 150–66

MacCulloch, D., *Reformation: Europe's house divided, 1490–1700*, London 2003

McDermid, J., 'Missing persons? Women in modern Scottish history', in Brother-stone, Simonton and Walsh, *Gendering Scottish history*, 37–45

Macfarlane, A., *The justice and the mare's ale: law and disorder in seventeenth-century England*, Oxford 1981

Mackay, L., 'Why they stole: women in the Old Bailey, 1779–1789', *JSH* xxxii (1999), 623–40

MacLean, M. and C. Carrell (eds), *As an fhearann (From the land)*, Edinburgh 1986

McLynn, F., *Crime and punishment in eighteenth-century England*, London 1989

McMahon, V., *Murder in Shakespeare's England*, London–New York 2004

Malcolmson, R. W., 'Infanticide in the eighteenth century', in Cockburn, *Crime in England*, 187–209

Mann, A. J., 'Embroidery to enterprise: the role of women in the book trade of early modern Scotland', in Ewan and Meikle, *Women in Scotland*, 137–51

Marland, H., 'Getting away with murder? Puerperal insanity, infanticide and the defence plea', in Jackson, *Infanticide*, 168–92

Marshall, R. K., *Virgins and viragoes: a history of women in Scotland from 1080 to 1908*, London 1983

Mathieson, W. L., *The awakening of Scotland: a history from 1747 to 1797*, Glasgow 1910

May, M., 'Violence in the family: an historical perspective', in J. P. Martin (ed.), *Violence and the family*, Chichester–New York 1978, 135–67

Mendelson, S. and P. Crawford, *Women in early modern England, 1550–1720*, Oxford 1998

Milgram, S. and H. Toch, 'Collective behaviour: crowds and social movements', in G. Lindzey and E. Aronson (eds), *The handbook of social psychology*, IV: *Group psychology and phenomena of interaction*, Reading, MA–London 1969, 507–610

Mitchison, R., 'The movements of Scottish corn prices in the seventeenth and eighteenth centuries', *Economic History Review* 2nd ser. xviii (1965), 278–91

———— and L. Leneman, *Sexuality and social control: Scotland, 1660–1780*, Oxford 1989

___ and L. Leneman, *Girls in trouble: sexuality and social control in rural Scotland, 1660–1780*, Edinburgh 1998

Morgan, G. and P. Rushton, *Rogues, thieves and the rule of law: the problem of law enforcement in north-east England, 1718–1800*, London 1998

Morris, A., *Women, crime and criminal justice*, Oxford 1987

Murdoch, A., 'The Advocates, the law and the nation in early modern Scotland', in W. Prest (ed.), *Lawyers in early modern Europe and America*, London 1981, 147–63

Parker, C., 'The moral agency and moral autonomy of church folk in the Dutch Reformed Church of Delft, 1580–1620', *Journal of Ecclesiastical History* xlviii (1997), 44–70

Peters, C., *Women in early modern Britain, 1450–1640*, Basingstoke 2004

Phillips, R., *Putting assunder: a history of divorce in western society*, Cambridge 1988

—————— 'Women, neighbourhood, and family in the late eighteenth century', *French Historical Studies* xviii (1993), 1–12

Phillipson, N. T., 'Lawyers, landowners, and the civic leadership of post-Union

Scotland: an essay on the social role of the Faculty of Advocates, 1661–1830, in eighteenth-century Scottish society', *JR* n.s. xxi (1976), 97–120

_____ 'The social structure of the Faculty of Advocates in Scotland, 1661–1840', in Harding, *Law-making*, 146–56

Piers, M.W., *Infanticide*, New York 1978

Pinchbeck, I., *Women workers and the industrial revolution, 1750–1850*, 3rd edn, London 1981

Place names and population in Scotland: an alphabetical list of populated places derived from the census of Scotland, Edinburgh 1967

Pollak, O., *The criminality of women*, Philadelphia 1950

Prevost, W. A. J., 'Letters reporting the rising of the Levellers in 1724', *Transactions of the Dumfries and Galloway Natural History and Antiquarian Society* 3rd ser. xliv (1967), 196–204

Prior, M., 'Women and the urban economy: Oxford, 1500–1800', in M. Prior (ed.), *Women in English society, 1500–1800*, London–New York 1985, 93–117

Quinault, R. and J. Stevenson (eds), *Popular protest and public order: six studies in British history, 1790–1920*, London 1974

Quinn, C., 'Images and impulses: representations of puerperal insanity and infanticide in late Victorian England', in Jackson, *Infanticide*, 193–215

Rabin, D., 'Bodies of evidence, states of mind: infanticide, emotion and sensibility in eighteenth-century England', in Jackson, *Infanticide*, 73–92

Radbill, S. X., 'A history of child abuse and infanticide', in R. E. Helfer and C. H. Kempe (eds), *The battered child*, Chicago 1968, 3–17

Reed, M. and R. Wells, *Class, conflict and protest in the English countryside, 1700–1880*, London 1990

Rendall, J., *The origins of the Scottish Enlightenment*, London 1978

_____ *The origins of modern feminism: women in Britain, France and the United States, 1780–1860*, Basingstoke 1985

Reynolds, S., 'Historiography and gender: Scottish and international dimensions', in Brotherstone, Simonton and Walsh, *Gendering Scottish history*, 1–18

Richards, E., *A history of the Highland Clearances*, I: *Agrarian transformation and evictions, 1746–1886*, London 1982

——— *A history of the Highland Clearances*, II: *Emigration, protest, reasons*, London 1985

_____ *The Highland Clearances: people, landlords and rural turmoil*, Edinburgh 2000

Roberts, M. and S. Clarke (eds), *Women and gender in early modern Wales*, Cardiff 2000

Rose, L., *The massacre of the innocents: infanticide in Britain, 1800–1939*, London 1986

Rose, R. B., 'The Priestly riots of 1791', *P&P* xviii (1960), 68–88

_____ 'Eighteenth-century price riots and public policy in England', *International Review of Social History* vi (1961), 277–92

Ross, E., ' "Fierce questions and taunts": married life in working-class London', *Feminist Studies* viii (1982), 575–602

Rowe, G. S. and J. D. Marietta, 'Personal violence in a "peaceable kingdom" ', in Daniels and Kennedy, *Over the threshold*, 22–45

Rublack, U., *The crimes of women in early modern Germany*, Oxford 1999

Rudé, G., *The crowd in history, 1730–1848*, London 1981

—— *The face of the crowd: studies in revolution, ideology and popular protest*, New York–London 1988

Ruff, J. R., *Crime, justice and public order: the sénéchaussées of Libourne and Bazas, 1696–1789*, London–Dover, NH 1984

—— *Violence in early modern Europe, 1500–1800*, Cambridge 2001

Rule, J., *Albion's people: English society, 1714–1815*, London 1992

Rushton, P., 'The matter in variance: adolescents and domestic conflict in the pre-industrial economy of northeast England, 1600–1800', *JSH* xxxv (1991), 89–107

Sanderson, E. C., *Women and work in eighteenth-century Edinburgh*, London 1996

Sauer, R., 'Infanticide and abortion in nineteenth-century Britain', *Population Studies: A Journal of Demography* xxxii (1978), 81–93

Sellar, W. D. H., 'Forethocht felony, malice aforethought and the classification of homicide', in Gordon and Fergus, *Legal history in the making*, 43–59

—— 'A historical perspective', in M. C. Meston and others (eds), *The Scottish legal tradition*, Edinburgh 1991, 29–57

Sharpe, J. A., 'Domestic homicide in early modern England', *HJ* xxiv (1981), 29–48

—— *Crime in seventeenth century England: a county study*, Cambridge 1983

—— '"Such disagreement betwyx neighbours": litigation and human relations in early modern England', in J. Bossy (ed.), *Disputes and settlements: law and human relations in the west*, Cambridge 1983, 167–87

—— *Crime in early modern England, 1550–1750*, Harlow 1984

—— 'Crime in England: long-term trends and the problem of modernization', in Johnson and Monkkonen, *The civilization of crime*, 17–34

—— *English witchcraft, 1560–1736*, London 2003

Sharpe, P., *Adapting to capitalism: working women in the English economy, 1700–1850*, Basingstoke 1996

Shaw, J., *The management of Scottish society, 1707–1764: power, nobles, lawyers, Edinburgh agents and English influence*, Edinburgh 1983

Shoemaker, R. B., 'The London "mob" in the early eighteenth century', *Journal of British Studies* xxvi (1987), 273–304

—— *Prosecution and punishment: petty crime and the law in London and rural Middlesex, c. 1660–1725*, Cambridge 1991

—— *Gender in English society, 1650–1850: the emergence of separate spheres*, Harlow 1998

—— *The London mob: violence and disorder in eighteenth-century London*, London 2004

Siegel, R. B., '"The rule of love": wife beating as prerogative and privacy', *Yale Law Journal* cv (1996), 2117-207

Simonton, D., *A history of European women's work: 1700 to the present*, London 1998

Sindall, R., *Street violence in the nineteenth century: media panic or real danger?* Leicester 1990

Slaven, A., *The development of the west of Scotland: 1750–1960*, London 1975

Smart, C., *Women, crime and criminology: a feminist critique*, London–Boston 1977

Smelser, N. J., *Theory of collective behaviour* London 1962

Smith, G. T., A. N. May and S. Devereaux (eds), *Criminal justice in the old world and the new: essays in honour of J. M. Beattie*, Toronto 1998

Smout, T. C., *A history of the Scottish people, 1560–1830*, London 1969

_____ 'Aspects of sexual behaviour in nineteenth-century Scotland', in A. A. MacLaren (ed.), *Social class in Scotland: past and present*, Edinburgh 1976, 55–85

Spencer Muirhead, J., 'Notes on the history of the solicitors' profession in Scotland', *Scottish Law Review* lxviii (1952), 25–36, 59–70

Spierenburg, P., 'Long-term trends in homicide: theoretical reflections and Dutch evidence, fifteenth to twentieth centuries', in Johnson and Monkkonen, *Civilization of crime*, 63–105

_____ 'How violent were women? Court cases in Amsterdam, 1650–1810', *Crime, History and Societies* i (1997), 9–28

Spraggs, G., *Outlaws and highwaymen: the cult of the robber in England from the Middle Ages to the nineteenth century*, London 2001

Stanko, E. A., *Everyday violence: how women and men experienced sexual and physical danger*, London 1990

Stein, P., 'Law and society in eighteenth-century Scottish thought', in N. T. Phillipson and R. Mitchison (eds), *Scotland in the age of improvement: essays in Scottish history in the eighteenth century*, Edinburgh 1970, 148–68

_____ 'Legal thought in eighteenth-century Scotland', in P. Stein (ed.), *The character and influence of Roman civil law: historical essays*, London 1988, 361–80

Stevenson, D., *Revolution and counter-revolution in Scotland, 1644–1651*, Edinburgh 2003

Stevenson, J., 'Food riots in England, 1792–1818', in Quinault and Stevenson, *Popular protest*, 33–74

_____ *Popular disturbances in England, 1700–1870*, London 1979

Stewart, M. M., '"In durance vile": crime and punishment in seventeenth- and eighteenth-century records of Dumfries', *Scottish Archives: Journal of the Scottish Records Association* i (1995), 63–74

Stone, L., *The family, sex and marriage in England, 1500–1800*, London 1977

_____ 'Interpersonal violence in English society, 1300–1980', *P&P* ci (1983), 22–33

Stretton, T., *Women waging law in Elizabethan England*, Cambridge 1998

Sweet, R., 'Introduction', to Sweet and Lane, *Women and urban life*, 21–42

_____ and P. Lane (eds), *Women and urban life in eighteenth-century England: 'on the town'*, Aldershot 2003

Symonds, D. A., *Weep not for me: women, ballads and infanticide in early modern Scotland*, University Park, PA 1997

Tausiet, M., 'Witchcraft as metaphor: infanticide and its translations in Aragón in the sixteenth and seventeenth centuries', in S. Clark (ed.), *Languages of witchcraft: narrative, ideology and meaning in early modern culture*, Basingstoke 2001, 179–96

Taylor, D., *Crime, policing and punishment in England, 1750–1914*, Basingstoke 1998

Thomas, M. I. and J. Grimmett, *Women in protest, 1800–1850*, London 1982

Thompson, E. P., 'The moral economy of the English crowd in the eighteenth century', *P&P* l (1971), 76–136

_____ *Customs in common*, London 1993

Thwaites, W., 'Women in the market place: Oxfordshire, *c*.1690–1800', *Midland History* ix (1984), 23–42

Tilly, C., 'Collective violence in European perspective', in H. D. Graham and T. D. Gurr (eds), *Violence in America: historical and comparative perspectives*, New York 1969, 83–118

Titus Reid, S., *Crime and criminology*, Hinsdale, ILL. 1976

Tobias, J. J., *Crime and industrial society in the nineteenth century* London 1967

Todd, M., *The culture of Protestantism in early modern Scotland*, New Haven–London 2002

Tomes, N., 'A "torrent of abuse": crimes of violence between working-class men and women in London, 1840–1875', *JSH* xi (1978), 328–45

Turner, R.H., 'Collective behaviour', in R. E. L. Faris (ed.), *Handbook of modern sociology*, Chicago 1964, 382–425

Ulbricht, O., 'Infanticide in eighteenth-century Germany', in R. J. Evans (ed.), *The German underworld: deviants and outcasts in German history*, London 1988, 108–40

Underdown, D. E., 'The taming of the scold: the enforcement of patriarchal authority in early modern England', in A. Fletcher and J. Stevenson (eds), *Order and disorder in early modern England*, Cambridge 1987, 116–36

Walker, D., *The Scottish legal system: an introduction to the study of Scots law*, Edinburgh 1992

Walker, G., 'Women, theft and the world of stolen goods', in Kermode and Walker, *Women, crime and the courts*, 81–105

_____ *Crime, gender and social order in early modern England*, Cambridge 2003

_____ and J. Kermode, 'Introduction', to Kermode and Walker, *Women, crime and the courts*, 1–25

Walter, J., 'Grain riots and popular attitudes to the law: Maldon and the crisis of 1629', in J. Brewer and J. Styles (eds), *An ungovernable people: the English and their law in the seventeenth and eighteenth centuries*, London 1983, 47–84

——— and K. Wrightson, 'Dearth and the social order in early modern England', *P&P* lxxi (1976), 22–42

Warner, J. and A. Lunny, 'Marital violence in a martial town: husbands and wives in early modern Portsmouth, 1653–1781', *Journal of Family History* xxviii (2003), 258–76

Watson, K., *Poisoned lives: English poisoners and their victims*, London 2003

Weisser, M., *Crime and punishment in early modern Europe*, Hassocks 1979

Wells, R. A. E., 'Counting riots in eighteenth-century England', *Bulletin of the Society for the Study of Labour History* xxxvii (1978), 68–72

Whatley, C. A., 'How tame were the Scottish lowlanders during the eighteenth century', in T. M. Devine (ed.), *Conflict and stability in Scottish society, 1700–1850*, Edinburgh 1990, 1–30

_____ 'Women and the economic transformation of Scotland, *c.* 1740–1830', *SESH* xiv (1994), 19–40

_____ *The Industrial Revolution in Scotland*, Cambridge 1997

_____ *Scottish society, 1707–1820: beyond Jacobitism, towards industrialisation*, Manchester 2000

Whetstone, A. E., *Scottish county government in the eighteenth and nineteenth centuries*, Edinburgh 1981

Whyte, I. D., 'Scottish population and social structure in the seventeenth and eighteenth centuries: new sources and perspectives', *Archives* xx (1993), 30–41

―――― *Scotland before the Industrial Revolution: an economic and social history c. 1050–c. 1750*, Harlow 1995

Wiener, C. Z., 'Sex roles in late Elizabethan Hertfordshire', *JSH* viii (1975), 38–60

Wiener, M., *Men of blood: violence, manliness and criminal justice in Victorian England*, Cambridge 2004

Williams, D. E., 'Were "hunger" rioters really hungry? Some demographic evidence', *P&P* lxxi (1976), 70–5

Wilson, N., 'The Scottish bar: the evolution of the Faculty of Advocates in its historical setting', *Louisiana Law Review* xxviii (1968), 235–57

Wiltenberg, J., *Disorderly women and female power in the street literature of early modern England and Germany*, Charlottesville, VA.–London 1992

Winslow, C., 'Sussex smugglers', in Hay, Linebaugh, Rule, Thompson and Winslow, *Albion's fatal tree*, 119–66

Wiskin, C., 'Urban businesswomen in eighteenth-century England', in Sweet and Lane, *Women and urban life*, 87–110

Wood, A., *The politics of social conflict: the peak country, 1520–1770*, Cambridge 1999

―――― *Riot, rebellion and popular politics in early modern England*, Basingstoke 2002

Wormald, J., 'Bloodfeud, kindred and government in early modern Scotland', *P&P* lxxxvii (1980), 54–97

Wrightson, K., 'Infanticide in earlier seventeenth-century England', *Local Population Studies* xv (1975), 10–22

Zedner, L., *Women, crime and custody in Victorian England*, Oxford 1991

―――― 'Women, crime and penal responses: a historical account', in M. Tonry (ed.), *Crime and justice: a review of research*, xiv, Chicago–London 1991, 307–62

Unpublished works

Davies, S. J., 'Law and order in early modern Stirlingshire', PhD diss. St Andrews 1984

Kilday, A.-M., 'Women and crime in south-west Scotland: a study of the Justiciary Court records, 1750–1815', PhD diss. Strathclyde 1998

Wasser, M. B., 'Violence and the central criminal courts in Scotland, 1603–1638', PhD diss. Columbia 1995

Index

Selkirk, 33n.
sexual assault, *see* rape
sexual morality, 61
Sheriff Court, 4, 27, 28, 32–4, 33n.,
    83–103
Sheriff officers, 28, 101, 110, 151
Shiel, loch, 101
'skimmington rides', *see* charivari
Smith, Adam, 153, 155
smuggling, 139
sodomy, 34
soldiers, 116. *See also* infanticide
Stair, Lord, *see* Dalrymple, James, 1st
    Viscount Stair
statutes: *see* Act of Union, Criminal
    Procedure Act, Heritable Jurisdictions
    Act, Infanticide Act, Murder Act,
    Patronage Act (1690), Patronage Act
    (1712), Riot Act, Robbery Act
Stewarton, 137
Stirling, 33n., 34
stouthrief, 130n., 130, 134, 139, 143.
    See also theft
strangulation, 45
Stranraer, 100, 114, 118
sugar-refining industry, 7
summary justice, 5
Surrey, 43, 55, 64, 81, 98, 100, 134
Sutherland, 120

Tayside, 114
textile industry, 7, 124
theft, 28–9, 34, 84; theft with violence,
    20. *See also* robbery, stouthrief
tobacco industry, 7
transportation, 34, 62, 109; petitioning for,
    62, 66
treason, 28, 34, 85; petty treason, 55, 55n.,
    56
Tweed, river, 23, 34, 42, 82, 104, 154

Union of Crowns (1603), 30
urbanisation, 7, 9

vagrancy, 139, 144–5
victims (of crime), 51–6, 52n., 74–6, 89,
    100–2, 115–16, 132, 136, 139; gender
    of, 23, 39, 52–4, 81–2 88–9, 95, 99,
    101–3
violence: attitudes to violent men, 55;

attitudes to violent women, 54–6; and
    crime, 2, 5; in the 'domestic sphere';
    in Europe, 69, 93, 101; inter-personal,
    28, 80–127; 'licensed', forms of, 89;
    persistence of, 10. *See also* assault,
    crimes against the person
violent threatening, 81

Wales, 7, 17, 116
Wallace, William, 15
weapons, 45–9, 53, 69–70, 91–2, 95, 99,
    103, 116, 122, 136, 137–8
West Kilbride, 136
West Lothian, 33n., 86
wet-nursing, 74
Wigtown, 33n., 91, 96, 137
Wigtownshire, 100, 114, 118
witchcraft, 17, 19, 46, 55n., 63, 63n., 152
women, 3; and crime, 1, 2, 3, 9, 11, 18–22,
    39, and criminal subordination, 20–4,
    and gendered leniency in court, 20,
    20n., 23, 62–3, 102, 113, 133–4,
    violence used by, 1, 3, 9, 21, 22, 40;
    and deviance, 19–24; and the domestic
    sphere, 22, 149–51; and the economy,
    12
women: in England, 13–14, 17, 82; and
    criminal behaviour, 18; and the law, 13;
    and social interaction, 14; and work, 13
women: in Scotland, 1, 9, 11, 14, 16;
    and assault, 80–103; characteristics of
    defendants, 148; and the committal of
    crime, 3, 11, 147–58; and contribution
    to the economy, 9, 16–17, 149–50;
    and criminality, 5, 5–7n., 84, 98, 101,
    147, 151–53, 156; and homicide,
    39–58, 41; and infanticide, 59–79; and
    justice, 33, 38; and the law, 16; and the
    legitimisation of criminality, 118–19,
    123–7, 152, 155–6; lowland women,
    and the use of violence, 5, 5–7n.; and
    militancy, 16, 18, 101–2; motives
    of defendants, 148; and popular
    disturbances, 104–27; and resett of
    theft, 140–2; and riot, 104–27; and
    robbery, 128–46; and social interaction,
    16–17; and the use of violence, 3,
    9, 39–58, 49–50, 59–103, 104–27,
    128–46, 147–58
Württemberg (Germany), 65n.